CW01395213

STRIKINGLY SIMILAR

Plagiarism and appropriation are hot topics when they appear in the news. A politician copies a section of a speech, a section of music sounds familiar, the plot of a novel follows the same pattern as an older story, a piece of scientific research is attributed to the wrong researcher ... The list is endless. Allegations and convictions of such incidents can easily ruin a career and inspire gossip People report worrying about unconsciously appropriating someone else's work. But why do people plagiarize? How many claims of unconscious plagiarism are truthful? How is plagiarism detected, and what are the outcomes for the perpetrators and victims?

Strikingly Similar uncovers the deeper psychology behind this controversial human behavior, as well as a cultural history that is far wider and more interesting than sensationalized news stories.

Roger Kreuz is an associate dean and Professor of Psychology at the University of Memphis, USA. He has written several books on language and communication for general audiences and writes a monthly column for *Psychology Today*.

This book was born out of an academic interest in how language use affects a person's identity and the shifting public attitudes regarding the concepts of plagiarism and appropriation, as well as over thirty years as a professor who has had first-hand experience with student plagiarism.

STRIKINGLY SIMILAR

Plagiarism and Appropriation from Chaucer to Chatbots

Roger Kreuz

CAMBRIDGE
UNIVERSITY PRESS

![CAMBRIDGE UNIVERSITY PRESS]

Shaftesbury Road, Cambridge CB2 8EA, United Kingdom

One Liberty Plaza, 20th Floor, New York, NY 10006, USA

477 Williamstown Road, Port Melbourne, VIC 3207, Australia

314–321, 3rd Floor, Plot 3, Splendor Forum, Jasola District Centre,
New Delhi – 110025, India

103 Penang Road, #05–06/07, Visioncrest Commercial, Singapore 238467

Cambridge University Press is part of Cambridge University Press & Assessment,
a department of the University of Cambridge.

We share the University's mission to contribute to society through the pursuit of
education, learning and research at the highest international levels of excellence.

www.cambridge.org
Information on this title: www.cambridge.org/9781009618328

DOI: 10.1017/9781009618335

© Roger Kreuz 2026

This publication is in copyright. Subject to statutory exception and to the provisions
of relevant collective licensing agreements, no reproduction of any part may take
place without the written permission of Cambridge University Press & Assessment.

When citing this work, please include a reference to the DOI 10.1017/9781009618335

First published 2026

Printed in the United Kingdom by CPI Group Ltd, Croydon CR0 4YY

A catalogue record for this publication is available from the British Library

A Cataloging-in-Publication data record for this book is available from the Library of Congress

ISBN 978-1-009-61832-8 Hardback

Cambridge University Press & Assessment has no responsibility for the persistence
or accuracy of URLs for external or third-party internet websites referred to in this
publication and does not guarantee that any content on such websites is, or will remain,
accurate or appropriate.

For EU product safety concerns, contact us at Calle de José Abascal, 56, 1°, 28003
Madrid, Spain, or email eugpsr@cambridge.org.

To the memory of Sam Glucksberg (1933–2022)

Nothing is sillier than this charge of plagiarism. There is no sixth commandment in art. The poet dare help himself wherever he lists – wherever he finds material suited to his work.
—*Scintillations from the Prose Works of Heinrich Heine* (1873)

A man can no more be completely original in that sense than a tree can grow out of air.
—George Bernard Shaw, Preface to *Major Barbara* (1905)

Plagiarists are purloiners who filch the fruit that others have gathered, and then throw away the basket.
—Horace Smith, *The Tin Trumpet* (1871)

I read Wolfe's new book *The Story of a Novel* and as usual he stole the whole damn thing from me. I am going to write and say will you please stop writing books you bastard.
—Jean Stafford, quoted in *The Interior Castle* by Ann Hulbert (1992)

Contents

Preface

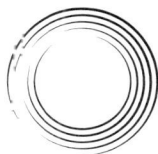

My interest in plagiarism was piqued by the research I conducted for *Linguistic Fingerprints*, my previous book on language and identity. In that work, I reviewed how researchers have invented methods for identifying unknown or anonymous authors by analyzing their language use, and my intent was to include a short description of how plagiarists could be identified through such means. That topic, however, felt like a digression from the main story that I wanted to tell, and I ended up scrapping what I had written. But it left me wondering about writers who plagiarize: whether they have anything in common, what their motivations are, and how likely they are to be caught. After completing my book on language and identity, I found myself searching for answers to these questions.

The more I read, the more intrigued – and frustrated – I became. I found lots of interesting cases online, but the stories were often incomplete. An episode of plagiarism usually makes it into a news cycle once, at the point of discovery. After that, the story vanishes from the headlines as the news cycle moves on to the Next Big Thing. The initial report is like a lightning flash illuminating a crime scene: it provides a quick glimpse of a complex story, but without any sort of resolution. Was the accusation of plagiarism true? Was it tried in the courts, or in the court of public opinion? Did the accused admit what they had done, or deny it, or offer some excuse? And what happened to them afterwards?

It occurred to me that if I did a little digging, I might be able to tease out some relatively complete stories lurking in newspaper archives and other online sources. In my naïveté, I thought there might be a few hundred such episodes in total, and that by cataloging and studying them, I could make some generalizations about the phenomenon of plagiarism.

I decided to create a database to keep track of my discoveries, as someone might do if they were collecting butterflies or old coins. I tagged each case in a variety of ways so that I could later, for example, pull up only French politicians who plagiarized their speeches, or American academics who cribbed while working on their dissertations. All this cataloging might be tedious, but the stories themselves were interesting, and I resolved to devote a summer to gathering my specimens.

Looking back, I'm astonished at how ignorant I was when I began this project. Without being aware of it, I had bought into some of the myths surrounding plagiarism, such as that the act is a relatively rare one – a transgression committed by panicky students or hack journalists. I also naïvely assumed that people typically plagiarize once, and then, racked with guilt, never transgress again. As it turns out, neither of these assumptions are correct.

To begin with, I had no idea how common the practice was. I quickly found dozens, then hundreds, and eventually thousands of cases. A project that I thought could be completed in one summer stretched into the following fall, winter, and spring. After ten months, I had cataloged over 4,600 cases, and I decided to stop – not because I had reached the end, but because I realized there was no end. By that point, however, I had unearthed plenty of raw material and knew that I could create a survey of appropriation in its many different forms and guises. I had also found accounts provided by the plagiarists themselves, their victims, and the public's reaction to these episodes.

I must confess that this odyssey has dented my faith in human nature. Like a veteran cop, I developed a hard-edged, cynical attitude, shaking my head and muttering to myself as I summarized case after case on my laptop. Toward the end, I developed the thousand-yard stare that combat veterans are said to acquire after they've witnessed too much carnage. My friends stopped asking me about the project because they knew I would fly into an impassioned monologue concerning the latest malfeasance I had unearthed.

Even though I eventually came to terms with how common plagiarism is, I'm still surprised by who has engaged in this practice. Yes, this group includes plenty of hacks and students. But they are joined by the highest elected officials of several countries, as well as Nobel and Pulitzer Prize recipients, bestselling authors and artists, and distinguished faculty at elite universities. Plagiarism: it's not just for mediocrities anymore.

When I wasn't logging cases of plagiarism, I was reading the literature devoted to the subject. But this didn't take nearly as much time. While scholars have written several texts for their fellow specialists on plagiarism during certain eras, like ancient Rome,[1] the eighteenth century,[2] or the Victorian era,[3] less common are more comprehensive accounts intended for a general audience.

The first such book to appear in English was *Literary Ethics*, written by H. M. Paull and published in 1928.[4] Paull's wide-ranging survey includes topics such as literary forgery, piracy, and censorship. One shortcoming of his approach, however, is that the discussion of plagiarism is relegated to a single chapter. The subject finally received star billing in 1952 when Alexander Lindey published *Plagiarism and Originality*.[5] This book provides an excellent treatment ranging from ancient Greek literature through the 1940s.

Thomas Mallon's *Stolen Words* followed in 1989.[6] His story of plagiarism is immensely readable, albeit somewhat idiosyncratic in its coverage. The author added a twelve-page update when the book was republished in 2001. Finally, Richard Posner's delightful *Little Book of Plagiarism* appeared in 2007.[7] It is aptly named: weighing in at a svelte hundred pages of large type on small pages, it is more of a long essay than a book-length treatment.

The coverage of plagiarism in these four volumes clearly reflects each author's avocation. Paull was a dramatist and Lindey was an attorney. Mallon is a novelist and essayist, whereas Posner is a judge and legal scholar. It seemed to me that a more psychologically informed account was needed to address important questions about appropriation. For example, do plagiarists have specific personality characteristics? What motivates people to steal the work of others? And perhaps most intriguingly, is unconscious plagiarism a real thing, or merely a facile excuse offered up by those caught red-handed?

There are also some curious gaps in earlier accounts of plagiarism. Perhaps most importantly, little has been written about the victims of appropriation – those writers, artists, and composers whose work has been commandeered without their knowledge or consent. And it's not always the victim who discovers the theft. Many cases of appropriation involve a third party who stumbles across the plagiarism and makes it known to the victim or to others. And as we will see, such altruistic whistleblowing is condemned at least as often as it is praised.

We like to tell our children – and ourselves – that cheaters never prosper, but how true is this sentiment? What are the long-term consequences of an accusation of plagiarism on someone's reputation or their career? The answer to this question depends on many factors, such as the individual's occupation, the circumstances of the discovery, and even the type of work being plagiarized. The cribbing of material for a commencement address, for example, is a Really Bad Idea, whereas most plagiarizing politicians survive such episodes – perhaps because people have such low expectations for elected officials to begin with.

It's a truism to say that the internet changed everything, but that doesn't make it any less true. It is certainly the case for many of the topics that I survey in this book. Mallon's account, published in the 1980s, when student plagiarism involved ordering a ghostwritten term paper through the mail, seems as dated as the era's leg warmers, or being a fan of the Culture Club. The internet brought the world to one's desktop and made it easier than ever to appropriate someone else's work.

Until the 1990s, plagiarism involved the actual effort of physically writing out or typing someone else's words. Computers have done away with the time-consuming drudgery of that step as well. As early as 1998, teachers were bemoaning the "copy and paste" plagiarism they had begun to see in their students' assignments.[8] And it truly had become just that easy: cribbing the work of others was as simple as highlighting some text on the screen and then pasting it into one's own document. This isn't possible in every case – Google Books, for example, doesn't allow it – but seemingly countless documents are available to be read – or ransacked – with the click of a mouse. And why even search for a good opening paragraph for your essay when ChatGPT is happy to construct one – or a dozen or more – for you?

The internet has made plagiarism far easier to commit, but it has also made appropriation much easier to recognize. A suspicious professor, for example, can use a search engine to determine whether a student's remarkably evocative turn of phrase is novel – or just taken from a novel. Even more powerful tools, like Turnitin, Grammarly, iThenticate, and their ilk can automate the process and check entire documents in the blink of an eye. These services aren't perfect – as we will see – but their widespread adoption in the education space probably does make would-be student plagiarists think twice before simply copying and pasting.

It is also the case that social media has made it easier than ever before to accuse someone of plagiarism. The hip-hop artist, avant-garde poet, or syndicated columnist can alert their followers on X (Twitter), Facebook, Instagram, or TikTok when they think that their work has been appropriated. And fans can alert their favorite artist or author about suspected plagiarism in the same way.

In my research on plagiarism and appropriation, I have relied on original sources as much as possible. These are typically journalistic accounts, which are valuable because they reflect the cultural attitudes of the times in which they were written. A newspaper article about a plagiarizing novelist in 1920, for example, reads somewhat differently than one written in 2020.

The most valuable resource by far proved to be *The New York Times*. The Gray Lady, as it is sometimes called, has functioned as a newspaper of record for many decades. But even more importantly for my purposes, it served as the "hometown paper" for Tin Pan Alley and the early film industry, both of which were hotbeds of plagiarism. And the *Times* still serves that hometown role in its coverage of Broadway and the US publishing industry – institutions that have generated their fair share of plagiarism scandals.

In addition, all the *Times*'s issues have been digitized, and the 15 million articles that its journalists have published – from its beginning in 1851 to today – are fully searchable online. Undoubtedly, the paper's editorial policies have changed through the years, but its coverage of appropriation provides a baseline for addressing certain questions, such as whether the overall rate of plagiarism has waned or waxed over time.

Tallying mentions of the word "plagiarism" each year in the *Times* is an admittedly crude yardstick, but it's better than nothing. It seems that the

1910s, as well as the 1940s through the 1970s, were periods of relatively low plagiarism, whereas rates during the 1920s and 1930s were higher. And the years from 2000 to the present have witnessed the highest rates of all: the number of articles mentioning plagiarism has been about eight times greater during this millennium than it was during the middle decades of the twentieth century. In the past decade, the word "plagiarism" appeared in the *Times* nearly 600 times, or about once every six days.

Two observations are worth making at the outset. The first is that plagiarism, as a term, is unusually problematic. As a label, it is both too broad and too vague. Actions that fall under this conceptual umbrella run the gamut from minor citation errors to the wholesale pilfering of entire texts. Many people assume that plagiarism is a binary, all-or-nothing sort of phenomenon, but in truth it is far from that.

A second observation is that appropriation is best described as a social and a cultural construct. During some historical periods, the practice was not viewed as especially problematic. Today, it is condemned on both moral and legal grounds, with the latter linked inextricably to modern notions of intellectual property. Plagiarism is not a crime per se, and those who seek relief or damages from the courts do so on the basis of copyright infringement. But even the notion of copyright has undergone significant change during the past century, clearly demonstrating the cultural fluidity of the concept.

An exploration of plagiarism's psychological and cultural aspects can help us make sense of what it is and why it happens so often. This is what I have tried to provide, and I hope that you find the cases I've included to be as fascinating as I do.

Acknowledgments

It's a pleasure to publicly thank those who, in various ways, helped to make this book a reality.

Katherine Kitzmann and Susan Fitzgerald were kind enough to read the first draft of my manuscript and to offer detailed feedback, as well as many, many suggestions for improvements. I also benefited greatly from the comments of three anonymous reviewers.

Ira Lightman and Ladrica Menson-Furr provided me with important clarifications on key issues, and I gratefully thank them for sharing their expertise with me.

The interlibrary loan staff of the McWherter Library at the University of Memphis was unfailingly helpful in tracking down articles, no matter how obscure, and the speed with which they provided what I needed was truly remarkable.

Writing a book while also attending to one's academic and administrative responsibilities requires a great deal of juggling and plate spinning. This would have been impossible without the ministrations of the excellent support staff that I am fortunate to work with. Stormey Warren and Jessica Abernathy truly deserve my thanks and my appreciation. I also acknowledge the support of Gary Emmert and Abby Parrill – two deans who have been wonderful to work for.

I'm indebted to my friends who listened patiently as I yammered on about this project over the past two years, particularly Keri Brondo, Gina Caucci, Bob Cohen, Katherine Kitzmann, Rick Marcus, Richard Roberts, and Deb Tollefsen.

Finally, Emily Watton at Cambridge University Press deserves special recognition for championing this project when it came her way. Her faith and support are why you are now reading what I have written.

Memphis, Tennessee, July 2024

CHAPTER 1

Setting the Stage

DEFINING PLAGIARISM

At the end of his weekly radio broadcast on January 5, 1936, Eddie Cantor made an intriguing announcement. The comedian, whose hour-long variety show was one of the most popular in the country, invited listeners to write essays of up to 500 words to answer the question "How can America stay out of war?". Cantor declared that he would personally establish a trust fund of $5,000 to pay for the expenses of the winner, or their designee, at the college or university of their choice. Given that tuition at Harvard University was only $400 per year during the Depression, the prize would easily provide the lucky recipient with the resources to complete an undergraduate degree.

Cantor announced that the winner would be decided by the presidents of the University of Chicago, Stanford, Vassar, and the City University of New York. The chosen entry, Cantor emphasized, would be the one deemed "the most constructive, sincere, and interesting. Fancy writing or technical knowledge," he made clear, was not a consideration. The deadline would be Washington's birthday, which was seven weeks away, and the winner would be announced on his program in early April.[1]

Not surprisingly, Cantor's offices in New York City were soon flooded with submissions: over 12,000 had arrived by the deadline. Entrants included high school students but also college students, faculty members, and elected officials.[2] The entries were reviewed by Cantor's staff, and 100 of these were passed along to the judges. During his April 5 broadcast, Cantor announced that the winner was Lloyd Lewis, a seventeen-year-old high school junior. He lived on a farm near Plattsburg, a village in north-west Missouri with a population of less than 2,000.[3]

Cantor arranged to have Lewis flown to New York City to accept the prize on his program. Having never traveled more than fifty miles from his family's farm, Lewis was enthralled by the sights and sounds of the Big Apple. His story was heartwarming – but it would not have a storybook ending.

The New York Times published excerpts of Lewis's essay, and a woman in New Jersey thought that the sentiment expressed sounded familiar. She checked and discovered that the excerpts matched an article that had been published four months earlier in *Peace Digest*. The original had been penned by Frank Kingdon, president of the University of Newark. The woman contacted Kingdon, who then tried, unsuccessfully, to reach Cantor. Kingdon informed a Newark newspaper, and they in turn contacted CBS and Cantor's manager.[4]

When confronted by reporters, Lewis readily admitted to having taken his essay from the article by Kingdon. His history teacher had given Cantor's theme to Lewis's class as an assignment, and he copied the essay between his farm chores. Lewis claimed he didn't understand that his entry had to be an original piece. "I thought you just were to send in the best essay you could find," he said. Lewis added, "If I had known, I would have written one myself."[5]

A chagrined Eddie Cantor allowed that Lewis had made an honest mistake. The following week, he awarded his scholarship to second-place finisher Owen Matthews, a nineteen-year-old Eagle Scout from Portland, Oregon.[6]

Although this episode occurred nearly ninety years ago, it's not hard to imagine a similar story playing out today. The concepts of intellectual property and plagiarism do not come naturally to anyone: they need to be taught.

A lack of familiarity with plagiarism as a concept has arisen in the courtroom as well. Such an episode occurred during the trial in Chicago of Gerald Frank, who was charged with copying from the French painter George Barbier. A decision by the jury was delayed when one of its members admitted that they didn't know the meaning of the word plagiarism.[7]

If we define plagiarism as the deliberate appropriation of someone else's words and ideas without acknowledgment or compensation, then it's fairly easy to articulate the two rules that guard against it. First, if someone wants to use the exact words of another writer, the words must be set off by quotation marks, accompanied by a citation of the original source. This can be provided via a footnote or an endnote, depending on the citation style being employed.

Second, the author can choose to paraphrase the original text. This requires the writer to restate the idea in their own words. Paraphrases don't take quotation marks, but a citation to the original work is still required. And that's it – that's all that is needed to avoid plagiarism.

These two rules may seem simple enough, but as with many things, the devil is in the details. For example, how many consecutive words can be taken from an original source before a citation is required? According to the World Association of Medical Editors, "plagiarism is when six consecutive words are copied" without attribution.[8] This seems reasonable – but almost every other single-digit number has been proposed as well. Mathieu Bouville, in his review of the issue, found sources claiming that the magic number is "two—three, four, or seven consecutive words."[9]

A lack of consensus on this issue is problematic because simple similarity detection software might have a relatively low threshold for matching word sequences, and this can result in false positives. For example, a Google search for the phrase "The bloody three-day battle of Gettysburg" yields about 700 results, including several books, although it's easy to imagine a student or a historian generating this six-word phrase on their own.

And issues surrounding paraphrasing are even more problematic than mere quotations. Expressing a complex idea in one's own words is hard, which is why student writers and non-native speakers of a language struggle with rephrasing. As a result, many writers end up engaging in so-called patch writing or mosaic plagiarism. This occurs when the writer maintains the same sentence structure as in the original and simply plugs in synonyms to replace some of the terms. This practice is also called "Rogeting" because those who engage in the practice often sound like they've swallowed a copy of *Roget's Thesaurus*.[10] In this way, an ordinary phrase like "the shadowy house" might be transmogrified into an awkwardly worded equivalent such as "the obscure habitation." In a student essay, such a phrase would be a red flag that its author is engaging in patch writing.

PLAGIARISM VERSUS ORIGINALITY

One way to define plagiarism would be to describe it as the opposite of originality. Instead of bringing something new into the world, the plagiarist duplicates the work of another and does so without attribution. Viewed in this way, plagiarism and originality could be thought of as binary labels, with all creative work pigeonholed into one category or the other. In practice, however, there exists a considerable degree of ambiguity. It might be better to characterize the two terms as endpoints on a continuum, and to assign other labels to cases that fall somewhere in between. People might appropriate the work of others for a variety of reasons, and some of these may not merit the scarlet letter of outright theft.

Consider, for example, the case of celebrity impersonators. In 1954, the actor Hal Holbrook created a one-man show in which he took on the persona of the elderly Mark Twain. The actor's transformation into the humorist involved a three-hour makeup routine as well as donning a three-piece white suit, bushy mustache, and white-haired wig.[11] During his performances, Holbrook would dispense the humorist's homespun wisdom in a quavering Southern drawl. After an appearance on "The Ed Sullivan Show," Holbrook began to perform his routine, titled "Mark Twain Tonight!," on a regular basis. He took his show to Broadway in 1966 and received an Emmy for a televised version of the routine during the following year.[12]

Was Holbrook appropriating from Twain? If so, he had plenty of company. During the 1870s and 1880s, several actors found employment impersonating the humorist, even as the real Twain was still active on the US lecture circuit.[13] And when Holbrook created his one-man show, the humorist had been dead for over forty years. Holbrook's performance shouldn't be characterized as plagiarism because he wasn't passing off Twain's *bon mots* as if they were his own. Everyone in Holbrook's audience understood that the man in the wig was channeling Twain, not stealing from him. His take on the humorist could best be described as pastiche: an affectionate tribute to the man's memory and work.[14]

But in 1975, a young actor named Michael Randall went beyond pastiche by performing a one-man show he called "Mark Twain Live!", and Holbrook sued him for plagiarism.[15] His claim was that Randall was cribbing from Holbrook's distinctive characterization of the humorist, and one that he had been honing for decades. Ultimately, the two men settled out of court: Randall was allowed to continue his performances but was forbidden to make use of Holbrook's take on Twain.[16] For Holbrook, at least, an impersonation of his impersonation was a step too far.

In comparison to pastiche, homage may not imitate the original source closely. Nevertheless, the spirit of the original may suffuse a performance to such a degree that the source of inspiration is unmistakable. The original artist may be flattered by the tribute. In other cases, however, the homage might be viewed as an infringement of the artist's intellectual property. This was the reaction, for example, of the Belgian choreographer Anne Teresa De Keersmaeker to Beyoncé's music video for "Countdown" in 2011.[17]

When artists draw on two or more sources for their creations, the resulting work can be referred to as bricolage (from the French bricoler, "to tinker," or "do it yourself").[18] The term is most frequently used in reference to mixed media in the visual arts but can also be applied more broadly. In music and the performing arts, the result might be described as a mash-up. And this is in keeping with Beyoncé's reply to De Keersmaeker: the singer maintained that her music video was "inspired" by artists such as "Brigitte Bardot, Andy Warhol, Twiggy, and Diana Ross" as well as by De Keersmaeker.[19]

Parodies are also derivative works that hew closely to an original, but in this case the intent is to satirize or to mock. It is also recognized as a form of fair use that is permitted by US copyright law. That's not to say that parodists haven't been taken to court, however, and we will return to this issue later in the book.

A cover version of a song, performed or recorded by a different artist, may also be quite similar to the original, and it requires negotiation between the would-be interpreter and whoever holds the work's copyright. Typically, a licensing fee is required. In some cases, a cover version may become much more popular than the original. For example, Whitney Houston's *I Will Always Love You*, recorded for a 1992 movie soundtrack, is a cover of a song written and recorded nearly twenty years earlier by Dolly Parton.[20] By 2022, Houston's version had sold more than 10 million copies.[21]

But even "original" works may not be truly original. A book or a film might be based on some earlier work, with previously established characters finding themselves in a new situation – as in a sequel – or in one that predates the original, as in a prequel. Hollywood has made extensive use of this tactic, since new intellectual property may be expensive to acquire and to market.

A successful film may give rise to a multi-work franchise. This is less of a financial risk than a totally new property, as there will be a built-in audience for such familiar, if derivative, efforts. This can make good economic sense, but audiences may not always care for such warmed-over fare if taken to extremes. When sequels draw too much from earlier works, they may be criticized as mere fan service, as in Marvel's 2019 release of *Avengers: Endgame*.[22]

Finally, let's consider the question of intent. In some cases, it's easy to conclude whether similarities between creative works are the result of pastiche, homage, or appropriation. Artists are often inspired by earlier works in their medium, and they expect others to be able to discern and to celebrate these resemblances. When critics of Johannes Brahms pointed out similar motifs in his First Symphony and Beethoven's Ninth, he is said to have growled *Das sieht jeder Narr* ("any fool can see that").[23]

Other cases of intent have proved to be exceptionally murky. Consider the case of a symphony completed by Austrian composer Hans Rott in 1880. Brahms's criticism of the young man's work is thought to have been a factor in Rott's descent into delusions of persecution. He died of tuberculosis in a psychiatric hospital at the age of twenty-five, and his symphony went unperformed until 1989. At that time, critics noted "quotations" from Rott's music in the symphonies of his conservatory classmate, Gustav Mahler. Mahler is known to have studied Rott's symphonic score, and some of the resemblances are striking, but musicologists are divided about what they mean.[24]

Some of the clues that we have are beguiling. Mahler is known to have heaped praise on Rott's memory, describing him as "a musician of genius ... who died on the very threshold of his career" and as "the founder of the new symphony as I myself understand it." But even though he became one of the leading conductors of his day, Mahler never made an effort to see Rott's work performed.[25]

Had Mahler been inspired by the work of his deceased classmate? Were the musical quotations intended as a tribute to him? Did Mahler unconsciously appropriate musical ideas that lodged in his mind when he studied Rott's score? And did he worry that a performance of Rott's symphony would expose these appropriations – unintentional or otherwise? Or did the two composers simply draw upon the same musical influences? It's impossible to say – but this example underscores how difficult it can be to draw conclusions when the evidence for appropriation is fragmentary.

PLAGIARISM OR COINCIDENCE?

A secret society. A globe-spanning conspiracy. The revelation that Jesus was married to Mary Magdalene. An individual who happens to be albino.

Some readers may recognize these plot points and details from Dan Brown's novel *The Da Vinci Code*, published in 2003, or the film starring Tom Hanks and Audrey Tautou. However, these elements also appear in *Sirkelens ende* ("Circle's End"), a thriller written by Norwegian author Tom Egeland and published in 2001, two years before Brown's bestseller.

At first blush, these similarities are striking. Does this mean that Brown plagiarized from Egeland? It seems unlikely. Egeland's novel was not translated into English – under the title *Relic* – until 2010, well after *The Da Vinci Code* was published. And Brown almost certainly did not read *Sirkelens ende*, as he isn't known to be fluent in Norwegian.

In addition, despite the similarities between the two books, the main characters and the story arcs are clearly different. In Egeland's thriller, the person with albinism is Bjørn Beltø, a professor of archeology and the story's protagonist. In Brown's, he is Silas, a murderous monk who plays a fairly minor role in the story. Brown's main character is Robert Langdon, a Harvard professor who studies art and symbols. Langdon had also appeared in Brown's previous book, *Angels & Demons*, which was published in 2000.

In Egeland's story, Beltø steals and hides an ancient relic. Brown's thriller begins with a murder at the Louvre. In Egeland's, most of the action takes place in Norway, London, and Israel. Brown's tale includes an interlude in London, but the story is principally set in Paris and Scotland.

In an interview, Egeland asserted that any similarities between the two books are pure coincidence, probably arising from the fact that he and Brown drew from the same sources, such as *Holy Blood, Holy Grail,*[26] a speculative work about a bloodline descended from Jesus, published in 1982. (The authors of that book did sue Brown, unsuccessfully, for copyright infringement.[27]) As it happens, Egeland made clear he was grateful for Brown's book, because it raised the visibility of his own novel.[28]

The human mind excels at detecting patterns, and it strains to do so even when there is no pattern to be found. We also tend to view coincidences with suspicion and assume there must be some underlying connection to explain them. This predilection serves us well most of the time, but it can also cause us to suspect appropriation when it is unwarranted. Coincidences, it seems, may be more common than we would think.

The New York Times, in its "Saturday Review of Books" on July 10, 1909, compared two recently published novels that possessed uncanny similarities. One was *By Their Fruits,* written by Australian-born novelist Rosa Campbell Praed. The other was *Michael Thwaite's Wife* by American author Miriam Michelson. Published about six months apart, their overall theme, plot points, and main characters were noted to be "almost identical."

Both novels are about twin sisters, one of whom represents goodness while the other embodies evil. And in both, the evil twin marries and then is ultimately replaced by the good twin. The reviewer concludes:

One can hardly think that here is a case of deliberate plagiarism – and yet, what is the explanation of so curious a coincidence as exists here in the work of two contemporary writers – one in England, the other in America – who have, in all probability, never communicated with each other?[29]

Or consider the case of British author William Golding. On the eve of Golding's receipt of the Nobel Prize in Literature in 1984, journalist Auberon Waugh published an article in *The Spectator*, a British weekly, about Golding's best-known novel. Waugh claimed that there were striking similarities between Golding's *Lord of the Flies*, published in 1954, and British writer W. L. George's *Children of the Morning*, which had been published nearly thirty years earlier, in 1926.

In both stories, children are marooned on a desert island. There is conflict as they split into groups. In both, a red-headed bully emerges as a leader. There is a fire. And in both, the story ends with the appearance of a navy cruiser – an American ship in George's story, and a British one in Golding's.

Waugh didn't accuse Golding of having deliberately plagiarized from George. Instead, he theorized that Golding had read George's story in his youth – he would have been fifteen when *Children of the Morning* was published – and that George's story had "an extraordinary subliminal effect on him." Waugh suggested that Golding should offer George's descendants a token of his appreciation, such as "a tin of pickled herrings," after he returned from the ceremony in Sweden.[30]

Golding was forced to defend himself from his hotel room in Stockholm. He told reporters that:

> As far as I can recollect I have never heard of this author or book, and it is most unlikely that I read it as a child. I cannot comment on the parallel plots until I have read *Children of the Morning* and reread *Lord of the Flies*, which I wrote more than a generation ago. The similarities must be coincidental. After all, there are a great many books in the world about a great many islands written by a great many authors.[31]

He continued, in a pricklier vein, with "I was awarded the Nobel Prize for a literary career which contains nine novels, not one." Golding's defensiveness is not surprising, as many critics, particularly those in the US, had been critical of the Swedish Academy's choice.[32]

Coincidental similarities also show up in places besides novels. In the world of comics, we have the curious case of Hairbutt and Hip Flask. Both creatures are anthropomorphic hippopotami, and both happen to be private detectives. Hairbutt the Hippo debuted in 1991, the brainchild of Australians Jason Paulos and Amerikah Bodine. Hip Flask appeared four years later, in 1995, and was the creation of British font designer Richard Starkings.

In 2001, when Bodine became aware of Hip Flask's existence, she accused Starkings of plagiarism. Given the remarkable degree of overlap – humanoid hippo private eyes – it's not surprising that Bodine assumed the worst. Starkings, however, protested that he was unaware of Hairbutt until 1998, when the character was brought to his attention by a reporter. At that point, he tried to differentiate the characters and dropped Hip Flask's private detective persona. Starkings has maintained that the similarities were "just a bizarre coincidence."[33]

As a final example, this time drawn from the world of music, consider the case of Tom Petty and Sam Smith. In 1989, Petty had a hit with "I Won't Back Down," released as a single from his "Full Moon River" album. And in 2014, Sam Smith released a song called "Stay with Me" on his first studio album. A cover version of Smith's song by Darkchild would go on to win a Grammy for Song of the Year in 2015.

Petty's publisher, however, noted similarities between the melodies and choruses of the two songs and contacted representatives for Smith. Although Smith claimed not to be familiar with "I Won't Back Down," he did admit that there was a resemblance, which he attributed to "a complete coincidence."[34]

Petty, for his part, was understanding, saying "All my years of songwriting have shown me these things can happen. Most times you catch it before it gets out the studio door but in this case it got by."[35] The two sides quickly came to an amicable settlement: Petty and his co-writer Jeff Lynne accepted Smith's offer of songwriting credits and 12.5% of the royalties from "Stay with Me."[36]

ORIGINS

The concept of plagiarism existed in classic antiquity, although it was not referred to by that term. The scholars of ancient Greece made use of words like κλοπή ("theft") and κλέπτειγ ("steal") to refer to the idea of literary appropriation.

Some of the targets of these accusations may be surprising. Aristoxenus of Tarentum, a philosopher of the fourth century BCE, accused Plato of cribbing most of *The Republic* from the writings of Protagoras. Aristoxenus's contemporary Alcinus claimed that Plato "borrowed heavily from Epicharmus, using his very words."[37] And a number of early Christians, such as Justin Martyr, accused Plato of copying Moses.[38]

During the second century CE, in a treatise titled *The True Word*, the Greek philosopher Celsus charged that Jesus had plagiarized his teachings from the writings of Plato. Although Celsus's treatise did not survive antiquity, we know about it through a refutation written by Origen of Alexandria, a third-century Christian scholar. (Origen's work, *Contra Celsus*, contains quotations that are extensive enough to allow a reconstruction of Celsus's arguments.[39])

The concept of literary appropriation was exported from ancient Greece to the Roman Republic. We see references to this concept by Terrence in the second century BCE and then by Cicero, Horace, and Pliny the Elder. To refer to appropriation, they employed Latin terms that were equivalent to those in Greek, such as *furtum* ("theft") or *surripere* ("to steal"). For example, Horace criticized a fellow poet for making himself beautiful with "stolen feathers."[40]

The first use of the term "plagiarism" in reference to literary theft is found in the writings of Martial, who lived during the first century CE. He is best known for his epigrams – terse, witty, and often acerbic observations about daily life in Imperial Rome. At one point, Martial discovered that Fidentis, a fellow poet, was reciting Martial's work as if it were his own.[41] In pleading with Quintianus, his patron, to intervene, Martial wrote:

hoc si terque quaterque clamitaris,	If you shout this three or four times,
inpones plagiario pudorem.	you will make the kidnapper ashamed of himself.[42]

Martial was metaphorically equating the thieving poet with a *plagiario*: that is, someone who kidnaps slaves or children. In thinking about his literary creations in this way, Martial might have been influenced by Ovid, who had likened the works of authors to their own children.[43]

After the collapse of the Western Roman Empire, concerns about literary plagiarism largely disappeared from European letters.[44] The focus shifted to the reshaping and refashioning of the work of earlier writers. The Dionysian notion of *imitatio* reigned supreme. In this context, copying was seen as a virtue, and it was originality that was suspect.

CHAUCER, SHAKESPEARE, AND FRANKLIN

If we examine the work of three authors, writing in the fourteenth, sixteenth, and eighteenth centuries, we can see that attitudes about appropriation were largely unchanging over this long period. Geoffrey Chaucer, considered the father of English literature, borrowed from writers of antiquity, such as Virgil, Ovid, and Boethius, as well as Dante and his near-contemporaries Petrarch and Giovanni Boccaccio. In some cases, he only recycled characters, plots, themes, or structures, but in others this appropriation was more direct. As Sherry Reames has pointed out, the "Second Nun's Tale" in *The Canterbury Tales* "bears an unusually close relationship to its sources. Every important detail in the narrative, and indeed almost every sentence, is paralleled in the Latin versions of the Cecilia legend."[45] The sources and analogues for Chaucer's work in general,[46] and *The Canterbury Tales* in particular,[47] have been extensively documented.

In one case, Chaucer took the notion of *imitatio* a step further. When he penned his epic poem *Troilus and Criseyde* in the 1380s, he relied heavily on Boccaccio's *Il Filostrato* but apparently felt compelled to attribute his material to a classical source. He refers to a "Lollius," although scholars have been unable to identify any author with that name. The modern consensus is that Lollius "is no more than a literary phantasm, a friend of Horace transformed by a medieval misreading into the author of a lost work on the Trojan war."[48] Technically, this makes Chaucer a fabricator as opposed to an appropriator. He may have been one of the first authors in English to make up a source – but he would not be the last.

Writing 200 years after Chaucer, Shakespeare also drew from Ovid and Boccaccio, as well as from a variety of other sources, such as Holinshed's

Chronicles and Chaucer himself. Shakespeare and Fletcher's *Two Noble Kinsmen*, for example, is essentially a reinterpretation of "The Knight's Tale."[49]

But none of this was considered unacceptable when Chaucer and Shakespeare were creating their works, and it is never characterized as plagiarism by scholars today. Instead, words like "source," or "borrowing," or "inspiration" are used. The prevailing attitude was that the works of other authors were fair game, as long as one improved on the original.

This can be clearly seen in Shakespeare's *Antony and Cleopatra*. For his play, the bard paraphrased from Thomas North's translation of *Plutarch's Life of Antony*'s description of Cleopatra and her barge. Shakespeare's version is vastly superior; as Richard Posner observed, "If this is plagiarism, then we need more plagiarism."[50]

Let us make a third and final jump forward in time, to 1732 and the American colonies. At the end of that year, Benjamin Franklin published a slender volume entitled *An Almanack for the Year of Christ 1733*. Franklin was a twenty-six-year-old printer who had taken over *The Pennsylvania Gazette* three years earlier and chose to publish this new venture using the pseudonym of Richard Saunders. *Poor Richard's Almanack*, as it came to be known, would appear annually for the next twenty-five years and proved to be exceptionally popular. Like other almanacs of the era, *Poor Richard* contained information on a variety of topics, such as weather forecasts, tables of tides, astronomical information, recipes, and poetic verse, but also proverbs and aphorisms. These terse and often cynical adages often appeared as filler at the end of a column of text. Many of them are still familiar:

"Fish and visitors stink in three days." (1736)
"Don't throw stones at your neighbours, if your own windows are glass." (1736)
"God helps them that help themselves." (1736)
"Haste makes waste." (1753)
"Early to bed and early to rise makes a man healthy, wealthy, and wise." (1757)

Today, Franklin's sterling reputation rests principally upon his roles as a founding father to his nation and his work as a scientist and inventor.

And the wit and wisdom of *Poor Richard* seemingly allows him to lay claim to the title of champion wordsmith as well. But does he deserve that distinction?

Franklin's printing enterprises flourished, and he retired fifteen years after establishing *Poor Richard*, giving him more time to pursue his manifold interests. However, he continued to compose the prefaces for the yearly editions of the almanac until 1757. In the final edition, "Richard Saunders" admitted that "not a tenth part of the wisdom was my own . . . but rather the gleanings I had made of the sense of all ages and nations."[51]

Although scholars like Carl Van Doren suspected that Franklin drew from writers like Dryden, Swift, and Rabelais,[52] the requisite heavy lifting – tracking down the exact sources – was performed by Robert Newcomb, in research for his 1957 dissertation. He found that Franklin had mined many different authors, but most of *Poor Richard*'s axioms came from the historian James Howell, physician Thomas Fuller, and the poet George Herbert. Franklin also drew from a posthumous work by the politician George Savile (Lord Halifax), Samuel Richardson, and French authors François de La Rochefoucauld and Michel de Montaigne.[53]

During Franklin's lifetime, publishers in Britain and the colonies habitually republished the work of others without attribution or compensation. Franklin was no better – but no different – from the others of his time. And as with Shakespeare, Franklin frequently improved on what he appropriated. As J. A. Leo Lemay describes it, Franklin would simplify and clarify. Whereas the originals were often formal and somewhat clunky, Franklin's renderings are vigorous and direct. For example, *Ray's Collection of English Proverbs*, from 1678, includes the adage "God restoreth health, and the physician hath the thanks." Franklin absconded with this sentiment but rendered it in *Poor Richard* as "God heals and the doctor takes the fee" (1736).[54]

THE MODERN VIEW EMERGES

We see the first stirrings of a new attitude about originality at the beginning of the sixteenth century. When the Italian engraver Marcantonio Raimondi started copying the woodcuts of Albrecht Dürer – including his unique AD monogram – the German artist lodged a complaint with the

Venetian government. Dürer's action is one of the earliest examples of what we would now call a copyright infringement lawsuit. Unfortunately for Dürer, the courts only prohibited Raimondi from copying the monogram: he was still free to reproduce and sell copies of Dürer's work. In modern parlance, Dürer retained his trademark, but his art was considered to be in the public domain.[55] (In a kind of karmic justice, however, Raimondi was later imprisoned for his reproductions of erotic images.[56])

The terms "plagiarism," "plagiarize," and "plagiarist" all made their debuts in the English language during the 1600s, although the first such form to be used – "plagiary," dating from 1598 – is now obsolete.

The last quarter of the 1600s witnessed a reawakening of interest in the concept of plagiarism. In 1673, the German philosopher Jakob Thomasius published *Dissertatio philosophica de plagio literario*, in which he argued that appropriation without attribution was morally wrong and equivalent to theft. Works like Van Almeloveen's *Plagiariorum Syllabus* of 1694 provided a catalog of appropriations by earlier Continental authors.[57] And Gerard Langbaine's *Momus Triumphans* – published in 1687 – performed the same service for literary texts written in English.[58]

At the same time, the meaning of the term "plagiarism" in English was shifting. Before about 1700, it referred to what is now called literary piracy, which is the unauthorized reproduction and selling of someone else's writing. Beginning in the eighteenth century, "plagiarism" was used in its modern sense, to refer to appropriation without attribution.[59]

It would be another century, however, before originality was truly seen as a virtue. It was during the Romantic period that artists came to be idolized, and this adoration raised them far above their station as mere craftspeople – which was how they had been regarded in the past. By the early nineteenth century, there were several authors who were able to support themselves solely by their writing. In America, these included Washington Irving, James Fenimore Cooper, and Edgar Allan Poe (albeit precariously). And in England, a similar list included William Makepeace Thackeray, George Eliot, and Charles Dickens. Dickens deserves special mention here, because his work was plagiarized on many occasions during his career.

Dickens's novels, incredibly popular from the start of his career, were serialized: that is, they initially appeared in weekly or monthly installments in popular magazines. For the monthly publications, it would take about a year and a half for an entire tale to appear in print. This provided an opening for unscrupulous publishers to capitalize on the public's interest – and impatience – to learn more about the Pickwick Club, Oliver Twist, or Nicholas Nickleby.

Dickens's most notorious *bête noire* was Edward Lloyd, a bookseller who also ran a literary sweatshop, paying writers a pittance to churn out serialized titles with fake titles like *The Penny Pickwick, Pickwick in America, Oliver Twiss,* and *Nickelas Nickelbery.*[60] Even worse, these weren't only knock-offs: Lloyd also undercut Dickens on price. The author was outraged, but the domestic copyright laws of his time were toothless, and the appropriation continued. Dickens was also popular in the US, but he received no royalties from the thousands of copies of his books that were sold there. It became clear to Dickens that it would take new laws to protect his livelihood.

In 1842, the author traveled to America to give readings of his works. He also took the opportunity to argue for an international copyright law that would protect his intellectual property outside of Britain. Dickens was surprised, and saddened, to discover that his entreaties largely fell on deaf ears. Americans liked their cheap pirated editions and resented his hectoring them about a moral obligation to provide authors with compensation.[61]

Dickens wasn't the only one to suffer from American indifference regarding the rights of foreign authors. A generation later, US publishers were busily churning out bootleg editions of the *Encyclopædia Britannica.* Charles Scribner's Sons, the authorized US publisher of the work, brought suit against Joseph Stoddart, a Philadelphia publisher who offered a pirated edition that was much cheaper than the legitimate version.

In 1879, when the case was heard by the Supreme Court, Justice Arthur Blair saw no problem with Stoddart's actions. He claimed that "To reproduce a foreign publication is not wrong. There may be a difference of opinion about the morality of republishing here a work that is copyrighted abroad, but the public policy of this country as respects the subject is in favor of such republication."[62] Stoddart's opinion, however, would not be the last word on this subject.

Allegations of plagiarism have resulted in controversies involving popular books and television shows, extended bouts of litigation involving the famous and the not-so-famous, and even public brawls. The following sections of this chapter provide a sampling of these disputes.

THE SLAP HEARD 'ROUND THE WORLD

At the 94th Academy Awards ceremony on March 27, 2022, comedian Chris Rock took to the stage to announce the award for the best documentary feature film. It was during those remarks that Rock made a joke at Jada Pinkett's expense. Her husband, actor Will Smith, marched up to the comedian and slapped him across the face on live TV. It was described by several media outlets as "The slap heard 'round the world."[63] But it wasn't the first time that this variation on Emerson's famous line had been used to describe a public wallop. The phrase had been employed ninety-one years earlier to describe another famous altercation – one that involved an accusation of plagiarism.

The principals in this earlier episode were Dorothy Thompson, Theodore Dreiser, and Sinclair Lewis. Literary feuds are not uncommon – famous writers have big egos – but this one escalated to a donnybrook that had eerie similarities to the later incident in Hollywood.

In 1927, a group of Americans was given a tour of Russia by the Soviet regime. The party included Thompson, a journalist who was head of the Berlin bureau of the *New York Evening Post*, and Dreiser, the novelist and avowed socialist. Based on her trip, Thompson published a series of articles about the new Soviet state in the *Post*, and these were collected into her 1928 book *The New Russia*. A month later, Dreiser also published an account of their tour, in the book *Dreiser Looks at Russia*. Thompson accused Dreiser of plagiarizing her articles "almost word for word" and threatened to sue him.[64] Dreiser made the improbable suggestion that she must have taken *his* notes from his Berlin hotel room.[65]

Earlier in 1928, Thompson had married the novelist Sinclair Lewis, who was awarded the Nobel Prize in Literature two years later. Dreiser, who was fourteen years Lewis's senior, had also been one of the finalists, and was widely seen as Lewis's primary competitor for that honor. There is no question that Dreiser was deeply disappointed at not getting the nod: one of his friends described him as "almost suicidal." Some believed that Lewis bested Dreiser only through "clever maneuvering," such as by making sure that his books were translated and published in Swedish.[66]

In March 1931, three months after the Nobels were awarded in Stockholm, a formal dinner was held at New York City's Metropolitan Club. The gathering was organized to honor the Russian novelist Boris Pilnyak. About thirty writers and critics were present for an evening of food, speeches, and cigars, and the gathering included both Lewis and Dreiser. At one point, host Ray Long called upon Lewis to speak, but he demurred. Instead, he said "I am very happy to meet Mr. Pilnyak. But I do not care to speak in the presence of one man who has plagiarized three thousand words from my wife's book on Russia." After an uncomfortable interval, several other attendees made remarks, and the incident seemed to be forgotten.

At the end of the evening, however, as the attendees were leaving, Dreiser and Lewis were seen talking together. Accounts vary, but Dreiser reportedly called Lewis a liar and a cheat. He then dared Lewis to repeat his allegation about plagiarism. When he did, Dreiser slapped him hard across the face. Lewis said it again and received a second strong blow. At that point, the two men were physically separated to prevent the episode from escalating. Afterwards, Lewis claimed he hadn't struck back only because he was forcibly restrained and said that he stood by his accusation.[67]

The bad blood between the two men continued. A week after the slapping episode, Dreiser claimed that he had been invited to pen the story of *Arrowsmith* before Lewis had. When asked about the assertion, Lewis was dumbfounded. He asked Paul de Kruif, the microbiologist who had assisted him with the novel, to help in refuting Dreiser's calumny.[68]

But had Dreiser truly cribbed from Dorothy Thompson's articles? The evidence is equivocal. At the time of Thompson's accusation, the newspaper columnist Franklin P. Adams reviewed both books and concluded there was a high degree of "verbal similarity" between them.[69] But in 1963, James Donald Adams, *The New York Times* book review editor and columnist, recalled sitting next to Lewis during the infamous dinner thirty years earlier. He opined that both Thompson and Dreiser "had drawn on the same news hand-out in Russia."[70] It's at least possible, therefore, that the similarities were the result of two writers mining the same source material.

As a final point of consideration, it's worth noting that Dreiser had been credibly accused of literary theft on three earlier occasions. He was alleged to have borrowed part of a fable by George Ade for his first book, *Sister Carrie*, published in 1900.[71] His 1925 novel, *An American Tragedy*, was criticized for directly incorporating material from court records and news articles without attribution. And two years before Thompson's claim, his poem "The Beautiful" was said to have nicked part of "Tandy," a story written by his friend Sherwood Anderson.[72] These earlier thefts don't mean that Dreiser was also guilty of borrowing from Thompson, but his history suggests that it wouldn't have been totally out of character for him.

DEEKS V. WELLS

A case of alleged plagiarism from the 1930s illustrates how difficult it can be to litigate a charge of appropriation against a well-known public figure.

In 1919, H. G. Wells began publishing *The Outline of History*, an illustrated story of humanity, from prehistory through the Great War. The work's forty chapters were serialized over the course of a year, then published together in two volumes comprising 1,300 pages. The prolific Wells, then in his early fifties, was still writing the speculative fiction he had become known for, such as *The Invisible Man* and *The War of the Worlds*. But he had also started publishing works on politics and sociological issues, as well as prophecies about the future.

Wells wasn't a historian: he had studied biology and zoology but was largely self-taught in other disciplines. Not surprisingly, therefore, his grand synthesis was criticized by professional historians, some of whom described it as "quite muddle-headed," "misleading," and "silly."[73] However, it was Wells's support for socialism and his acceptance of Darwin's theory of evolution that rankled many readers, especially those in the US. Even though Wells was writing sixty years after the publication of *On the Origin of Species*, the adoption of his *Outline* as a college textbook in Kansas proved to be controversial.[74] The book met with an even chillier reception in Tennessee, where the state legislature banned it from public libraries in 1925.[75]

In Canada, the book was read with great interest by a former college teacher and journalist. Florence Deeks of Toronto became aware of

Wells's *Outline* in late 1920, when she read a glowing review in the magazine *Saturday Night*. She immediately purchased a copy – and was horrified. Deeks had spent the years of World War I laboring over her own history of the world, with the goal of putting the role of women into proper perspective. She submitted her manuscript, titled *The Web of the World's Romance*, to Macmillan of Canada in July 1918, but heard nothing from the company for nine months. At that point, she was informed it had been rejected, and she retrieved her manuscript.

Upon reading the *Outline*, Deeks unwrapped the copy of her typescript that Macmillan had rejected. She found evidence that it had been handled extensively. Some pages were creased and others had been dog-eared. And as she carefully compared her *Web* to the *Outline*, she became convinced that Wells had plagiarized from her typescript.

Deeks spent many months meticulously documenting the pattern of similarities that she found. Overall, the plan of the two works was the same, although Wells had dispensed with her emphasis on women's place in history. In many instances, she found similar words arranged in the same sequence. In addition, several historians compared the works at her request, and they reported similar omissions and, in some cases, even the same errors in both.[76]

Wells had written his *Outline*, consisting of some 400,000 words, in only nine months – an astonishing feat. However, this timeline is plausible because he was known to be a prodigious writer who relied on his wife Catherine to turn his longhand scrawls into clean typescript. And the title page of the *Outline* listed four eminent scholars whom Wells had relied on for "advice and editorial help."[77] Despite the criticism from other professional historians and from politicians, the book became a bestseller: over the next decade, more than two million copies went into print, and the royalties made Wells a wealthy man.[78]

In 1925, Deeks initiated a lawsuit against Wells and Macmillan, in which she sought a half million dollars in damages from the defendants.[79] However, it would take nearly five years for the case to be heard in court, as both sides made changes in their legal counsel.[80] For his part, Wells strenuously denied ever having seen the manuscript of Deeks's book, much less using it as a plan for his own.

The trial finally began in June of 1930. Deeks's counsel needed to convince the Honorable William E. Raney that the similarities between the two books were not mere coincidence, and that Macmillan of Canada had sent her manuscript to England, where Wells made use of it for his *Outline*. The plaintiffs called three historians as expert witnesses to buttress the first part of their case, and the defense called on one of their own.[81]

Some evidence did support the plaintiff's claims. John Saul, the Macmillan employee who took receipt of Deeks's manuscript, had at one point told a golfing buddy that the typescript was sent to New York and then on to England although he later said that it had never left Toronto. Wells's panel of experts, cited on the title page, had conducted no research for the book and wrote none of the *Outline*: they served as little more than consultants. And Wells never produced the longhand original of his manuscript, but only a typescript of his book. Catherine Wells, who had typed the work for her husband, would have been able to provide details about the workflow, but she had passed away three years before the trial began.[82]

It's worth noting that Wells had been accused of plagiarism previously. His 1895 novel, *The Wonderful Visit*, was noted to have similarities with Grant Allen's *The British Barbarians*.[83] And in 1901, the Irish novelist Robert Cromie accused Wells of "practically lift[ing] the first nine chapters" of his 1890 book, *A Plunge into Space*, for *The First Men in the Moon*. Wells, for his part, said he had never heard of Cromie or his book.[84]

After hearing the arguments made by attorneys on both sides, Judge Raney ruled that the case be dismissed. He concluded there was no evidence that the *Web* manuscript had found its way abroad. The plaintiff was also held responsible for costs. Raney referred to Deeks's quest for justice as an "obsession," and claimed that "this action ought not to have been brought."[85] Deeks was disappointed by the outcome but undeterred. She chose to represent herself at an appeal to the Ontario Supreme Court in May of 1931, pleading her case before four judges. But this too was unsuccessful.[86]

Deeks turned to the British courts for redress, again serving as her own counsel. At the end of the October 1932 trial before three judges of the Judicial Committee of the Privy Council (JCPC), she was told for a third time that she had not convinced the court. It was pointed out that collections of historical facts will inevitably have similarities, but that this is not proof of appropriation. "Neither Miss Deeks nor Mr. Wells was present at the beginning of the world," she was told.[87]

Convinced of the righteousness of her cause, Deeks appealed to the JCPC for a rehearing, but her request was denied. In April of 1933, she petitioned her sovereign, King George V, and then the secretary of state for the Home Office, who pronounced her entreaty "frivolous." As a final Hail Mary, she sent a personal letter to the King in May of 1933, again to no avail. After nearly a decade of tilting at windmills, Florence Deeks had exhausted her legal options.

For his part, Wells seemed primarily concerned with the cost of the litigation. A report published after the British trial claimed that Wells had spent $10,250 defending himself – which would be over $200,000 today.[88]

For decades, *Deeks v. Wells* was little remembered, but a 2000 book by historian A. B. McKillop revived interest in the case. Written as narrative nonfiction, it paints a sympathetic portrait of Deeks as a courageous David doing battle against Macmillan and Wells's Goliath. Wells is depicted, not inaccurately, as a dissolute, self-indulgent libertine. McKillop even suggests that Sir Richard Gregory, an astronomer with close ties to Wells, his lifelong friend, and to Macmillan, could have served as the critical conduit for delivering Deeks's manuscript. And McKillop points out, more than once, that the sexist attitudes of the era – in both society and the courts – helped to make Deeks's quest for justice a quixotic one.

But are those the right conclusions to draw? McKillop had interpreted the Deeks case through a historical lens. Law professor Denis Magnusson's take was somewhat different. His 2004 article makes the crucial point that the case and subsequent appeals were heard by judges and not by a jury. Judges would be inclined to require a higher standard of proof regarding infringement: similarities that could sway a jury might be insufficient for those conversant with copyright law. Judge Raney found no paragraphs or even sentences that were the same in both works, and historical facts and information are not protected by copyright.

In addition, without tangible proof of Deeks's manuscript leaving Macmillan's custody, it becomes difficult to argue that it was ever seen by Wells. Magnusson concludes that, given the lack of evidence of substantial similarity or access, Deeks's argument was weak and the case was decided correctly. Finally, Magnusson found no evidence that sexism played a major role in the outcome. Canadian society was undoubtedly more sexist a century ago than it is today, but this seems to have had no bearing on either the length of the Deeks's trials or the written decisions.[89]

GONE WITH THE WIND

Margaret Mitchell's *Gone with the Wind* has been controversial – and tremendously popular – since its publication in 1936. The thousand-page novel, which took the Atlanta native ten years to write, garnered Mitchell the Pulitzer Prize for Fiction. And the 1939 film version, starring Vivien Leigh and Clark Gable, has become iconic. But Mitchell was also accused of plagiarism, and disputes over the book's intellectual property have continued into the twenty-first century.

A few months after *Wind*'s publication, Susan Lawrence Davis filed suit against Macmillan, Mitchell's publisher, for copyright infringement. A dozen years earlier, Davis had released *Authentic History of the Ku Klux Klan, 1865–1877*.[90] The Alabama native had based her book on material provided by her father and others involved in the foundation of the Klan. Davis asked for an eye-popping $6.5 billion in damages, claiming that Mitchell had incorporated "whole pages" from her book, as well as histor-ical information and terms such as "carpetbagger" and "scalawag."[91]

Mitchell, in responding to the suit, claimed to have never heard of Davis's book until the suit was brought. Davis sought an out-of-court settlement, but Macmillan refused to cooperate. Both Mitchell and her publisher felt that the publicity of a court trial would be helpful for *Wind*'s sales.[92] The case was heard by Judge Henry W. Goddard, who dismissed the suit in July 1937. He pointed out that the Klan history contained "no plot or story," and facts about the Civil War and its aftermath were in the public domain.[93]

Later that year, Mitchell was herself the plaintiff in a case brought against theatrical producer Billy Rose. She claimed infringement based on a musical number that had been staged at the Fort Worth Frontier Fiesta. Rose initially claimed that his revue wasn't based on Mitchell's novel. In response to the suit, he said, "We have a Southern plantation. There have been Southern plantations before. We burn a house, but houses were burned before Margaret Mitchell was born. The rest is music and dancing."[94] Six months later, however, Rose had a change of heart and decided to settle out of court. He sent Mitchell a letter of apology and $3,000 – about $65,000 today – as compensation.[95]

Tragically, Margaret Mitchell was struck and fatally injured by a drunk driver in 1949. She was only forty-eight years old when she died. Her husband, John Marsh, passed away three years later, and the rights to Mitchell's novel passed to her brother, Stephens Mitchell. When Stephens passed away in 1983, the estate was inherited by his sons, Eugene and Joseph Mitchell.

Anticipating – and fearing – the expiration of the book's copyright in 2011, the heirs made the controversial decision to authorize a sequel to Mitchell's novel.[96] The author they chose was Alexandra Ripley, who had previously written historical novels set in the South.[97] *Scarlett: The Sequel to Margaret Mitchell's 'Gone with the Wind'*, was published in 1991. Ripley's book was panned by some critics, with *The New York Times* describing it as "disastrous."[98] Nevertheless, it became a bestseller. Another authorized sequel, *Rhett Butler's People* by Donald McCraig, met with a friendlier reception in 2007.[99]

The creators of unauthorized works based on *Gone with the Wind* have faced vigorous legal challenges from Mitchell's estate, although the heirs' track record has been mixed at best. They were successful, for example, in preventing a theater in Atlanta from mounting a stage production titled *Scarlett Fever*. Its creators described the 1979 play as a spoof or parody, but a district court found that the production hewed too closely to Mitchell's novel and the MGM film. As a derivative work, it infringed on the book's copyright. The court ruled for the plaintiffs, granting an injunction against performances of the play.[100]

Soon after the successful litigation of *Scarlett Fever*, a new threat to Mitchell's legacy materialized. In 1982, French author Régine Deforges published a novel titled *La Bicyclette bleue*. The author was sued by the American Trust Bank, holders of Mitchell's world rights, because of the novel's substantial similarity, in its first seventy pages, to *Wind*. Deforges herself freely admitted taking her inspiration from Mitchell's novel. The plaintiffs sought five million francs – more than $2 million today – from the author. Initially, a French court sided with the plaintiffs: the trial judge declared Deforges's work to be "an illicit reproduction," although damages were reduced to two million francs (more than $800,000).[101] However, Deforges appealed the ruling, and the judgment was reversed a year later. In a striking contrast to the original decision, the appeals court described Deforges's work as "an original intellectual creation."[102] The novel would eventually sell millions of copies in France.

Finally, in 2001, the country music songwriter Alice Randall created a stir with her novel *The Wind Done Gone*, a story set in Mitchell's world but told from the point of view of the plantation's enslaved men and women. In March of that year, lawyers for the Mitchell estate sought an injunction to block Houghton Mifflin, Randall's publisher, from releasing the book. The estate characterized Randall's novel as an unauthorized sequel, with fifteen characters in common, as opposed to a parody, which would have been considered fair use. The injunction was granted.[103] However, Houghton Mifflin appealed and had the injunction overturned.[104] And in May, the estate settled the case, requesting that a donation be made by the publisher to Morehouse College.[105] All of the legal wrangling raised the visibility of Randall's book, and initial sales were brisk.[106] Each copy of the novel bore a prominent red seal labeling it as "An Unauthorized Parody."

We live in a world that has become balkanized with regard to copyright status, and this has affected Mitchell's legacy as well. Due to a revision in US copyright law, ninety-five years must elapse before a book enters the public domain. As a result, protection for *Wind* has been extended until 2032. In the European Union, however, the rule is seventy years after the author's death, and *Wind* lost its copyright protection in those countries in 2020.

And in Australia, Mitchell's novel entered the public domain in 1999, as that country's protection extends for only fifty years after the death of the author.[107] As a result, an unauthorized sequel titled *The Winds of Tara*, written by Texas author Katherine Pinotti, cannot be legally published or purchased in the US – but no restrictions exist Down Under, where the novel was released by Fontaine Press. (At the time of this writing, copies of the 400-page paperback can be found on eBay starting at $170.)

"HAVE GUN, WILL TRAVEL"

For an example of how difficult it can be to accuse a large corporation of plagiarism, consider the case of Victor DeCosta. He was quite a character – literally. Born in Massachusetts in 1908, he worked as a cowboy and rodeo rider in Texas in his younger days. He eventually moved to Rhode Island, became a heavy equipment mechanic, and had five children.[108] But he never lost his love for the Wild West.

Starting in 1947, DeCosta began making appearances at parades, horse shows, and charities. Riding a black stallion, he dressed in black cowboy attire and sported a rakish mustache. His costume included a gun holster emblazoned with a silver knight chess piece.[109] At one of his events, someone in the crowd shouted "*paladino*" at him. DeCosta liked the term, which means "champion" in Italian. He adopted the English form of the name, Paladin, as his moniker.[110] Over the years, DeCosta distributed tens of thousands of business cards that featured the knight piece. Each bore the words "Have Gun Will Travel, Wire Paladin," followed by a post office box number in Rhode Island.

In September of 1957, ten years after DeCosta created his persona, CBS began airing a Western called "Have Gun – Will Travel." The series was a hit for the network and 225 episodes were produced over six seasons. Richard Boone starred as a character named Paladin, a West Point graduate and cavalry veteran of the Civil War. Paladin found employment by taking on clients seeking a private investigator, an expert gunslinger – or both.

Each episode of "Have Gun" began with a close-up of the holster of Paladin's Colt single-action Army revolver, emblazoned with the figure of a chess knight in platinum. Paladin dressed in black and sported a mustache. He drummed up business by passing out calling cards that featured the knight piece and the words "Have Gun Will Travel, Wire Paladin, San Francisco."[111]

DeCosta was unaware of his televised doppelgänger until a family dinner in the fall of 1957, when a sibling mentioned that they had seen Victor on a program the night before. Astonished, DeCosta made a point of tuning in to "Have Gun" the following Saturday and was astounded. He immediately began to seek legal representation.

Screenwriters Herb Meadow and Sam Rolfe, the creators of "Have Gun," maintained they had come up with the Paladin character on their own. They claimed to have never visited the parts of New England where DeCosta made his appearances. And the business card's motto? Meadow and Rolfe said it was derived from "Have tux, will travel," a showbiz saying that had been circulating for years,[112] and one used as a title by Bob Hope for a book he published in 1954.[113] Any similarities between the television character and DeCosta's alter ego, the network claimed, were accidental and coincidental.

Because DeCosta hadn't copyrighted his character or his cards, he chose to sue CBS for misappropriation. His case, however, wasn't heard until almost a decade later, in 1966. A jury found for the plaintiff and awarded DeCosta $150,000 ($1.4 million today). CBS appealed the decision, and an appeals court set aside the verdict two months later. Even though there was evidence of appropriation, the appeals court concluded that DeCosta's "pure" character had never appeared in an incorporated work. As a result, the law didn't provide him any protection.[114] In addition, DeCosta couldn't prove financial damages, since he had never charged for his appearances as Paladin.[115] The case was appealed to the Supreme Court, but the justices declined to review it.[116]

A few years later, DeCosta took another run at CBS by alleging that the network had infringed on his character's trademark. Once again, he was successful in the initial trial: the judge found that the defendants had "intentionally misappropriated the property of the plaintiff."[117] But a year later, an appeals court overturned the lower court's ruling. Trademark infringement, the appeals court declared in 1975, requires confusion on the part of the public. The chief judge ruled that the plaintiff had failed to demonstrate "that the public had been deceived."[118]

A third round of litigation occurred in the early 1990s. In 1977, DeCosta registered for trademark protection for the Paladin character and his card, then filed suit against Viacom International, the distributor of "Have Gun" in syndication. In September of 1991, a jury in Providence found Viacom guilty of violating DeCosta's trademark. He was awarded $1 million in compensation for his loss and $2.5 million in punitive damages, for a cool sum of $3.5 million (nearly $8 million today).[119]

Victor DeCosta died in January of 1993 at the age of eighty-four, sixteen months after the Viacom verdict.[120] He had spent thirty-four years and the bulk of his savings trying to obtain compensation for the appropriation of his Paladin character. When interviewed after finally triumphing in court, he declared: "The money to me is secondary at my age. I just wanted to get justice. I'm a stubborn old man. When I own something, I don't allow nobody to steal it."[121] Unfortunately for him, he did not live long enough to receive the money he had been awarded at trial, and it passed to his heirs instead.

CHAPTER 2

The Plagiarism Hunters

COPYRIGHT TRAPS

Lillian V. Mountweazel, the American photographer, was born in Bangs, Ohio, in 1942. After dabbling in fountain design, she found her true passion behind the camera. Mountweazel became known for photographic essays of offbeat topics, such as Parisian cemeteries and the letterboxes of rural America. Sadly, her promising career was cut short in 1973, when she died in a conflagration while working for *Combustibles* magazine.[1]

This terse accounting of Mountweazel's brief career can be found nestled between entries for "Mount Vernon" and "Mount Wilson Observatory" in the fourth edition of the *New Columbia Encyclopedia*, published in 1975. But not a word of it is true – Mountweazel didn't meet an untimely, albeit ironic end, and she wasn't a photographer. In truth, she never existed: everything in the biographical entry was fabricated by the editors. But why would such an authoritative reference work include an entirely fictitious article?

Welcome to the world of copyright traps. They are employed because there is a long history of encyclopedists, lexicographers, and cartographers cribbing from one another. However, this type of plagiarism can be difficult to prove. Facts can't be copyrighted, and a definition for a simple concept like "chair" doesn't allow for a lot of leeway. A dictionary entry would need to mention that chairs have a seat, a back, legs, and possibly arms, but it would be difficult to prove that an entry including those attributes had been poached from an earlier wordlist.

As a result, the editors of reference works have taken to adding fictitious words, concepts, and place names to their wares in order to protect their intellectual property. The specter of a fraudulent entry is intended to deter would-be poachers: should such an entry reappear in some later compilation, the creator of the made-up material can accuse the pirate of infringing on copyrighted content.[2]

There are various kinds of copyright traps, with names like "canary traps" or "honeytokens," but they are commonly referred to as Mountweazels, in honor of the *Columbia Encyclopedia's* phantom photographer. And although this term was coined relatively recently, the concept of a copyright trap is far older.

Consider the fanciful entry "jungftak," which appeared in the 1943 edition of *Webster's Twentieth Century Dictionary*. The editors defined this as "a Persian bird, the male of which had only one wing, on the right side, and the female only one wing, on the left side; instead of the missing wings, the male had a hook of bone, and the female an eyelet of bone, and it was by uniting hook and eye that they were enabled to fly – each, when alone, had to remain on the ground."[3] This counterfeit entry certainly gets extra credit for originality.

Or how about fake telephone numbers? A 1991 Supreme Court case involved such duplicitous digits. The Rural Telephone Service Co. of Kansas had published a directory for its subscribers that intentionally included four fictitious listings.[4] Feist Publications, another directory company, sought to license Rural Telephone's list but was refused. Feist used the list anyway, and when the new directory was found to include the fake numbers, Rural Telephone sued for infringement. Even though Feist had been caught red-handed, the Supreme Court ruled against Rural Telephone. In her opinion, Justice Sandra Day O'Connor appealed to the doctrine that facts cannot be copyrighted, and that even a large collection of such facts, like a phone directory, cannot be protected.[5]

Mountweazels have been found in all types of reference works. Rupert Hughes's 1903 *Musical Guide* contains an extensive alphabetical list of musical terms, with the final entry being "zzxjoanw." (Hughes helpfully explains that it's pronounced like "shaw.") He also informs the reader that it derives from the Māori language and can refer to a drum, a fife, or a conclusion.[6] Hughes's guide was republished several times, but the veracity of the entry doesn't seem to have been questioned until 1976, when Peter Cohen pointed out its many suspicious elements: the unlikely pronunciation (like the exclamation "pshaw"), the multiplicity of meanings, and the fact that dictionaries of Māori don't include it. Cohen describes the entry as a hoax, but Hughes may have intended it to serve as a copyright trap.[7]

There is even such a trap lurking in perhaps the world's most distinguished reference work. When the compact edition of the *Oxford English Dictionary* was released in 1971, a review written by commentator William F. Buckley included the rumor that it contained "a spurious word of the editors' super-secret devising, so that their grandchildren might know the contemporary estate (sic) of plagiarism."[8] It is unknown if the phantom word has been discovered.

This tradition of including false entries has continued into the twenty-first century: a fake word was added to the *New Oxford American Dictionary* in 2001. That dictionary's editor, however, let slip that the impostor was a word beginning with the letter "E." With that clue, a team of linguistic sleuths determined that the impostor was "esquivalience" (defined as the shirking of one's duties). And this trap did snare at least one victim: the word was incorporated into the online Dictionary.com, although it has since been removed.[9]

Copyright traps have also been employed by mapmakers who add "paper towns" or "trap streets" to their products to protect their intellectual property. For example, Google added a place named "Argleton" to the English county of Lancashire, but it's not clear whether this was intended as a copyright trap or was simply an error, and it no longer appears on Google Maps.[10]

The best-known paper town is the fictitious village of Agloe, supposedly located in Delaware County in New York state. It was inserted into a map produced by the General Drafting Company in 1937. In this case, however, life imitated art: a general store bearing the name was said to have opened at that location a few years later.[11] When Agloe later appeared on a map produced by Rand McNally, General Drafting threatened to sue, but McNally argued that the paper town had become real.[12] The case of Agloe may sound familiar because it appears prominently in a 2008 young adult novel *Paper Towns* by John Green, as well as in the 2015 film based on the book.

High-tech examples of copyright traps can be found in microscopic designs etched into integrated circuits. These were painstakingly added by chip designers to protect their company's intellectual property. This chip art, visible only through a microscope, might feature patterns, images, or even messages.[13] In 1984, US copyright law was revised to explicitly cover chip masks, and as a result such artwork was no longer needed. Galleries of these minuscule masterpieces can still be found online, however.[14]

The web pages that make up the internet consist of code that is visible for all to see – as well as to appropriate. An example of this was alleged to have occurred in 2001, when coders for the Scientology organization Narconon were accused of helping themselves to the design and layout of the popular British e-magazine *Urban75*. The similarities between the two websites could have been chalked up to coincidence. However, the designer of *Urban75* claimed that the Narconon website included his bespoke JavaScript programming – designed for pop-up windows – even though it wasn't used by the site. In this case, the nonfunctional code was the smoking gun suggesting that appropriation had occurred – although the executive director for Narconon stated that he didn't think infringement took place.[15]

There have been other cases in which plagiarists have outed themselves by including unique details in their derivative works. In 1698, for example, the French cartographer Nicolas de Fer executed a map of North America. It includes a charming detail: a cartouche of industrious beavers constructing a dam near present-day Niagara Falls. This element, however, also appears in an engraving produced seventeen years later by the English cartographer Herman Moll. Moll didn't give de Fer credit, but the inclusion of the dam-building scene in his "Beaver Map" reveals the source of Moll's handiwork.[16]

In 1942, the feature columnist Beth Brown wrote an article for *Cosmopolitan* about Clara Barton, the founder of the American Red Cross. Unfortunately for Brown, she relied a little too heavily on Mercedes De Acosta's unpublished screenplay about Barton, titled *Angel in Service*. De Acosta had decided to spice up Barton's straitlaced life by inventing fictitious characters for her screenplay, including a love interest named Tom Maxwell – a moniker bestowed in honor of De

Acosta's favorite brand of coffee. Brown credulously incorporated these details into her story about Barton, and De Acosta prevailed in a plagiarism suit that she filed against Brown and the magazine.[17]

THE SECRET OF NIH

Technology has made it easier than ever to engage in plagiarism – but the same is also true of plagiarism detection. In the early 1990s, a government employee developed a computer program designed to identify unattributed appropriation. And its use to sniff out academic plagiarism would lead to a series of controversial accusations, a great deal of acrimony, and even a hunger strike.

As with many projects that end up going off the rails, cell biologist Ned Feder and chemist Walter Stewart began their work with the best of intentions. The scientists were employed by the National Institutes of Health (NIH) in Bethesda, Maryland, where they initially collaborated in studying the nerve cells of snails. Over time, however, the focus of their work shifted to ferreting out scientific misconduct, even though they weren't affiliated with the NIH office tasked with identifying fraud.

By the time their work was featured in a 1988 article in *The New York Times*, the pair had made both friends and enemies in the scientific establishment. Their investigative work had resulted in several high-profile discoveries of questionable research ethics and had won them praise from members of Congress. The article in the *Times* also noted – perhaps prophetically – their "fanatical" devotion to this task.[18]

In 1992, Stewart created a tool to augment the duo's arsenal of fraud detection methods: a computer program that partly automated the search for instances of potential plagiarism. Their microcomputer, when fed papers that the researchers had digitized, could be programmed to identify thirty-character sequences that were identical between two papers.[19] (Stewart chose this number so that the program would ignore lengthy but generic sequences, like "deoxyribonucleic acid," but still detect relatively short instances of copying between two texts.)[20] The device became known as their "plagiarism machine." It would prove to be the duo's most important legacy, but it was also responsible for their downfall.

In 1990, at an academic meeting in Illinois, a professor of literature named Robert Bray described similarities he had discovered between an Abraham Lincoln biography written in 1952 by historian Benjamin Thomas and one published twenty-five years later by Stephen B. Oates, a professor at the University of Massachusetts Amherst.[21] Oates strongly disputed the accusation and pointed out that he and Thomas had made use of the same source materials.[22]

The issue was taken up by the American Historical Association (AHA), which launched an investigation into the plagiarism charge. Oates criticized the investigation as partisan and compiled a 200-page rebuttal.[23] Nearly two dozen of Oates's colleagues reviewed his response and signed a statement asserting that the accusation was without merit.[24]

Concerned that the AHA might exonerate Oates, the historian Michael Burlingame approached Stewart and Feder at NIH and asked if they might use their software to analyze the two Lincoln biographies. Questions had also been raised about possible plagiarism in other books that Oates had written – biographies of Martin Luther King Jr. and William Faulkner published during the 1980s – and Burlingame requested that the duo analyze those texts as well. Stewart and Feder digitized the three biographies by Oates as well as sixty-three books that the historian might have copied from in creating his own accounts of the lives of the three men.

In early 1993, after four months of labor, Stewart and Feder submitted to the AHA a 1,400-page review of Oates's work. They had found, they claimed, 175 instances of overlap in Oates's book on Lincoln, 240 in his book on the life of King, and another 200 in his tome on Faulkner. Their conclusion was simple: Stephen Oates was a serial plagiarist.

The AHA, however, was not convinced by this form of evidence. "Computer-assisted identification of similar words and phrases in itself," the Association declared, "does not constitute a sufficient basis for a plagiarism or misuse complaint."[25] Later that year, the AHA issued a nebulous ruling that neither fully exonerated nor censured Oates: there were similarities of expression in the two Lincoln biographies, but the Association chose not to characterize these correspondences as plagiarism. The equivocal nature of the report's conclusions satisfied no one.[26]

Furious, Oates counterattacked. Why, he asked, had two government employees, in the service of the National Institute of Diabetes and

Digestive and Kidney Diseases section of the NIH, spent months of their employer's time investigating books by historians, who had never received government funding? Oates took his complaint to the NIH and to sympathetic members of Congress, including Senator Paul Simon. In a letter to the director of the NIH, Simon observed, "I don't see where the action by these two gentlemen fits into NIH's mission in any way."[27]

The Oates controversy threw into sharp relief an ongoing debate about what, exactly, constitutes plagiarism. Is it the appropriation of a particularly vivid or apt expression from someone else's writing? Or is it the appropriation of a sequence of words? This was, after all, what Walter Stewart's program was designed to hunt for. And if plagiarism is defined as cribbing consecutive words, then how many must be taken before the author crosses a line and commits theft? As we saw in Chapter 1, there are no agreed-upon answers to such questions.[28]

But the story of Stewart and Feder doesn't end there. The NIH's budget is controlled by Congress, and there was political pressure at the Institute to rein in the work of two employees who seemed to have gone rogue. In response, in April 1993, the so-called fraud-busters were reassigned to new duties: Stewart was transferred to a new laboratory, and Feder was tasked with reviewing grant proposals submitted to the Institute. Their old offices were shuttered and their voluminous files locked away. Believing that their work in ferreting out misconduct was more important than their new responsibilities, neither man was happy about their assignments.[29]

Stewart was particularly aggrieved, believing that he and Feder had been denied due process and any chance to appeal the reassignment. He was also concerned that they were not allowed to finish work on nearly two dozen open cases of misconduct they had been investigating. Stewart decided to protest the NIH's decision in a dramatic and public way by going on a hunger strike – a highly unusual action for a scientist to take. After three weeks of consuming only water, Stewart had shed twenty pounds, and he told a reporter for *The New York Times* that he was growing weaker.[30]

On the twenty-fifth day of Stewart's hunger strike, the Department of Health and Human Services (HHS), of which NIH is a part, said they would review the reassignments. Stewart, however, chose to continue his fast, even though he was approaching the point where his actions might have serious medical consequences.[31] After thirty-three days without food, Stewart had lost thirty pounds and his blood pressure was dangerously low. A physician implored him to end his strike, as did his supporters in Congress. With other whistleblowing scientists taking up his cause and fasting for twenty-four hours each, Stewart felt he had made his point and ended his strike.[32]

Ultimately, neither Stewart nor Feder was successful in challenging their reassignments. An investigation by the General Accounting Office failed to find evidence that HHS had retaliated against them in violation of the Whistleblower Protection Act. As a result, the two men continued their work on scientific fraud on their own time.[33] Feder left the NIH in 2006 and joined the Project on Government Oversight (POGO), which allowed him to continue investigating scientific misconduct.[34]

In hindsight, Stewart and Feder's plagiarism machine can be seen as a proof of concept, demonstrating that the power of computers could be harnessed to ferret out textual piracy. More sophisticated versions of their early efforts would soon make themselves felt in classrooms, boardrooms, and the publishing industry.

THE PLAGIARISM POLICE

A handful of people have gained notoriety as plagiarism hunters, detectives, or sleuths. It doesn't appear that anyone has ever consciously sought out such a job title, however. Instead, these are individuals who find themselves taking on a particular role due to circumstance. They do seem to share certain personality characteristics, however: they are often described as meticulous, driven, and obsessive, but otherwise their backgrounds are varied. Thumbnail sketches for five of the best-known follow.

* * *

British spy novelist Jeremy Duns seems to have had his conversion experience in late 2011, when he reviewed an advance copy of *Assassin of Secrets* by debut novelist Q. R. Markham. Duns was initially impressed and declared the mystery novel to be an "instant classic."[35] However, an online allegation of plagiarism by a James Bond fan caused Duns to reassess his opinion. After scrutinizing the text, he claimed that "the whole book had been stitched together from passages taken from a range of spy novels published in the last 30 years," including a six-page stretch copied from *License Renewed*, a Bond novel by John Gardner.[36] Markham's publisher, Little, Brown & Company, ended up recalling the book's 6,500-copy print run,[37] and Markham, whose real name was Quentin Rowan, apologized to Duns and the authors that he had borrowed from.[38]

In the same month, Duns called attention to similar passages in Lenore Hart's *The Raven's Bride* and *The Very Young Mrs. Poe*, published in 1956 by Cothburn O'Neal. Duns characterized Hart's novel as "unbelievably plagiarized,"[39] but Hart claimed the resemblance was due to both novelists making use of the same sources.[40] And in this case, Hart's publisher, St. Martin's Press, defended their author: her book was not recalled.

Duns took to his blog in 2013 to complain about Nate Thayer's "25 Years of Slam Dunk Diplomacy,"[41] claiming that the account of Dennis Rodman's visit to North Korea had been "massively and unambiguously" plagiarized from Mark Zeigler's "The Oddest Fan," which appeared in the *San Diego Union-Tribune* seven years earlier.[42] In his defense, Thayer wrote that "every reference in the story was properly cited and the overwhelming amount was obtained through old fashioned legwork where I personally contacted dozens of sources and interviewed them."[43] An article about the affair in the *Columbia Journalism Review* concluded that Thayer's attributions were "sloppy," but argued that this was not the same as plagiarism[44] – demonstrating, once again, the ambiguity of that loaded term.

* * *

It was in January of 2013 that poet Ira Lightman began his career as a poetry sleuth. After coming across online speculation that a prizewinning poem by Christian Ward might not be original, Lightman proved that "The Deer at Exmoor" was plagiarized from a poem by Helen Mort.[45] (Ward, for his part, issued an apology, claiming he had merely modeled his effort on Mort's and had mistakenly submitted "a premature draft" to the competition.[46])

As time went by, Lightman began to receive tips about other suspicious cases, and he found that he enjoyed this sort of detective work. Later that year, for example, Lightman demonstrated that "dozens" of verses by Australian poet Graham Nunn were "blatant rip-offs." (Nunn, for his part, posted a "vague defense" to his blog.[47])

A few months later, American poet Charles Hartman was alerted that one of his poems had shown up in an online venue. "A Little Song," which Hartman had published in 1974, had been transformed into "Dead Wife Singing" by the English poet David Morgan.[48] It was Lightman who assembled a team, via Facebook, that quickly uncovered a dozen more appropriations by Morgan, with at least one theft dating back to the 1980s. Caught dead to rights, Morgan apologized and vowed that he would copy no more.[49]

And in 2015, Lightman played a role in proving that Sheree Mack had plagiarized from poets Ellen Phethean and Joan Johnston. Mack initially admitted to "slackness and carelessness" but later described the experience as "a public lynching."[50] The following year, Lightman came across an online posting about Pierre DesRuisseaux, the recently deceased Canadian Parliamentary Poet Laureate. A Facebook group called "Plagiarism Alerts" claimed that that DesRuisseaux had appropriated from Maya Angelou. Lightman confirmed the claim, and also discovered that thirty of the forty-seven poems in DesRuisseaux's volume, *Tranches de vie*, drew heavily from other poets, including Tupac Shakur. The book was withdrawn by the publisher, but no public statement was made.[51] And in 2020, Lightman claimed that Australian poet Judith Beveridge borrowed phrases from others for several of her works and had done so "for decades." Beveridge admitted to the borrowing and expressed regret "for not being more scrupulous." [52]

The poet Sheenagh Pugh once told Lightman that "plagiarists never do it just once,"[53] and his experiences with poetry appropriators have convinced him of the truth of Pugh's observation.

* * *

In 2004, Tom Matrka was a doctoral student in mechanical engineering at Ohio University, specializing in research on thermal conductivity. As he read the work of his advisor's previous students, he discovered a thesis that recycled fifty pages from an earlier student's work. Over the course of several months, he spent hours in the library and eventually identified nearly thirty theses that contained plagiarized content, sometimes including the exact same typographical errors and misspelled words as in other theses.

When Matrka reported what he had found to the school authorities, no action was taken until a review committee verified a twenty-year pattern of "rampant and flagrant plagiarism" in the school's mechanical engineering program. Altogether, thirty-nine problematic theses were identified.[54] One student's degree was revoked, and other graduates were asked to rewrite the problematic sections of their theses. Some of the faculty advisors were sanctioned, and one faculty member's contract was not renewed.[55]

* * *

In 2013, Stanford microbiologist Elisabeth Bik typed a few sentences from her published work into a search engine and discovered her words popping up in an online book chapter. What started out as idle curiosity led to more checking, and ultimately the discovery of thirty biomedical articles with significant attribution issues. Bik contacted the editors of the journals in question and succeeded in getting some of the cribbed papers retracted. She then expanded her focus to identifying problematic images in published research.[56]

Bik began finding images that had been stretched, flipped, rotated, or otherwise manipulated – a common practice in papers with falsified or fabricated data. This pursuit caused her to leave her academic post so that she could ferret out scientific fraud full-time. By the end of 2022, she had examined the contents of about 100,000 papers and had identified about 6,500 with duplicated images or other serious problems. She has been successful in having nearly a thousand of these faked papers retracted.[57]

* * *

As we have seen, plagiarism sleuths typically specialize in their fields of expertise, like spy novels, poetry, mechanical engineering, or microbiology. This was not the case for Stefan Weber. The Austrian academic became radicalized when, in 2005, he discovered that a large portion of his dissertation had been appropriated by Joachim Fels, a German theologian. Weber's persistence led to a university investigation, which resulted in Fels having his doctorate revoked. Fels, for his part, claimed that his failure to cite Weber was due to "an editorial mishap" and was not intentional.[58] The Fels case garnered a good deal of attention, and, like the poetry sleuth Ira Lightman, Weber began receiving tips about other suspected cases, which often involved politicians.

One of these was Christine Aschbacher, the Austrian Labor Minister. The problems that Weber identified in her master's and doctoral theses caused Aschbacher to resign her position in 2021.[59] Later that year, Weber accused Annalena Baerbock, a co-leader of Germany's Green Party, of plagiarizing for her book about national renewal.[60] In response, Baerbock claimed to have used "publicly available sources" but that "it would have certainly been better if I had worked with a list of references."[61] The Green Party politician, who was a candidate for chancellor, ended up finishing third, with 15 percent of the vote, in that fall's federal election.

In May of 2022, Weber targeted Diana Kinnert, who had been a rising star in Germany's Christian Democratic Union (CDU). He accused Kinnert of over 200 instances of improper or missing citations in books she had published in 2017 and 2021. Kinnert apologized for her carelessness.[62]

However, not all of Weber's accusations have been on target. In 2007, he took Johannes Hahn, the Austrian Minister of Science and Research, to task for problematic citations in his dissertation. Hahn was cleared of that charge in 2011,[63] and went on to serve as the European Commissioner for Budget and Administration.

Not surprisingly, many of the plagiarism hunters' subjects have been highly critical of their accusers. Bik, in particular, has come under fire from her detractors. She's been referred to as a "witch hunter" and subjected to online harassment. However, she has also received the support of thousands of her fellow scientists who signed petitions on her behalf.[64] And Weber has essentially become a hired gun who charges clients up to $400 per hour for his sleuthing services.[65] Although the ethical issues involved in plagiarism detection can be complex, the work also appears to be lucrative.

BLOWING THE WHISTLE ON THE WHISTLEBLOWERS

In some cases, it isn't the plagiarist who is vilified. Instead, it's the person who calls attention to the appropriation who gets the blame. Typically, this happens when a whistleblower's revelation creates bad PR for an institution. When an author is accused of plagiarism, for example, it's not unusual for their publisher to rally to their defense, often going so far as casting aspersions on the accuser. Similarly, a charge of plagiarism against an elected official may result in pushback from other leaders. Some of the most vitriolic reactions, however, have occurred when accusations of plagiarism are made against student athletes.

In September of 1999, Linda Bensel-Meyers, an English professor at the University of Tennessee, had had enough. As the director of her department's first-year composition program, she witnessed many student athletes receiving special treatment by the school. She finally decided to go public with her concerns, claiming that the university had engaged in a pattern of academic fraud, with the goal of maintaining athletic eligibility, for nearly forty students, most of whom were football players. The abuses included altered grades, exemptions from probationary status, and instances of plagiarism. In the latter case, she reported that tutors for the Athletics Department were writing papers for several of their student athletes.[66]

At the beginning of the 2000 football season, Bensel-Meyers informed the NCAA that three of the football team's freshman players had submitted essays that bore striking similarities to one another. This was, she claimed, the tip of the iceberg of the school's "institutional plagiarism" problem.[67] An investigation resulted in one-game suspensions for four players, although no NCAA rules were found to have been violated.

Given the near-religious fanaticism of Volunteer fans in Knoxville, it's not surprising that Bensel-Meyers experienced significant backlash. She found herself the target of lawsuits, and said that the controversy put a strain on her marriage. She received curses and threats from more rabid Vol fans. Colleagues began to anonymously contribute to a legal defense fund for her.[68] By the following year, her marriage had ended, and only one member of the UT faculty was publicly supporting her.[69] In 2003, after receiving death threats that mentioned her kids, she decamped from Knoxville to join the faculty at the University of Denver.[70]

A decade after the episode in Tennessee, another high-profile case came to light at the University of North Carolina (UNC) at Chapel Hill. In this instance, the whistleblower was investigative journalist Dan Kane of Raleigh's *The News & Observer*. His inquiries uncovered a host of problems involving athletes and academic fraud at UNC. Like Bensel-Meyers at Tennessee, Kane documented unauthorized grade changes and even fake classes that were designed to benefit the school's student athletes.

The problems came to light at UNC in 2010. Michael McAdoo, a football linebacker, was found to have violated NCAA rules by accepting too much assistance from a tutor for a term paper assignment. (Specifically, McAdoo's tutor was found to have written the paper's footnotes and bibliography for him.) Seeking reinstatement, McAdoo filed suit against UNC, which led to his assignment being made public. The document was scrutinized by an anonymous supporter of North Carolina State – an intense rival of UNC's – who found it to be "a compendium of plagiarized material."[71] Kane, the investigative reporter, became aware of the claims about McAdoo's paper and verified the appropriation: his analysis found that 39 percent of the twenty-one-page paper's content had been taken from other sources.[72] This led to a broader journalistic investigation, with *The News & Observer* requesting student records that the university refused to supply, citing privacy concerns.

Kane's reporting raised issues concerning another student athlete, wide receiver Erik Highsmith. He was found to have plagiarized for a course blog by appropriating material originally written by a group of eleven-year-old children.[73] The plagiarism issues were part of a larger cheating scandal that eventually came to light. The scandal led to the resignations or firings of four Chapel Hill employees, as well as the imposition of NCAA sanctions against the school.[74]

Like Bensel-Meyers at the University of Tennessee, Kane was subjected to threats of violence from angry Tarheel fans who believed that he had a vendetta against UNC. Kane's refusal to be intimidated led to his receiving the Frank McCulloch Award for Courage in Journalism in 2015.[75]

Finally, at Florida State University in 2013, it was Christina Suggs, a doctoral student, who stepped forward to complain about the pressure she received to overlook plagiarism by student athletes. Suggs, who was serving as a teaching assistant in an online hospitality course, claimed that Chris Casher, a defensive end, "copied every portion of his project" and provided no citations. The course instructor allowed Casher to redo the assignment. (Casher, for his part, did not respond publicly to Suggs's accusation.)

In other cases involving student athletes, no action was taken at all. As reported by *The New York Times*, the work of three other members of the football team also "contained page after page of text lifted verbatim from websites."[76] To Suggs, the lack of consequences for plagiarism was a clear example of favoritism benefiting the school's student athletes.

After she reported these and other issues, school officials stated that a "leading law firm" had investigated and discovered no infractions of NCAA rules. The university did cancel some of the online hospitality courses and made changes to increase the rigor of others. However, the school officials stated that the changes were not the result of Suggs's allegations.[77]

As the fall 2013 semester came to an end, Suggs was told that her position as a teaching assistant would not be continued. The reason given was that she had not accrued enough credit hours with the business school. For her part, Suggs believed the reason was her allegations against the student athletes and the subsequent investigation. She decided to leave the university before obtaining her doctorate, even though that had been her dream for several years.[78]

* * *

The dangers of giving commencement speeches will be discussed in Chapter 6, but one example is described here because it also involves blaming the whistleblower.

In May of 2019, the principal of Parkersburg High School, Kenneth DeMoss, delivered remarks at his school's annual commencement ceremony. At a party after the event, graduating senior Abigail Smith overheard someone say that DeMoss's speech sounded like one that had been given by the actor Ashton Kutcher. After searching online, Smith found that her principal's address bore a striking similarity to the remarks made by Kutcher in accepting Nickelodeon's 2013 Teen Choice Ultimate Choice Award.

Smith, who had been the school's speech and debate team captain, was surprised and disappointed. She spliced together a video to illustrate the "several near-verbatim sections" in the two addresses, which she then uploaded to social media. Not long afterwards, DeMoss contacted Smith and asked her to take the video down. He told her that he hadn't plagiarized Kutcher because he had used examples from his own life. When Smith refused to delete the video, DeMoss enlisted a teacher to ask her to do so. Once again, she refused, claiming that "If I am held to a standard, I believe that my administrators and faculty should also be held to the same standard."[79]

DeMoss then sent a letter of explanation to the senior class and their parents, stating in part that he had received no compensation of any kind for his remarks, although he allowed that he was "not as specific as I should have been" to give credit to the original source. He also posted the letter to Facebook but later deleted it. He did apologize at a county Board of Education meeting, and the board voted to suspend him for five days without pay. (The same group had given DeMoss a Principal of the Year award a few weeks earlier.)

In reporting the episode, *The Washington Post* pointed out that Kutcher's Teen Choice remarks had racked up more than 3.5 million views on YouTube, so the principal should have realized that some of his students might recognize it. But it was the reaction of some of the parents that is the most puzzling. In online comments, a few refused to admit that DeMoss had acted inappropriately. Instead, they focused their ire on Smith, who they criticized for "snitching" and "being vindictive."[80] Smith, for her part, maintained that "I just wanted people to know the truth."[81]

ACADEMIC MISCONDUCT

In November of 1988, the career of Dr. Shervert Frazier was derailed by an allegation of plagiarism. At the time, the sixty-seven-year-old physician was one of the most prominent psychiatric researchers in the country: a faculty member of the Harvard Medical School, he was also the director of its affiliated McLean Hospital. In addition, Frazier had recently completed a two-year stint as the director of the National Institute of Mental

Health (NIMH) – the primary federal agency for funding research on psychological disorders. Directing the NIMH is considered the "top job in American psychiatry."[82] He was a highly effective administrator and fundraiser and thought of as a role model for his junior colleagues at the hospital.

Frazier was also a prolific contributor to the scientific literature, with nine books and ninety journal articles and book chapters to his credit.[83] One of these journal articles, however, would serve as the catalyst that would seriously damage his reputation – at least temporarily – and nearly end his career.

Frazier's plagiarism was discovered in April of 1988 by Paul Scatena, a graduate student at the University of Rochester. He had been reviewing the literature on phantom limb pain, a brain phenomenon in which amputees experience unpleasant sensations from a missing arm or leg. Scatena came across a 1970 review article by Frazier and noticed some inaccuracies in the article's citations. He then experienced a strong sense of *déjà vu*: it seemed as if he had read one of the paragraphs in the paper before. Scatena's hunch turned out to be correct, as a check revealed that the passage in question had appeared in a *Scientific American* article in 1961.[84]

Was this an isolated instance of carelessness, or a hint that other problems lurked in the psychiatrist's writings? Over several weeks, the graduate student checked other articles by Frazier and discovered additional instances of appropriation. In total, Scatena found plagiarized material in four papers written between 1966 and 1975. The material that Frazier had borrowed came from two journal articles and a previously published book.[85]

In August, Scatena mailed his findings to the dean of the Harvard Medical School, where a faculty conduct committee investigated and verified Scatena's claims about Frazier's appropriation. Appearing before the committee, Frazier accepted the findings but claimed that the borrowing had been unintentional. Under pressure from his dean, Frazier resigned his positions – the directorship of McLean Hospital and his Harvard professorship – the day before Thanksgiving.[86]

Reactions to Frazier's transgressions and to his forced resignation were mixed, and the *Times* published several letters that weighed in on both sides of the issue. Several members of the psychiatric community argued that Frazier's punishment was simply too severe. Any instances of sloppy scholarship over a decade earlier, they argued, had to be weighed against his prominence in the field and his contributions to psychiatry. Plagiarism is wrong, one colleague opined, but copying material for a review article or two isn't as bad as falsifying or fabricating data, and so a lesser punishment, such as a reprimand, would have been appropriate.[87] Other letter writers praised Harvard for doing the right thing: one commented that "To condone, minimize or explain away such behavior sends the wrong message and besmirches a noble profession."[88]

In deciding on their course of action, officials at Harvard had to consider the potential damage to the school's reputation. Other episodes of academic misconduct had transpired during the previous decade, and the school's response to these had been criticized as both too little and too late. As a result, the officials may have felt that they had no choice but to respond forcefully to the allegations against Frazier.[89]

Equally important may have been the desire to avoid the appearance of hypocrisy. The dean of the Medical School, Daniel Tosteson, was quoted as saying, "Our university rules are pretty harsh. You can't be a student and plagiarize. Are we to say it's O.K. for a professor?"[90]

The allegations against Frazier made waves in part because of the prominence of the individual who stood accused. In addition, some of the psychiatrist's defenders were unhappy that the *Times* chose to run the story on its front page, under the headline "Eminent Harvard Professor Quits Over Plagiarism, University Says."[91] Stories about academic misconduct rarely make page one of the Gray Lady, and front-page stories about plagiarism are rarer still.

That's not to say that the *Times* hasn't weighed in on such conduct in the past. A century earlier, in July of 1885, the paper ran a half-dozen stories about Charles Kendall Adams, a professor of history at Cornell and a leading candidate to assume the university's presidency. His bid for the position, however, was dealt a serious blow when an alumnus claimed that Adams's 1874 book, *Monarchy and Democracy in France*, had been "appropriated largely" from Henry Thomas Buckle's *History of Civilization in England*, published in 1857.[92]

Allegations that Adams had cribbed from Buckle first appeared in the pages of *The Nation* in 1875, and the *Times* reprinted that magazine's side-by-side excerpts from the two books, as well as some apparent borrowing from de Tocqueville's *Memoir and Remains*. The *Times* also reported that in a later issue of *The Nation*, Adams had defended himself by pointing out that he and Buckle had drawn on the same sources, such as the writings of the French philosopher Helvétius. "That their language [in the two books] should correspond," Adams claimed, "was no more strange than when two reporters should use the same expression in reporting or abstracting the same speech." And Adams ascribed his unattributed quotations from de Tocqueville as being due to his great familiarity with that author's work, which led to "unconscious memory" and writing "without thinking of the source from which they had come into his mind."[93]

The *Times* published its article about Adams's appropriations on the day that the Board of Trustees met to vote on the next president of Cornell. (The paper later noted that before the bundles containing this issue were distributed in Ithaca, "every available copy . . . was engaged by certain parties.") At the board meeting, outgoing president Andrew White made a two-hour speech in which he denounced the claims made against Adams. In addition, he extolled the candidate's qualifications to serve as the school's new leader. After such an oration, it should come as no surprise to learn that the trustees duly elected Adams as Cornell's new president.[94]

The *Times*, which had been championing another candidate – one preferred by Cornell alumni residing in New York City – had difficulty coming to terms with this outcome. Over a month after the new university president was chosen, the paper ran another story about Adams's appropriations, this time from the work of French philosopher Paul Janet. In the final sentence of the article, it was noted that Adams's *Monarchy and Democracy in France* – the publication that had caused his difficulties – was dedicated to his close friend, former president Andrew White.[95]

During the Adams presidency, Cornell's student body doubled in size and its law school was established. His repeated clashes with the school's faculty, however, led to his resignation seven years after assuming the leadership role. Adams decamped for the University of Wisconsin, where he served as its president for nine years. He passed away a year later, in 1902 at age sixty-seven. Obituaries that ran in *The Publisher's Weekly*[96] and in *Science*[97] made no mention of the plagiarism allegations, nor does the entry about him in Wikipedia.

And what was the fate of Shervert Frazier, the Harvard physician accused of plagiarism a century later, in the 1980s? Three months after his resignation, he was reappointed to McLean Hospital as a staff psychiatrist, but without faculty status at Harvard.[98] And in 1998, ten years after his ouster as director, the hospital held a dinner in his honor. The event raised over a million dollars in donations for the Shervert H. Frazier Research Institute, which opened in 1992. He retired from McLean in his late eighties and died in March of 2015 at age ninety-three. Unlike Adams, however, Frazier's plagiarism was given prominent mention in his *Boston Globe* obituary.[99]

The divergent outcomes for Shervert Frazier and Charles Kendall Adams illustrate the convoluted nature of plagiarism allegations within the academy. They also reveal the complexity of the factors involved, such as the nature of the accusations, an individual's academic prominence, institutional considerations, and coverage by the media. These all play a role in determining how such allegations are investigated and adjudicated, as well as the long-term effects on the accused's career and reputation.

STUDENT PLAGIARISM

It was a late evening in mid December of 1990, and I was working in my college office, trying to tie up some loose ends at the end of the semester. The sound of approaching footsteps in the quiet building intruded on my train of thought. A moment later, a manila envelope appeared under my office door. With a sudden thrust from the other side, it slid across the floor. The footsteps retreated down the hallway, and I was left alone with a most unwelcome holiday gift.

I already knew what the envelope contained because of an earlier telephone conversation. The caller, his voice nervous and hesitant, informed me that a student in my graduate course had plagiarized part of the term paper she had submitted. As proof of this claim, the caller – who identified himself only as another student – would provide me with a photocopy of the research article she cribbed from for her assignment.

I hadn't yet read the student's paper, but when I did, I quickly realized that I would have been suspicious even without my late-night visitor and the damning evidence slipped under my door. The student's grades had been marginal, and her previous written assignments were poor. The verbiage in the term paper was more of the same – except for several articulate passages that glittered like diamonds amid her own tortured prose. And when I examined these well-written sections, I found that they had been copied word for word from the journal article provided by her classmate.

This was my first experience with student plagiarism. I was a young assistant professor and uncertain how to proceed, so I contacted the student and asked her to come see me. Showing her the two documents, I requested that she explain the remarkable similarity of thought on display. The student denied having plagiarized the article for her paper, but I told her that I had no choice but to give her a failing grade for the assignment. She accepted my decision with equanimity but asked that I not tell anyone about what she had done.

In mid January, after the holiday break, I received a call from the plagiarist's dean, asking me why the student had performed so poorly in my class. I explained what had transpired with a certain degree of trepidation. He then asked to see the evidence that supported my allegation of plagiarism. Once he had reviewed the two papers, the dean confided that this was not the first time the student had run into such difficulties. I later learned that she had been terminated from her graduate program.

My experience is hardly unique. Most of my faculty colleagues have had similar experiences during their careers – except perhaps for the cloak-and-dagger of an anonymous phone call and a large brown envelope. My vivid memories of that event, now decades in the past, serves as a reminder of how troubling these episodes can be for those of us who must adjudicate them.

Student plagiarism at the collegiate level is such a serious issue because it is a violation of the institution's code of conduct, and this can lead to suspension or expulsion. In retrospect, I was fortunate in my first brush with appropriation: I had in my possession the document that the student had plagiarized from, and the evidence was incontrovertible. But what do instructors do when they only suspect that appropriation has taken place?

In many cases, they do nothing. Instructors find confronting students about their apparent plagiarism to be quite stressful,[100] and without clear proof, it isn't unusual for them to give students the benefit of the doubt. Sloppy or inadequate citation isn't good, but invoking the academic equivalent of the death penalty may seem disproportionate. It's not unusual, for example, for an instructor to allow the student to resubmit their assignment.

Although the internet has made copy-and-paste plagiarism easier than ever before, it has also led to the development of new tools to detect such copying. These include text-matching services that can scan a submitted document and compare it to a vast number of papers available online, as well as many more that exist behind paywalled academic databases.

The best-known of these is Turnitin, which is used by several thousand educational institutions. Most colleges have been making use of such services for many years. My own university, for example, made Turnitin available to faculty in 2005. As a result, today's undergraduates have grown up in a world in which a presumption of guilt has always been a given.

Although such companies are often referred to as providing plagiarism detection, the truth is that they can only generate a similarity score with one or more other documents, leaving it up to the instructor to decide whether it is high enough to cause concerns. Clearly, a paper that contains 40 percent matching text is more problematic than one with only a 10 percent overlap score, but how much is too much? Such decisions are left up to the course instructor.

It has also become common for universities to require students to submit their master's theses or doctoral dissertations to Turnitin. Predictably, some students have balked at this, either because they are opposed to the company's business model or because they don't want their work to become part of Turnitin's proprietary database.[101]

Students also have the ability to submit their work to Turnitin to obtain a similarity score. This may alert them to unintentional plagiarism and allow them to correct such issues before submitting assignments to their instructor. However, it also allows them to game the system: if a course syllabus states that papers with a similarity score over 25 percent will not be accepted, some students will reduce the amount of appropriated content until they achieve a score of 24 percent.

The widespread adoption of Turnitin has led to a cottage industry of tricks designed to evade the company's similarity algorithms. Some, like substituting look-alike letters from other alphabets or the insertion of white space between characters,[102] are issues that can be identified and thwarted algorithmically.

Another dodge involves using services variously referred to as word, text, or article spinners. These are intended to evade identification by replacing terms with synonyms. This can, however, lead to the impression that a student has swallowed a thesaurus. (Some readers may recall an episode from the television show *Friends*, in which Joey writes a letter of recommendation to an adoption agency to support Monica and Chandler. Unfortunately, he makes overzealous use of his word processor's synonym function. This leads to verbiage in which he describes the couple as "humid prepossessing *Homo sapiens* with full-sized aortic pumps" instead of "warm nice people with big hearts.") And a text spinner is happy to transform "Martin Luther King" into "Martin Luther Prince."[103] Needless to say, instructors become suspicious when they see such constructions.

How accurate are these similarity detection services? No system is foolproof, and faculty who employ them are haunted by the possibility of false positives. Given that a charge of plagiarism can lead to serious consequences, instructors are justifiably concerned about their error rates.

In the wake of plagiarism allegations against Harvard president Claudine Gay in December 2023 and Neri Oxman the following month, the author and game designer Ian Bogost decided to try training the plagiarism microscope on his own work. Writing for *The Atlantic*, he described using iThenticate to analyze his 68,000-word dissertation, written twenty years earlier. iThenticate, which is owned by Turnitin, is primarily used by corporate clients such as government agencies, publishers, and large businesses. It was reportedly used by the Biden campaign during his bid for the presidency in 2020.[104]

Bogost was confident that iThenticate would give his thesis a clean bill of health and was shocked when it returned a score of 74 – in other words, nearly three-quarters of his *magnum opus* had been copied from sources in iThenticate's database. Had Bogost plagiarized the majority of his dissertation?

It turned out that he hadn't. Bogost had written and published a book based on his thesis, and many of the false positives stemmed from that work, or from reviews and commentary based on it. And after excluding his own published work as well as the dissertation's bibliography and quoted material, the similarity score fell to 9. He eventually reduced the score to zero, but only after devoting hours of work to checking dozens of false positives.[105] Clearly, this is a labor-intensive process and not something that the instructor of a large class could do.

Although it's unlikely that a student's similarity score will be inflated by previous writing, there is still the moral quandary of self-plagiarism. This issue was brought to the fore in a 2013 letter submitted to Chuck Klosterman, the ethicist for *The New York Times*. The writer asked if it was ethical to submit the same paper in two different college courses. Is this simply a smart use of one's time – or is it cheating? Klosterman decreed that the student was lazy but not duplicitous.[106] Predictably, this response was met with howls of protest from those who disagreed with his assessment.[107]

DUBIOUS DISSERTATIONS

On February 16, 2011, the German newspaper *Süddeutsche Zeitung* published a report by Andreas Fischer-Lescano, a law professor at the University of Bremen. The article alleged that Karl-Theodor zu Guttenberg, the German Minister of Defense, had plagiarized parts of his doctoral dissertation, which he had submitted to the University of Bayreuth in 2007. Although Guttenberg initially called the charge "absurd," within a few days he acknowledged that he had made "serious mistakes" in his dissertation.[108]

Guttenberg had been a rising star in Chancellor Angela Merkel's cabinet: he was young, charismatic, and popular with the press. The accusation, however, led to widespread protests in Germany, and Bayreuth revoked his doctorate a week after the initial allegation.[109] And only a week after that, Guttenberg resigned from his post and his seat in the Bundestag.[110] The episode led to the coining of the term "guttenbergen," a German neologism for committing academic plagiarism.[111] But it also had far more serious consequences.

In the US, the completion of a doctorate – which requires an original work of scholarship – confers the title "doctor of philosophy" (PhD) upon the degree recipient. Students might refer to their college professor as "Dr. Smith," but the honorific isn't used socially. Physicians who earn medical degrees are considered to be the "real" doctors. In Germany, however, a PhD has considerable cachet: the honorific becomes part of one's name (*Herr Doktor* or *Frau Doktor Schmidt*) and is even printed on one's passport.[112] As a result, any fakery involved in obtaining the high-status credential is viewed particularly unfavorably.

One outcome of the Guttenberg scandal was the formation of VroniPlag Wiki – a crowdsourced collaboration established to ferret out and expose plagiarism in German dissertations.[113] "Vroni" is a German nickname for "Veronica," and the website was named after Veronica Sass, the daughter of a long-serving Bavarian politician. Sass had earned her doctorate at the University of Konstanz, and her dissertation was the first one that the online organization called into question. Sass's degree was subsequently revoked.[114]

VroniPlag Wiki invites the public to anonymously submit tips about suspect dissertations. If at least 20 percent of a thesis is found to contain plagiarized content, it is added to the website. The appropriations for each dissertation are graphically depicted as a kind of barcode: vertical stripes on a horizontal band indicate which pages are problematic. Stripes that are darker, wider, and more frequent indicate greater amounts of appropriation. Instead of using document similarity software, which can result in false positives and misses, suspect theses are checked manually against potential source texts by a large network of anonymous contributors.[115]

Within weeks of setting up shop, VroniPlag Wiki contributors discovered what seemed to be serious issues with a dissertation submitted by Matthias Pröfrock to the University of Tübingen in 2007. Initially, he admitted that he might have made some inadvertent mistakes in his thesis.[116] But in fact, half of the document's pages contained nonattributed text, including information that had been copied from Wikipedia. Pröfrock, who had been elected to the state parliament of Baden-Württemberg that spring, had his degree revoked.[117]

In May of 2011, VroniPlag Wiki called into question a dissertation by Silvana Koch-Mehrin, who was then serving as the vice-president of the

European Parliament. Unlike Pröfrock, Koch-Mehrin chose not to make a public statement regarding the charges.[118] A subsequent investigation by the University of Heidelberg documented more than 120 problematic sections spread across 80 pages of her 2001 thesis, and the university revoked her doctorate.[119]

Another member of Merkel's cabinet was felled by a VroniPlag investigation in early 2013. In this case, it was Annette Schavan, who had earned her doctorate from Heinrich Heine University Düsseldorf in 1980. Schavan, who had served as Merkel's Minister of Education and Research for seven years and was close to the German Chancellor, denied that she had copied the work of others.[120] However, a university investigation confirmed the VroniPlag allegations and stripped her of her degree.[121]

Two years later, it was Ursula von der Leyen's thesis that came under scrutiny. Like her predecessor Karl-Theodor zu Guttenberg, she was serving as the nation's Minister of Defense. Von der Leyen had completed a medical dissertation in obstetrics at the Hannover Medical School in 1990, and VroniPlag concluded that the degree of her plagiarism was "moderate." Von der Leyen claimed that she was innocent of the charges.[122] An investigation by her alma mater found "obvious flaws" but concluded that "the pattern of the plagiarism does not indicate a fraudulent intent." Von der Leyen kept her degree – and her position in the German cabinet.[123] (She would go on to become President of the European Commission.)

But in early 2019 – during the fourth and final Merkel cabinet – yet another federal minister found herself under the VroniPlag microscope. This time it was Franziska Giffey, the Minister of Family Affairs, who had earned her doctorate from the Free University of Berlin in 2010. An initial review by her alma mater concluded that Giffey's plagiarism was "minor," but she resigned her office in May of 2021 after a second review was conducted.[124] The Free University revoked her doctorate the following month, making her the third member of a Merkel cabinet to resign due to allegations of plagiarism.[125] Giffey, for her part, stated that the attribution errors "weren't intentional or planned." She also continued with her campaign to become the mayor of Berlin, and six months after losing her doctorate, she won her election.[126]

By May of 2021, after ten years of operation, VroniPlag Wiki had documented 211 plagiarized dissertations. Fewer than twenty of these had been written by individuals with connections to politics,[127] but, as we have seen, that number included some of Germany's most prominent appointed officials.

What does this tell us about the incidence of academic misconduct in Germany? One point to consider is that a majority of Merkel's cabinet members possessed doctoral degrees. At the time of her second cabinet, for example, eleven of her fifteen ministers held a doctorate.[128] (Merkel herself has a PhD in quantum chemistry, which she earned in 1986 in East Germany.) And as of 2013, approximately 25,000 doctorates were awarded annually in Germany – about twice as many, per capita, as those earned in the US.[129] Given these numbers, perhaps we shouldn't be surprised that three federal ministers were called out for attribution issues in their theses.

How does this compare with the rate of dissertation plagiarism seen in other countries? Researcher Dora Clarke-Pine addressed this question by randomly selecting 120 psychology dissertations from a variety of institutions in the United States. If plagiarism is arbitrarily defined as the copying of ten or more consecutive words without attribution, then Clarke-Pine found that 80 percent of the theses in her survey contained plagiarized material. And if the criterion is loosened to the copying of five or more consecutive words – once again, without attribution – then the authors of all 120 theses were guilty of appropriation.[130]

Debora Weber-Wulff, a member of the VroniPlag project, believes that German universities have simply chosen to ignore the problem for far too long.[131] And the same is undoubtedly true in the US, since institutions of higher learning have no incentive to identify student plagiarists or their too credulous dissertation advisors. Quite the opposite is true, since a plagiarism scandal can adversely affect a college's reputation. And while the situation may be serious in Germany and America, it pales in comparison to what has transpired in Eastern Europe.

DOUBTFUL DEGREES

In March of 2006, two fellows at the Brookings Institution in Washington, DC went public with their analysis of an academic thesis that Vladimir

Putin supposedly authored nearly a decade earlier. The thesis was submitted for a Candidate of Economic Sciences degree, which is roughly equivalent to the PhD in Western countries. As a result, the President of Russia is technically Doctor Putin.

The ex-KGB officer submitted his 218-page document to the Saint Petersburg Mining Institute in 1997, during his time as Deputy Chief of the Presidential Staff to Boris Yeltsin. The title of the thesis is "Mineral and Raw Materials Resources and the Development Strategy for the Russian Economy"[132] – a topic seemingly far removed from Putin's undergraduate training in law, or the counterintelligence and surveillance work he engaged in with the KGB.

Brookings fellows Clifford Gaddy and Igor Danchenko reported that the thesis's author relied heavily on a Russian translation of *Strategic Planning and Policy*, a 1978 textbook written for US business schools by professors William King and David Cleland. In the second chapter of Putin's thesis, they found "more than 16 pages of text copied virtually word for word." In addition, a half-dozen tables and diagrams were "lifted directly or slightly modified from the textbook with no attribution whatsoever." And the business textbook was the only source that Gaddy and Danchenko checked, so other parts of the thesis may have been copied from other sources.[133]

Finally, the Brookings fellows expressed considerable doubt that the work had been written by Putin himself. They asserted that it was "clearly the product of some diploma-mill type operation," making the actual plagiarist Putin's ghostwriter.[134]

In 2018, the ghost's identity was revealed. Olga Litvinenko, the daughter of the rector of the Saint Petersburg Mining Institute, claimed that her father had literally cut and pasted the thesis together during the summer of 1997. During a vacation at his dacha, Vladimir Litvinenko photocopied paragraphs out of books and then glued the sections onto pages as his fourteen-year-old daughter watched. "I saw all this. It happened right before my eyes," she told a reporter for *Radio Free Europe*.[135]

A system that regulated the conferral of academic degrees was largely abandoned at the time of the dissolution of the Soviet Union in the early 1990s, and Russia became the Wild West with regard to advanced degrees. As in Germany, doctorates carry considerable social prestige, and many upwardly mobile professionals and politicians chose to acquire one through less than legitimate means. Websites offered dissertations written to order in about a month and for as little as $1,500. "You can just pay the money and forget about it, and then they'll bring you your diploma at home," one whistleblower alleged.[136]

The plagiarism epidemic in Russia was publicly acknowledged by Prime Minister Dmitri Medvedev in 2012, when he admonished high school and college students about the evils of copying materials found on the internet. Igor Fedyukin, a deputy minister of education and science, was asked to explore the magnitude of the problem. He led a group that examined twenty-five history dissertations, chosen at random from the well-respected Moscow Pedagogical State University. The group found that "all but one were at least 50% plagiarized, with some as much as 90% copied from other sources."[137]

The straw that broke the camel's back, however, was the 2012 appointment of an unqualified but politically well-connected historian to head a distinguished institute for mathematics. Outraged Russian academics took action, calling the appointee's dissertation into question. In this way, the Dissernet project was born.[138]

Like VroniPlag Wiki, Dissernet is an amorphous group of activists who are intent on exposing academic corruption. Unlike the VroniPlag group, however, the initial process of checking theses for plagiarism has been automated. A computer program compares each dissertation against all the others in an online Russian archive. When theses with suspiciously high degrees of overlap are discovered, members of the group manually check the two documents.

As with VroniPlag, the Dissernet collaborators release their results online. As of mid 2016, the group claimed to have identified about 5,600 suspicious dissertations. Approximately one-quarter of these, or nearly 1,300, had been fully investigated and verified as problematic. These include about 40 dissertations ostensibly authored by members of the State Duma – the lower house of the Federal Assembly of Russia.[139]

Perhaps the most egregious example alleged by the Dissernet collaborative concerns the thesis of Duma member Igor Igoshin, who was awarded the Doctor of Sciences degree in 2004. His thesis was a wholesale appropriation of an earlier dissertation on the manufacture of chocolate. Igoshin's *magnum opus*, however, concerns beef production. Igoshin – or his ghostwriter – simply overlaid a meaty vocabulary atop the confectionary prose. The word "chocolate" was replaced by "meat," "white chocolate" was transformed into "Russian beef," "regular milk chocolate" was replaced by "imported beef," and so on.[140] (It should be noted that Igoshin referred to Dissernet's claims as "absurd"[141] and that there was no official finding of plagiarism or a court ruling in this case.)

Fraudulent dissertations aren't only a problem in Russia: similar issues abound in countries that were once part of the USSR or the former Soviet bloc. A 2019 report, for example, found that Ukraine "has dozens of private firms that offer ghostwritten dissertations for sale."[142]

In Romania, Prime Minister Victor Ponta was accused in 2012 of plagiarizing his law dissertation: it was alleged that more than half of his 432-page thesis was copied.[143] (Ponta denied having plagiarized, but gave up his doctorate two years after the allegations surfaced.)[144] And when he was the acting Prime Minister of the country in 2015, Gabriel Oprea was accused of plagiarizing his law thesis. Although he accused the author of the plagiarism report of lying,[145] Oprea was stripped of his degree in 2016.[146] They were joined by Prime Minister Nicolae Ciuca in 2022, who had his military science dissertation called into question: nearly a third of its pages, it was claimed, contained appropriated material.[147]

Farther south, in the Balkans, plagiarism scandals involving government officials have contributed to student protests. In 2014, the dissertation of Nebojša Stefanović, Serbia's Minister of Internal Affairs, was called into question by Serbian academicians based in the UK.[148] Shortly thereafter, issues were also raised regarding the thesis of Siniša Mali, the mayor of Belgrade. Mali denied the charge and in 2018 was promoted to the position of Minister of Finance by Prime Minister Ana Brnabić. These and other scandals led to a twelve-day student blockade of the Rectorate of the University of Belgrade during the summer of 2019.[149]

A similar series of events played out in neighboring Albania. In 2018, Taulant Muka, an epidemiologist who had been trained in the Netherlands, claimed that several politicians had plagiarized their theses, including members of Prime Minister Edi Rama's cabinet. The accusations, along with increases in tuition, led to the Second Students

Movement, which culminated in boycotts and the occupation of academic buildings in early 2019.[150]

Although some academic reforms were adopted in both countries, government officials credibly accused of plagiarism largely escaped any negative consequences. For example, although Siniša Mali had his degree revoked in 2019 by the University of Belgrade,[151] he retained his position as Minister of Finance and became the Deputy Prime Minister of Serbia in 2022. And in Albania, only one of seven accused politicians forfeited their position.[152] In both countries, the protests by students show that they realize how academic corruption reduces the value of the legitimate degrees they are working so hard to earn.

CHAPTER 3

Unconscious Plagiarism

MARK TWAIN

On December 3, 1879, the publishers of *The Atlantic Monthly* held a breakfast and reception at the Brunswick Hotel in Boston. The event was organized to honor Dr. Oliver Wendell Holmes, who had celebrated his seventieth birthday that summer. Holmes had given *The Atlantic* its name at its founding, twenty-two years earlier, and his contributions to the magazine's pages had helped to ensure its success.[1]

In attendance at the breakfast were many of the authors who had written for *The Atlantic* over the years. Poems were read in Holmes's honor, and several attendees were called upon to make speeches. The remarks of one guest included an arresting confession: Mark Twain admitted to having plagiarized from the event's guest of honor.[2]

Twain was no stranger to charges of plagiarism during his career. During the years before the celebration for Holmes, he was engaged in a long-running dispute with the novelist Charles Heber Clark. Accusations of appropriation flew back and forth between the two men. And a decade later, Clark would accuse Twain of lifting the plot for *A Connecticut Yankee in King Arthur's Court* from his novelette *The Fortunate Island*.[3] But Twain had always stoutly defended himself when charged – that is, until he accused himself of having stolen from the good doctor.

The ore that Twain had mined came from *Songs in Many Keys*, published in 1862.[4] We know that Twain read Holmes's volume in 1866, because he mentioned the collection of poems in a letter to his publisher. At the time, he was employed as a correspondent for the *Sacramento Union* and was reporting from Hawaii. Having contracted saddle boils after days of hard riding, he was forced to convalesce in Honolulu. Confined to a hotel room for two weeks, Twain was said to have "read the book to rags."[5]

Three years later, in 1869, Twain published his first book, titled *The Innocents Abroad, or The New Pilgrim's Progress*. The work describes the humorist's prolonged excursion to locations in Europe and Palestine during 1867. The book was well received and greatly enhanced Twain's visibility as a humorist. It is still considered "the most popular travel book ever written by an American."[6]

In his remarks at Holmes's celebration, Twain related how a friend had complimented him on his travelogue's dedication. Twain confessed to a fondness for it as well. But then the friend continued with "I always admired it, even before I saw it in *The Innocents Abroad*." Shocked, Twain demanded to know where he had encountered it previously. His friend claimed that it bore a strong resemblance to the dedication appearing in *Songs in Many Keys*. According to Twain, the pair ducked into a bookstore to find a copy of Holmes's collection. And in his speech, the chagrined author asserted that "I had really stolen that dedication, almost word for word." Recalling his convalescence in Hawaii and his reading and rereading of Holmes's poetry, he concluded that he must have "unconsciously stole[n] it."[7]

It might be helpful, at this point, to compare the two dedications to determine the extent of Twain's borrowing. This is Holmes's wording:

TO

THE MOST INDULGENT OF READERS,

THE KINDEST OF CRITICS,

MY BELOVED MOTHER,

ALL THAT IS LEAST UNWORTHY OF HER

IN THIS VOLUME

IS DEDICATED

BY HER AFFECTIONATE SON.[8]

And this is Twain's:

TO

MY MOST PATIENT READER

AND

MOST CHARITABLE CRITIC,

MY AGED MOTHER,

THIS VOLUME IS AFFECTIONATELY

INSCRIBED.[9]

In one sense, the inscriptions are strikingly similar, with the same ideas expressed in the same order. Laudable characteristics of the reader are followed by those of the critic, the mother, and finally the dedication itself. But the appropriation is clearly not "almost word for word," as Twain claimed. Whereas Holmes's mother is "indulgent," "kindest," and "beloved," Twain's is "patient," "charitable," and "aged." (It could be argued that Holmes's description is the more flattering of the two.) There is no mention in Twain's dedication of the unworthiness of the volume. The concept of affection appears in both, but this is undoubtedly a sentiment commonly expressed in dedications of this sort.

In his remarks at the breakfast, Twain went on to relate how he sent Holmes a letter of apology. Holmes responded that no harm had been done and furthermore stated he "believed we all unconsciously worked over ideas gathered in reading and hearing, imagining they were original with ourselves."[10]

The most interesting aspect of this episode may be the willingness of both authors to attribute Twain's appropriation to the workings of his unconscious mind. For men of letters of the 1870s, the possibility of unconscious plagiarism seems to have been taken as a given. But was this a sentiment that was widely shared?

* * *

A dip into the archives of *The New York Times* reveals many appeals to unconscious plagiarism from the late nineteenth century. The following two are illustrative.

In December of 1890, we find the case of one John M. Criley, a student at Wittenberg College in Ohio. Speaking on the topic of "The Agitator and His Mission," Criley was judged the winner of the school's annual oratory contest. The second-place finisher, however, accused Criley of having "cribbed" his twenty-two-sentence speech from a book by Wendell Phillips, the noted orator and abolitionist. At a trial held by the school's faculty, Criley admitted to having read Phillips's book, and allowed that he might have "absorbed some of it and might have unconsciously used some of it." Although the faculty found him innocent of the charge of plagiarism, he was not allowed to advance to a state-wide competition. The equivocal ruling suggests that not all of Criley's inquisitors were willing to accept his explanation.[11]

And an article from October of 1879 reports the case of George C. Lorimer, a Baptist pastor in Chicago. He was accused of liberally borrowing from a sermon delivered the previous year by Joseph Parker, a preacher in London. In a public letter of explanation, Lorimer noted that "My memory is such that pretty nearly everything I read adheres frequently in the words of the author, and unconsciously becomes part of my mental furniture." In his defense, the pastor claimed that he would "not have been so stupid to purposely infringe on the property of a writer so well and favorably known."[12] Apparently, his congregation accepted this explanation: his 1904 obituary describes a successful career leading churches in Chicago, Boston, and New York City.[13]

Just as with Twain's remarks at the Boston breakfast, the college student and the Baptist pastor saw no need to explain the idea of unconscious plagiarism, so it seems to have been firmly established by the 1870s. But where had this idea come from?

* * *

As we have seen, the concept of plagiarism can be traced to the writings of Martial in the first century CE. But to borrow and not be consciously aware of having done so? That idea seems to have arisen more recently.

The concept of the unconscious is associated by many with Sigmund Freud, but the idea predates psychoanalysis. Furthermore, on the day that Twain confessed his appropriation to Holmes's guests, Freud was a twenty-three-year-old student engaged in compulsory military training. The completion of his medical degree from the University of Vienna lay two years in his future.[14] To find the origins of the unconscious, we must turn to a now-obscure German philosopher – and to his English plagiarist.

The notion of unconscious processes has existed, in one form or another, since ancient times: it appears, for example, in the writings of

Galen (second century CE) and Plotinus (third century CE). But in its modern form, it was fleshed out by the German idealist philosophers such as Johann Gottlieb Fichte and in particular by Friedrich Wilhelm Joseph Schelling. Samuel Taylor Coleridge brought Schelling's ideas to the attention of the English-speaking world. And as it happens, the English poet, best known for *The Rime of the Ancient Mariner*, was discovered to have plagiarized Schelling's ideas about the unconscious in his *Biographia Literaria* of 1817.[15] According to the Scottish philosopher Lancelot Law Whyte, "By 1850 [the term 'unconscious' as] both adjective and noun were extensively used in Germany, and were moderately common in England."[16]

Twain is certainly not the only person to claim having appropriated without being aware of it, and the following sections provide some additional examples of this phenomenon.

HELEN KELLER

Few stories are as heartwarming or as inspirational as Helen Keller's. Born in Alabama in 1880, Keller suffered a bout of illness at nineteen months that left her unable to see or to hear. Over the next few years, she developed a series of gestures – commonly called home signs – that allowed her to communicate, in a limited way, with her family.

Seeking a way to provide their daughter with an education, her parents contacted an institution for the blind in Boston. Its director asked one of the school's alumni, Anne Sullivan, to become Keller's teacher. Sullivan began her work shortly before the child turned seven. She tried to teach her the names of things by employing a manual alphabet. This involved tracing out each word, letter by letter, onto the palm of the girl's hand.

Progress during the first few weeks was slow, because the child didn't seem to grasp the concept of words. But in an episode made famous by the 1962 movie *The Miracle Worker*, Keller suddenly made the connection between the cold liquid running over one hand and Sullivan spelling out "water" in the other. After that, Keller became a sponge for everything that Sullivan could teach her.[17]

And for many, this story is the extent of their knowledge about Helen Keller – a courageous woman who triumphed over adversity. But while still a child, she was involved in a plagiarism scandal that cast a shadow over her young life, and also seriously damaged the reputation of her teacher.

A year after her breakthrough with Sullivan, Keller was enrolled at the Perkins School for the Blind – her teacher's alma mater. During a break from school when she was eleven, Keller wrote a short story as a birthday gift for Michael Anagnos, the school's director. Titled "The Frost King," it explains the leaves changing color during autumn as the work of fairies painting them. Impressed by his pupil's effort, Anagnos arranged to have the story published in the January 1892 issue of the school's alumni journal, *The Mentor*.[18] The work was reprinted in *The Goodson Gazette* in West Virginia, where one of that paper's readers noticed a strong resemblance to a story by Margaret Canby.[19]

In 1873, Canby had published a collection of stories titled *Birdie and His Fairy Friends: A Book for Little Children*. The volume consists of thirteen stories about a young boy – Birdie – who lives in a cottage in the country with his parents. Some of the stories describe his adventures with fairies; in others, Birdie is told stories about these magical creatures. One story, in which Birdie's mother tells him about the Frost Fairies, bears a striking similarity to Keller's.[20] In a later issue, the *Gazette* published the two stories side-by-side, and the resemblances are clear.

Canby's "The Frost Fairies" is nearly 2,000 words long, and the following excerpt, describing King Frost, provides a sense of its style:

> You must know that this king, like all other kings, has great treasures of gold and precious stones in his palace; but being a good-hearted old fellow, he does not keep his riches locked up all the time, but tries to do good, and make others happy with them.[21]

Keller's "The Frost King" is a story of less than 1,200 words: it is shorter than Canby's because it doesn't include Birdie's interactions with his parents. The following lines are those that parallel Canby's description:

> You must know that King Frost, like all other kings, has great treasures of gold and precious stones; but as he is a generous old monarch he

endeavors to make right use of his riches. So wherever he goes he does many wonderful works.[22]

The similarities are obvious, and there are many more besides. In both stories, the fairies hear "the tinkling of many drops falling through the forest, and sliding from leaf to leaf." In both "Their fears were well founded, for their long absence had alarmed the king." And in both, King Frost declares that "My treasures are not wasted if they make little children happy." Clearly, Keller had somehow appropriated Canby's tale as her own. But when confronted by Anagnos, the girl said she had no memory of having encountered "The Frost Fairies" previously. And when the director questioned Sullivan, she emphatically denied any familiarity with the story.

Sullivan made inquiries to discover how Keller had been exposed to Canby's work. She learned that Sophia Hopkins, a faculty member at the Perkins School, owned a copy of Canby's book and that it was she who had read the volume to Keller during a visit to Hopkins's home in Brewster, Massachusetts during the summer of 1888.[23] In the next issue of *The Mentor*, Anagnos published an editorial note explaining that Keller's story was "at least to some extent, a reproduction" of Canby's work, and that Keller had been exposed to it three years before she had sent "The Frost King" to him as a birthday present.[24]

In his note, Anagnos referred to Keller's actions as plagiarism, but this characterization was challenged by several prominent supporters of the child, including Alexander Graham Bell – a prominent figure in the deaf community – and Mark Twain. As we have already seen, Twain believed in the possibility of inadvertent plagiarism. In a letter he wrote to Keller in 1903, Twain stated:

> Substantially all ideas are second-hand, consciously and unconsciously drawn from a million outside sources and daily used by the garnerer with a pride and satisfaction born of the superstition that he originated them. Whereas there is not a rag of originality about them except the little discoloration they get from his mental and moral calibre and his temperament, which is revealed in characteristic phrasing.[25]

"The Frost King" affair became even more fraught when one of Anagnos's teachers told him about a conversation she had with Keller. The teacher claimed to have learned that it was Sullivan who had read Canby's story to her. In her autobiography, however, Keller reported telling the teacher "most emphatically that she was mistaken."[26]

Prior to this allegation, Anagnos had been sympathetic toward Keller. But the teacher's assertion seems to have turned the director against both the child and Sullivan. He convened a hearing to determine whether Keller had consciously plagiarized her story and selected eight members of the school to serve as a jury. After subjecting the girl to a lengthy interrogation, the jury's vote was a tie. The episode, however, destroyed the remaining bonds of trust that Keller and Sullivan had with Anagnos, and the two left the Perkins Institute soon thereafter.[27]

No matter whether Hopkins or Sullivan had read "The Frost Fairies" to Keller, a remarkable aspect of the episode was her ability to recall it with such fidelity three years later. In her autobiography, Keller stated that she did "not recall a single circumstance connected with the reading of the [Canby] stories" but that "the language was ineffaceably stamped upon my brain."[28]

This retentiveness seems to have been a general aspect of the workings of Keller's mind. When she first started reading embossed books on her own, she recalled:

> Read I did, whether I understood one word in ten or two words on a page. The words themselves fascinated me; but I took no conscious account of what I read. My mind must, however, have been very impressionable at that period, for it retained many words and whole sentences, to the meaning of which I had not the faintest clue; and afterward, when I began to talk and write, these words and sentences would flash out quite naturally, so that my friends wondered at the richness of my vocabulary.[29]

For many years, the plagiarism episode affected Keller's self-confidence about her writing. A decade after the controversy, she wrote:

> Indeed, I have ever since been tortured by the fear that what I write is not my own. For a long time, when I wrote a letter, even to my mother, I was seized with a sudden feeling of terror, and I would spell the sentences over

and over to make sure I had not read them in a book. Had it not been for the persistent encouragement of Miss Sullivan, I think I should have given up trying to write altogether.[30]

In the years following "The Frost King" episode, Keller's achievements were remarkable. She learned to speak intelligibly and to "hear" others by placing a hand to their lips. With the steadfast assistance of Sullivan, she graduated from Radcliffe, becoming the first deaf and blind person to complete a college degree. She became an activist for the rights of women and people with disabilities and wrote over a dozen books.[31] And in 1968, at the time of her death at age 87, she was one of the most admired women in America.[32] The accusation of plagiarism had darkened Keller's childhood, but she was able to overcome it during an incandescent adulthood.

ROBERT LOUIS STEVENSON

The Scottish author Robert Louis Stevenson penned many short stories and a dozen novels during his brief literary career. Today, he is remembered chiefly for two works that are strikingly different in character. One of these is the gothic novel *Strange Case of Dr Jekyll and Mr Hyde*, and the other is *Treasure Island*, a coming-of-age adventure story. Stevenson's tale of privateers and buried treasure appeared in serial form in a children's magazine during 1881 and 1882. It was released in book form the following year and has been a tentpole of the young adult literary canon ever since.

Stevenson died young, falling victim to a stroke in Samoa at the age of 44. He and his wife Fanny had moved to the Polynesian island four years earlier. In 1894, a few months before his death, he returned to the subject of *Treasure Island* by writing a short account of its genesis. It started with the drawing of a map of the eponymous island, and this fired his imagination. As he studied his cartographic handiwork, he wrote:

The future characters of the book began to appear there visibly among imaginary woods; and their brown faces and bright weapons peeped out upon me from unexpected quarters, as they passed to and fro, fighting, and hunting treasure, on these few square inches of a flat projection. The

> next thing I knew, I had some paper before me and was writing out a list of chapters.[33]

It would be, he declared, "a story for boys; no need of psychology and fine writing."[34]

In addition, Stevenson identified the sources for certain elements in his story. Long John Silver's parrot, he asserted, had been appropriated from Defoe's *Robinson Crusoe.* The skeleton pointing to the treasure? That came from Poe's *The Gold-Bug.* But these borrowings did not trouble him: "they are trifles and details; and no man can hope to have a monopoly of skeletons or make a corner in talking birds."[35]

What did concern Stevenson, however, was a source that he had not been consciously aware of. He writes:

> It is my debt to Washington Irving that exercises my conscience, and justly so, for I believe plagiarism was rarely carried farther. I chanced to pick up the "Tales of a Traveller" some years ago, with a view to an anthology of prose narrative, and the book flew up and struck me: Billy Bones, his chest, the company in the parlor, the whole inner spirit and a good deal of the material detail of my first chapters – all were there, all were the property of Washington Irving. But I had no guess of it then as I sat writing by the fireside, in what seemed the springtides of a somewhat pedestrian inspiration; nor yet day by day, after lunch, as I read aloud my morning's work to the family. It seemed to me original as sin; it seemed to belong to me like my right eye.[36]

Tales of a Traveler was written by Geoffrey Crayon, the pen name used by Washington Irving. Today, he is best remembered for "Rip Van Winkle," and "The Legend of Sleepy Hollow." His *Tales of a Traveler* was published in 1824. The final section of Irving's collection, titled "The Money Diggers," consists of five linked stories. One of these is titled "Kidd the Pirate" and is a slight work of seven pages. It briefly sketches the life and execution of the notorious Scottish privateer, William Kidd, and subsequent searches for his buried pirate booty. Two longer stories follow – "The Devil and Tom Walker" and "Wolfert Webber, or Golden Dreams" – and they contain passing references to Kidd and buried treasure as well.[37]

However, as with Twain's debt to Oliver Wendell Holmes, it seems that Stevenson overstated his debt to Washington Irving. Irving's stories do not contain "the whole inner spirit and a good deal of the material detail" of *Treasure Island*, as Stevenson claimed, but rather the unadorned trifles that he would weave into his own story of buccaneers and buried riches. What vexed Stevenson the most, it seems, was his inability to remember having absorbed these details from Irving's stories.

In his confession, however, Stevenson never explicitly states that he read Irving's book before writing his own. It may be that the similarities he perceived with *Tales of a Traveler* are the result of both men having used a common source. Most likely, that source was Charles Johnson's *A General History of the Robberies and Murders of the Most Notorious Pyrates*, a collection of biographies published in 1724. Stevenson makes a passing reference to "Johnson's 'Buccaneers'" in his account of *Treasure Island*'s origins, and the names of two of *Treasure Island*'s characters – Ben Gunn and Israel Hands – appear to have come from Johnson's work.[38] There may have been unconscious appropriation, but Stevenson may have misidentified its source.

VLADIMIR NABOKOV

The publication of *Lolita*, by Russian American author Vladimir Nabokov, was a literary event that almost never happened. Unhappy with his tale of a middle-aged man obsessed by a young girl, Nabokov attempted, on more than one occasion, to consign his draft to the flames of a trash barrel. Each time, it was the intervention of his wife Véra that saved the work.[39] Unable to find an American publisher, Nabokov arranged to have his novel debut with a French firm in 1955. A positive notice by Graham Greene in England was followed by its 1958 publication by Putnam in the US, where it became a bestseller.[40]

What was Nabokov's inspiration? One source seems to have been the 1948 abduction of eleven-year-old Florence Sally Horner by the pedophile Frank La Salle. He took his young victim on a twenty-one-month cross-country odyssey from New Jersey to California. Arrested and convicted of rape, La Salle died in prison sixteen years later. He did, however, outlive his abductee: Horner died at the age of fifteen in a highway accident. Véra Nabokov explicitly denied that the Horner case was an influence, but since the abduction is mentioned in chapter 33 of *Lolita*, her husband was clearly aware of it.[41]

If we peel back another layer of the strata forming Nabokov's literary career, we find his Russian novella *Volshebnik* ("Enchanter"). In that story, a middle-aged man is besotted by a young French girl. She is the daughter of a widow whom the man marries to gain access to her progeny. Nabokov wrote *Volshebnik* in Paris in 1939, and although he thought he had destroyed the manuscript a version resurfaced twenty years later, after the publication of *Lolita*. Translated into English by his son Dmitri, the work was published in 1986, nine years after his father's death.[42] Moving further back in time, we find a two-paragraph synopsis of *Lolita*'s plot in his novel *Dar* ("The Gift") written in the late 1930s while he was living in Berlin.[43]

And in the spring of 2004, German author Michael Maar claimed to have hit literary bedrock.[44] In a book released the following year, Maar showed that Nabokov's novel bore a number of similarities to a short story published in Germany in 1916. Written by Heinz von Eschwege under the pen name Heinz von Lichberg, it describes a middle-aged traveler who becomes infatuated with a young girl. She is the daughter of the pension owner where the traveler is staying. And the name of the girl, and of von Lichberg's story? Lolita.[45]

When von Lichberg s story was published, Nabokov was still a teenager, attending school in Saint Petersburg. But six years later, following the Russian Revolution and his studies at Cambridge, Nabokov joined his family in Berlin, where they had relocated in 1920. He lived in that city for the next fifteen years. Could Nabokov have read von Lichberg's story during that time? The tale was published in a collection of von Lichberg's stories titled *The Accursed Gioconda*, and the book would certainly have been available to Nabokov during his years in Berlin. Maar also discovered that the two men resided in the same area of the city, and that his landlady was related to von Lichberg.[46]

Apart from the subject matter and the girl's name, the two stories share little else. Von Lichberg's *Lolita* is a slim work of eighteen pages and fewer than 4,000 words. It is set in Germany and Spain. Nabokov's novel weighs in at over 110,000 words, and its story unfolds primarily in New

England. The protagonist in von Lichberg's tale tells an overwrought, supernatural story that reads like a tale penned by E. T. A. Hoffman – an author alluded to in the initial lines of his story. Other than the young ages of the girls and their shared name, the two Lolitas have little in common. As Maar put it, "Nothing of what we admire in the novel *Lolita* is already to be found in the tale; the former is in no way deducible from the latter."[47]

But Maar also directed our attention to another story in von Lichberg's 1916 collection – one titled *Atomit*. Here there are similarities to *The Waltz Invention,* a play that Nabokov published in Russian in 1938. (An English translation by Dmitri appeared in 1966.) In both stories, a weapon of great destructive power is offered to a government ministry. And the name of Nabokov's protagonist – Salvator Waltz – is reminiscent of two of the characters in von Lichberg's *Lolita*: Aloys and Anton Walzer (the German word for "waltz").

Although Maar made clear he didn't consider these similarities to be instances of plagiarism, some of the media's reporting was not as nuanced. An article in *The Guardian* about Maar's research was headlined "Novel Twist: Nabokov Family Rejects Lolita Plagiarism Claim."[48] In the minds of some readers, this may have created an unfortunate linkage between unethical appropriation and the novel's author.

Are the correspondences between these stories a form of homage – a tip of the hat by one author to another? It seems unlikely in this case. Von Lichberg joined the Nazi party in 1933 and worked for the Reich's military intelligence service during the Second World War. Nabokov's wife Véra was Jewish, and the family relocated from Berlin to Paris in 1937. They were forced to flee when the Germans invaded in 1940. Nabokov's brother Sergey remained in France and died in the Neuengamme concentration camp. The author's antipathy toward Germany and the Nazis, therefore, would seem to preclude tribute as a motivation.

Were the correspondences with von Lichberg's stories merely a string of coincidences, or some kind of personal literary joke? After all, Nabokov was well known for creative wordplay and subtle allusions in his literary creations. But if a joke is so obscure that it takes nearly fifty years to uncover, what is the point of making it at all?

A more likely explanation, and one suggested by Maar, is that the resemblances may be the result of unconscious plagiarism. Nabokov was known to be a voracious reader. He could have easily swept up the details in von Lichberg's stories and – without even realizing it – made use of them years later. Nabokov biographer Brian Boyd quoted the author as saying that he "liked to gather bits of straw and fluff for years before [he] built his nest."[49] And this echoes an observation by J. R. R. Tolkien, who wrote that a story "grows like a seed in the dark out of the leaf-mold of the mind: out of all that has been seen or thought or read, that has long ago been forgotten, descending into the deeps."[50]

In 2017, the literary theorist Delia Ungureanu discovered a possible connection between *Lolita* and two works by Salvador Dalí. The first of these was a story titled *Rêverie*, appearing in a French magazine in 1931. The plot has similarities to *Lolita*: a middle-aged man lusts after a twelve-year-old girl, although in this case the widowed mother is a willing accomplice. In Dalí's version, the girl's name is "Dulita." Nabokov might have encountered the story while living in Paris, and it could have served as a source of inspiration for *Enchanter*, as mentioned earlier.[51]

Dalí's nymphet reappears more fully realized, as "Dullita" in his memoir *The Secret Life of Salvador Dalí*. Published in 1942, it was reviewed by *The New Yorker* the following year, at a time when Nabokov was writing for that magazine. Dalí's memoir includes a footnote that references *Rêverie*.[52] If Nabokov read Dalí's book or was guided by it to his earlier story, these could have served as some of the raw material that eventually grew, "like a seed in the dark," into *Lolita*.

GEORGE HARRISON

Charges of plagiarism by composers and musicians are at least as common as they are for authors. Perhaps the most notorious case of this sort was the suit brought against George Harrison. In November of 1970, a few months after the breakup of the Beatles, the former "quiet" member of the group released his solo triple album *All Things Must Pass*. One of the singles from that album, "My Sweet Lord," became a hit for Harrison, but it would go on to cast a long and litigious shadow over his career.

Harrison began composing the song in December of 1969, following a concert date in Copenhagen. According to one account, Harrison asked Delaney Bramlett, another musician on the tour, how he would start a gospel song. "Delaney started scatting on 'Oh My Lord,' [with] Bonnie [Bramlett] and Rita Coolidge chorusing 'alleluia.' Harrison had his concept" for the song that became "My Sweet Lord."[53]

After returning to the UK, Harrison and keyboard player Billy Preston worked on refining the raw material from the jam session.[54] Preston released his own interpretation of the song shortly before Harrison's, but it was the former Beatle's version that became a hit and established his reputation as a solo artist.

Others remembered the jam session in Copenhagen differently. Delaney Bramlett recalled seizing Harrison's guitar and playing the tune of "He's So Fine" while singing "Oh my Lord, I just wanna be with you." Bramlett was surprised when Harrison's song was released the following year: he contacted the former Beatle and said that he hadn't intended for Harrison to use the song's melody. Harrison replied "Well, it's not *exactly* the same." According to Bramlett, Harrison assured him he would receive a writing credit for "My Sweet Lord," but he never did.[55]

But the dispute between Harrison and Bramlett might not be as important as the fact that "He's So Fine" had been written eight years earlier by another artist. Ronnie Mack had composed "He's So Fine" for the Chiffons as a reworking of a song he had originally composed for the Tokens. Released in the spring of 1963, the group's first single became a sensation and sold over a million copies. Mack, who had become the quartet's manager, died at the end of that year from Hodgkin's lymphoma. He was only twenty-three years old.

When Harrison's song was released eight years later, its similarity to the Chiffons' hit was widely noted. In the spring of 1971, country singer Jody Miller released a cover of "He's So Fine" that employed a slide guitar like Harrison's, accentuating the resemblance between the two songs.[56] Even during the recording session for "My Sweet Lord," keyboardist Bobby Whitlock found himself singing "He's so fine, wish he was mine" – a line from the Chiffons' hit. But when Whitlock pointed out the resemblance to Harrison, he was told "Well, we'll work that out."[57]

The rights to "He's So Fine" were owned by Bright Tunes Music Corporation, and the publisher filed suit against Harrison for copyright infringement in February of 1971. A trial was delayed because Bright Tunes went into receivership before being acquired by former Beatles business manager Allen Klein. The band members' split with him had been acrimonious, and Klein was now a party in the suit against his former client. Harrison tried to settle out of court by offering Bright Tunes $148,000 – half the amount the song had earned in the US and Canada, and nearly $800,000 today – but Klein rejected the offer.[58]

Five years after the suit was filed, the case was finally heard in a New York City courtroom. The presiding judge, Richard Owen, happened to have a musical background: as a hobby, he composed operas.[59]

In court, both Harrison and keyboardist Billy Preston admitted to having heard "He's So Fine," and given the song's popularity in the UK, they would have been hard pressed to say otherwise.[60] However, Harrison maintained that the principal source of his inspiration was the gospel song "Oh Happy Day," an arrangement of an eighteenth-century hymn. This version, recorded by the Edwin Hawkins Singers, had been released in 1968 and became a worldwide hit the following year.[61] The problem with this claim is that "My Sweet Lord" sounds a lot more like "He's So Fine" than it does "Oh Happy Day."

In his analysis, Owen began with the overall structure of the two songs. "He's So Fine" is composed of two motifs: a three-note sequence the judge designated as A, and a four-note sequence he labelled B. Both songs had at least one A motif and at least one B motif. In other words, neither of the motifs was unique to that song, so their use by Harrison did not constitute infringement. What Owen focused on instead was the order of the motifs in each song. Their pattern in "He's So Fine" is A-A-A-A-B-B-B-B, one that Owen asserted was "highly unique." In comparison, the pattern of motifs in "My Sweet Lord" is A-A-A-A-B-B-B-T. T is a transitional element that has the same length as motif B. In addition, the last repeat of B in Mack's song makes use of a grace note, which also appears in Harrison's T. Finally, Owen asserted that "the harmonies of both songs are identical."[62]

Based on previous decisions in federal cases, a ruling of copyright infringement requires that two criteria be met: the defendant must have had access to the original work, and a substantial degree of similarity must exist between the two.[63] In his ruling in September of 1976, Owen ruled that both criteria had been satisfied. The critical passage is worth reproducing in full:

> I conclude that the composer, in seeking musical materials to clothe his thoughts, was working with various possibilities. As he tried this possibility and that, there came to the surface of his mind a particular combination that pleased him as being one he felt would be appealing to a prospective listener; in other words, that this combination of sounds would work. Why? Because his subconscious knew it already had worked in a song his conscious mind did not remember. Having arrived at this pleasing combination of sounds, the recording was made, the lead sheet prepared for copyright and the song became an enormous success. Did Harrison deliberately use the music of "He's So Fine"? I do not believe he did so deliberately. Nevertheless, it is clear that "My Sweet Lord" is the very same song as "He's So Fine" with different words, and Harrison had access to "He's So Fine." This is, under the law, infringement of copyright, and is no less so even though subconsciously accomplished.[64]

Simply put, the judge concluded that ignorance of one's muse is no excuse. Infringement, be it conscious or unconscious, is a violation of the intellectual property belonging to someone else. Harrison was ordered to pay $2.13 million in damages, which would be about $11.4 million today. This amount was later reduced to $1.6 million ($8.5 million).

A couple of months after the judge's ruling, Harrison released the album *Thirty Three & 1/3*, which included "This Song" – his sardonic take on the protracted litigation. His lyrics assure the listener that his song doesn't "infringe on anyone's copyright," that his "expert tells me it's okay," and that "this tune has nothing *bright* about it."

In 1978, ABKCO Music, which Klein now owned, acquired Bright Tunes's interest in "He's So Fine" for $587,000 (about $3.1 million). In further litigation during 1981, Owen ruled that Klein shouldn't benefit from his purchase, since it created a conflict of interest between the businessman and Harrison.[65] Owen reduced the damages Harrison had to pay still further, to $587,000 – the amount that Klein had spent to purchase the rights to "He's So Fine" in the first place.[66] By paying that amount to his former manager, Harrison was able to acquire the rights to Ronnie Mack's song.

Other disputes related to profits from "My Sweet Lord" resulted in additional litigation between Klein and Harrison, and these cases dragged on for several more years.[67] Matters were finally settled in 1998 – twenty-seven years after the original lawsuit had been filed. Harrison succumbed to cancer three years later at age fifty-eight. Despite his creative work as a member of the Beatles and his accomplishments as a solo artist, articles about Harrison's life invariably mentioned the dispute over "My Sweet Lord" and Owen's ruling on unconscious plagiarism.[68]

THE SUBCONSCIOUS COPYING DOCTRINE

The ruling that George Harrison unconsciously plagiarized "He's So Fine" was a significant event in American jurisprudence. But the decision in that case didn't create a new judicial standard. Judge Owen was guided by a precedent that had been established some fifty years earlier, in a little-known but highly consequential infringement case. The precedent would become known as the subconscious copying doctrine.

In 1919, Ben Selvin, a well-known bandleader, recorded "Dardanella," which became the bestselling tune in the US during the following year. The song employed an ostinato accompaniment that was unusual in popular music of the period. It consisted of a repeating musical pattern of eight notes.

Soon after "Dardanella" faded from memory, Jerome Kern's *Good Morning Dearie* opened on Broadway.[69] The musical comedy included a number titled "Kalua," which also made use of a distinctive ostinato accompaniment. Music publisher Fred Fisher, who had written the lyrics for "Dardanella," filed suit against Charles Dillingham, the musical's producer, for infringement, although his request for an injunction was denied.[70]

Fred Fisher Inc. v. Dillingham was heard by Judge Learned Hand in 1924. Although his *Show Boat* wouldn't premiere for another three years, Kern was already a well-known composer of songs and successful stage works. He denied the charge of plagiarism, and even the judge thought it was unlikely that someone of Kern's stature would stoop to thievery from a novelty song.[71] Kern's biographer, however, noted that the composer did little to endear himself to Judge Hand: while on the witness stand, he was unable to control his temper and spewed bitter and caustic remarks.[72]

The judge believed that Kern must have heard "Dardanella" during its brief but incandescent heyday. But he rejected the idea that the composer would have risked his reputation by deliberately appropriating the song's distinctive accompaniment. He concluded there was only one explanation for the striking similarity of the two compositions. In his decision, Hand wrote:

> Whether he [Kern] unconsciously copied the figure, he cannot say, and does not try to. Everything registers somewhere in our memories, and no one can tell what may evoke it. On the whole, my belief is that, in composing the accompaniment to the refrain of "Kalua," Mr. Kern must have followed, probably unconsciously, what he had certainly often heard only a short time before. I cannot really see how else to account for a similarity, which amounts to identity.[73]

Hand realized that he was blazing a new legal trail, adding:

> On the issue of infringement this conclusion is enough. The point is a new one, but I think it is plain. The author's copyright is an absolute right to prevent others from copying his original collocation of words or notes, and does not depend upon the infringer's good faith. Once it appears that another has in fact used the copyright as the source of his production, he has invaded the author's rights. It is no excuse that in so doing his memory has played him a trick.[74]

Despite ruling for the plaintiff, Judge Hand characterized the suit as "a mere point of honor, of scarcely more than irritation, involving no substantial interest. Except that it raises an interesting point of law, it would be a waste of time for every one concerned."[75] Consequently, he awarded the plaintiff only $250 (about $4,500 today) – the minimum amount allowed by law. But with this ruling, the subconscious copying doctrine became part of US jurisprudence.

The notion of unconscious plagiarism could have been appealed to in other infringement cases during the following years, but there seems to have been a general reluctance to invoke it. Litigators may have concluded that it was too difficult to convince a judge or jury that invisible and unknowable forces were responsible for appropriation.

Nevertheless, the subconscious copying doctrine did form the basis of a 1936 appeals court decision in *Sheldon v. Metro-Goldwyn Pictures Corp.* In that case, MGM's movie "Letty Lynton" was found to hew too closely to the play "The Dishonored Lady." In other cases, however, the possibility of access by the defendant was less clear, or the works in question were not considered sufficiently similar.

Following its application in the Harrison case, the subconscious copying doctrine played a role in *Three Boys Music v. Bolton*. In 1991, Michael Bolton and his co-writer Andrew Goldmark had a hit with "Love Is a Wonderful Thing." They were sued for infringement by The Isley Brothers, who had released a song with the same title in 1966. The R&B group alleged that Bolton's song employed a chorus that was similar to their own.

Bolton maintained he had never heard the Isley Brothers' song, and the track does qualify as reasonably obscure: it never entered the Billboard Top 100 and enjoyed only limited airplay. The song was released as a 45-rpm single and didn't even appear on an album until 1991, a year after Bolton and Goldmark had written their song.[76] Therefore, a major issue in the 1994 trial was one of access: could Bolton have ever heard the Isley Brothers' recording? At trial, the pop singer was forced to admit he was a big fan of the R&B group and also confessed to collecting their albums.

Bolton's position was also weakened by the existence of a tape from one of the artists' recording sessions. On it, Bolton can be heard asking Goldmark whether their composition was too similar to Marvin Gaye's "Some Kind of Wonderful." This was evidence, the plaintiffs argued, that Bolton was worried he was copying from other musicians.[77]

All of this was enough to convince a Los Angeles jury to find for the plaintiffs, who were awarded $5.4 million in damages (nearly $11 million today), with Sony Music, Bolton's label, on the hook for most of that amount.[78] The jury's decision was upheld by a federal appeals court six years later. In its ruling, the court opined that "It is entirely plausible that two Connecticut teenagers [Bolton and Goldmark] obsessed with rhythm and blues music could remember an Isley Brothers' song that was played on the radio and television for a few weeks, and subconsciously copy it."[79]

Following the ruling by the Ninth Circuit Court of Appeals, a petition was made to the Supreme Court in 2000. However, the justices declined to hear it.[80] At the time of this writing, it remains the largest settlement ever awarded for musical copyright infringement.

Some legal scholars have been troubled by the application of the subconscious copying doctrine when the works in question are "temporally remote."[81] "Dardanella" had its moment in the sun a year before Kern's musical comedy, and "My Sweet Lord" was preceded by "He's So Fine" by seven years. In both cases, it could be argued that the original works were still "in the air" when the alleged plagiarists were fermenting their own musical ideas. But Bolton's song followed the release of the Isley Brothers' single by twenty-five years. If the unconscious mind has no statute of limitations, then it becomes difficult to draw a bright line between appropriation on the one hand and inspiration on the other.

SELF-PLAGIARISM

In February of 1980, the Knack released an album titled . . . *But the Little Girls Understand.* It was a follow-up to their first record, *Get the Knack*, which had come out only eight months earlier. The band's debut effort had been a huge success, with its first single "My Sharona" rocketing to the top of the Billboard Hot 100 and remaining there for six weeks. "Good Girls Don't," another single from that album, also charted, rising as high as number eleven on the Billboard list.

. . . *But the Little Girls Understand* did not enjoy the same level of success as *Get the Knack*. "Baby Talks Dirty," the album's first single, charted only as high as number 38 on Billboard, and other singles from the album performed even worse. Was it a case of sophomore slump, in which a sterling debut is followed by a less-than-stellar encore?

The song "Baby Talks Dirty," in particular, was criticized as being a "transparent rewrite" of "My Sharona."[82] And as its co-writer, Doug

Fieger put it, "Had that song come out on a fifth album, I think people would have said 'Oh, they've gone back to their roots. They take the 'My Sharona' riff to another place.' But as it was, people were gunning for us."[83] In other words, it seems that the Knack were criticized for sounding too much like ... the Knack.

In a way, stealing from oneself seems like a surefire recipe for success. After all, if the public likes a given artist's work, shouldn't that artist continue to give their fans more of the same? In reality, self-plagiarism of this kind doesn't always work. One problem is that the public can be fickle, and tastes can change. In addition, major hits like "My Sharona" can quickly wear out their welcome through overexposure.

Musical groups that remain popular for many years often go through a continual process of experimentation and development. Reinvention, rather than repetition, may be the reason that such groups remain popular over time. The Beatles are a good example of this progression. As their songs evolved from bubblegum pop to psychedelic-inspired rock, they probably lost some fans, but undoubtedly gained many others who were intrigued by their growth as musicians.

Besides the loss of fans' interest, self-plagiarism can have other draw-backs, as musician John Fogerty discovered. He was a co-founder of Creedence Clearwater Revival (CCR), a group that enjoyed tremendous success in the late 1960s and early 1970s. After that, the musician struck out to establish a solo career. The rights to Fogerty's *oeuvre* with CCR, however, were owned by Fantasy Records' owner Saul Zaentz. And in 1984, when Fogerty recorded "The Old Man Down the Road" for Warner Bros., he was sued by Zaentz on the grounds that the song sounded too much like the 1970 CCR hit "Run through the Jungle." As *The New York Times* put it, "Mr. Zaentz sued Mr. Fogerty for plagiarizing himself – to the tune of $140 million"[84] (over $400 million today). Although Fogerty ultimately prevailed in court, the litigation dragged on for years and cast a shadow over his career.[85]

More recently, Kelly Clarkson accused her co-writer Ryan Tedder of plagiarizing himself on their 2009 single "All I Ever Wanted." Earlier that year, Beyoncé had released "Halo," a song on which she had also worked with Tedder. When Clarkson listened to the two songs in succession, she discovered that the backing track, which includes "somber piano, crashing drums, and hand-claps," was similar on both.[86] Clarkson felt that she had to go public with her concerns to avoid a charge of plagiarism by Beyoncé. Tedder, for his part, characterized Clarkson's claims as "both hateful and absurd."[87]

Not all stories of musical self-plagiarism end badly, however. When composer Giacomo Puccini premiered "Madama Butterfly" at La Scala in February of 1904, the audience nearly rioted, in part because it was seen as borrowing too heavily from his earlier "La Bohème." [88] Puccini withdrew the piece, substantially revised it, and mounted it three months later at Brescia, to great acclaim.[89] It is now one of the most frequently performed of all operas.

Authors, like musicians, can run into trouble when they recycle their earlier material. In 2012, Jonah Lehrer was accused of plagiarizing blog posts for *The New Yorker* from his earlier writing for *The Wall Street Journal*, *Wired*, and other outlets.[90] This led to the discovery that Lehrer had fabricated quotes attributed to Bob Dylan for his bestselling book *Imagine: How Creativity Works*.[91] In a statement, Lehrer apologized to his editors and his readers and resigned from *The New Yorker*. His publisher, Houghton Mifflin, was forced to recall all copies of *Imagine* from booksellers.[92]

Another case of an author's self-plagiarism involves the British writer Enid Blyton. She was both unbelievably prolific and incredibly popular. During a forty-six-year career, she penned more than 700 books for children.[93] Instead of writing according to a plan or conducting research for her stories, however, she relied solely on her imagination, leaving her vulnerable to committing inadvertent plagiarism and also self-plagiarism. As Robert Druce put it, "That she did so [plagiarize] is very clear: just as it is frequently easy to recognize the literary sources outside her own work, so it is easy to see how, in each genre she attempted, individual stories circle over a strictly limited number of plots and settings."[94]

How do authors respond to readers who accuse them of recycling their work? When an indignant fan wrote to Raymond Chandler in 1952 to accuse him of self-plagiarism, he readily agreed with his correspondent. One part of his lengthy reply is particularly illuminating:

> Writers like Dashiell Hammet and myself have been widely and ruthlessly
> imitated, so closely as to amount to a moral plagiarism, even though the

law does not recognize anything but the substantial taking of a plot. I have had stories taken scene by scene and just lightly changed here and there. I have had lines of dialogue taken intact, bits of description also word for word. I have no recourse. The law doesn't call it plagiarism. Against this background you must pardon me if I find it a little bit ludicrous that you should object to my using what is mine in the way that seems to me most suitable and most convenient. If my earlier stories had been published in a magazine of prestige and significance, the situation would have been rather different.[95]

Filmmakers have also been taken to task for repeating themselves. When *Old School* hit theaters in 2003, a critic accused Ivan Reitman of plagiarizing from *Animal House*, the movie on which he had served as a co-producer twenty-five years earlier.[96] (Reitman is not known to have publicly responded to this claim.)

The same issue can bedevil prolific cartoonists. Between 1950 and 2000, Charles Schulz drew a new *Peanuts* comics strip every day, publishing nearly 18,000 over his career. These included two nearly identical strips, distributed on June 11, 1987 and January 20, 1996. In the earlier strip, Snoopy is standing next to a mailbox, perusing a letter. "Dear Contributor," the letter begins. "We are returning your worthless story. It is the dumbest story we have ever read. Please don't send us any more. Please, Please, Please!" In the final panel, Snoopy is smiling and relaxing under a tree, thinking "I love to hear an editor beg."

The strip published nine years later has three panels instead of four, and by its end, Snoopy is atop his doghouse in front of a typewriter. The letter describes his story as "stupid" instead of "worthless" – but otherwise the two strips are identical, right down to the thrice-repeated "please, please, please." [97] Schulz clearly liked this idea, and it seems to have occurred to him twice.

INADVERTENT PLAGIARISM

As we have seen, unconscious plagiarism is appropriation without awareness. In this way, it is fundamentally different from run-of-the-mill plagiarism, in which a person deliberately commandeers someone else's words or ideas. Researchers who study the phenomenon typically refer to it as cryptomnesia or as inadvertent plagiarism. Cognitive psychologists who study the phenomenon have often characterized it as the result of a memory error – a bookkeeping mistake made by one's mental accountant. This can result in a genuine belief that an idea, a phrase, or a melody is the product of one's own mind instead of someone else's.

All of us have experienced memory failures of this type at one time or another. You might, for example, tell a friend an amusing story, only to have them indignantly reply that they told *you* the same anecdote a few days earlier. Or an idea that a business executive overhears becomes, a short while later, their brainstorm for a marketing scheme – much to the chagrin of the rank-and-file employee who initially proposed it. How and why do such mistakes happen?

As we go about our daily lives, we file away the things that happen to us as one type of memory. In other cases, we might only imagine or fantasize about something, and these episodes also become memories, albeit remembrances for events that never truly happened. And then there are the events that happen to other people. These can become memories as well, but in some cases, they might be misremembered as things that happened to us. To account for cases like these, many researchers have made use of a conceptual framework proposed by psychologist Marcia Johnson and her collaborators. It is referred to as the source-monitoring framework.[98]

To explain this approach, let's consider a concrete example. Did you really lock your front door before leaving for work this morning, or did you only think about it but fail to do so? As you nervously reflect on this during your morning commute, you remember that there was a bee buzzing around the doorknob, and that you shooed it away before inserting your key in the lock. Being able to recall *perceptual* details of an episode, such as the sight and sound of the bee, gives you confidence that you truly locked the door as opposed to merely thinking about it. The source-monitoring framework states that the more sensory details we can recall, the more confident we can be that a given memory is real.

Reflective processes are also at work when we attempt to recall something, and the source-monitoring framework specifies two of these.

Heuristic decisions are those that are fast and automatic ("Well of course I locked the door – I always do!"). But such snap judgments are more likely to be inaccurate. Systematic decisions, on the other hand, are deliberate, time-consuming, and effortful. But if you laboriously reconstruct the chain of events as you prepared to leave your apartment, you are more likely to correctly recall whether or not you locked the door.

The scientific study of inadvertent plagiarism began in 1989 with the pioneering work of psychologists Alan Brown and Dana Murphy. They made use of a technique called exemplar generation, which will be familiar to anyone who has seen the TV game show *Family Feud*. Groups of four research participants were assigned categories such as "musical instruments" or "articles of clothing." Each participant was required to produce an appropriate answer, such as "flute" or "shirt" when it was their turn to respond. In total, each participant supplied four exemplars for four different categories, and they were not allowed to repeat any of the other members' answers. By the end, each participant provided sixteen responses and heard forty-eight more generated by the others.

Afterwards, each participant was asked to write down the exemplars they had provided for each category, as well as four completely new items that had not been supplied by the others. If a participant generated a "new" item that had been produced by another participant during the study, it was considered an instance of inadvertent plagiarism. And across three experiments, a majority of the participants made such errors.[99] These results inspired other researchers to determine how and why such errors occur.

In the initial study by Brown and Murphy, the research participants recalled items shortly after they had been generated. In real life, however, inadvertent plagiarism can occur long after one has been exposed to this information. In later studies, the participants were asked to return to the lab a day, a week, or three months later to recall the information. The results were consistent: as the length of time increased, so did incidents of inadvertent plagiarism.[100] It is important to note that this doesn't begin to approach the years or even decades that might elapse before real-world plagiarism occurs, but it does suggest that inadvertent appropriation can occur shortly after exposure and becomes more likely as time goes by.

It's also the case that the appropriation of single-word category members is a pale analogue of real-world cryptomnesia, in which ideas, melodies, or entire literary plots are misperceived as the products of one's own mental processes. To address this limitation, other studies have made use of creative idea generation, such as "How can traffic accidents be reduced?"[101] or to generate alternative uses for common objects, such as a brick or a paper clip.[102] These studies also found substantial rates of inadvertent plagiarism.

The source monitoring framework makes predictions about factors that should affect the identification of a memory's origin, and these conjectures have been largely supported by laboratory studies. In the Brown and Murphy study, for example, inadvertent plagiarism was higher for items named immediately prior to a given participant's own turn. The impending need to respond is thought to temporarily diminish the attention paid to these items, and this makes identifying their source more difficult later.[103]

In addition, source monitoring predicts that perceptual similarity should make it more difficult to accurately recall the source of information. To test this, some studies have manipulated the gender of the participants assigned to the groups producing the category exemplars. When these groups consist of people of the same sex as opposed to mixed-sex groups, the rates of inadvertent plagiarism are nearly twice as high.[104] When others are perceived as similar to ourselves, the cognitive system loses a perceptual cue that helps us keep track of who said what.

Another prediction of the source monitoring framework is that inadvertent plagiarism should become more common as one grows older. The prediction is based on prior research showing that older adults are less skilled at making use of contextual information. This includes the location of objects or the format in which something is learned – for example, whether they are told something by the experimenter or see it projected on a screen.[105]

Does inadvertent plagiarism increase with age? The evidence is mixed. One study did find a higher incidence among participants in their early seventies compared to those in their late teens and early twenties. And by using a variety of cognitive measures, the researchers were able to identify the source of the participants' difficulties. They found that poorer episodic recall – a deficit in recalling past experiences – and decreased working memory capacity, such as the ability to remember a telephone number, were responsible for the older participants' poorer performance.[106] However, a later study that included somewhat younger older adults – those in their mid to late sixties – failed to find a difference in rates of inadvertent plagiarism when compared to participants in their early twenties.[107] The two studies differ in other respects as well, which makes direct comparisons between them difficult.[108]

Even the effect of mood on inadvertent plagiarism has been investigated. This is because the source monitoring framework predicts that happiness is associated with more error-prone heuristic decision processes. Sadness, on the other hand, tends to invoke systematic decision processes that tend to be more accurate. In two experiments, Amanda Gingerich and Chad Dodson induced mood states by having participants write about particularly happy or sad personal experiences for a few minutes. As predicted, the sad participants engaged in less inadvertent plagiarism than those who were happy.[109]

Rates of self-plagiarism are typically fairly low in inadvertent plagiarism studies. In this context, self-plagiarism is defined as providing an earlier response of one's own when asked to generate new examples of a category or an idea. This is also consistent with the source monitoring framework, since self-generated material is typically embedded in a rich set of distinctive retrieval cues.[110] These cues enhance recall and result in fewer memory errors.

Other researchers have taken a different tack by directly asking people about their inadvertent plagiarism experiences. Anne-Catherine Defeldre asked 200 younger adults to recall and describe an episode of inadvertent plagiarism they had experienced. About half were able to do so, and the results were consistent with the source memory framework. For example, same-sex plagiarism was reported far more often than opposite-sex plagiarism. In addition, self-plagiarism was uncommon, suggesting that we have better source memory for our own mental products than for those of others.[111]

Extrapolating the results of these laboratory studies to real-world phenomena can be problematic. Misremembering the source of individual words is clearly not the same as appropriating sentences, ideas, or plot elements. The extant research, however, clearly supports the idea that appropriation can occur without conscious awareness. But as we have seen, the law finds those engaging in "subconscious copying" to be as culpable as those who engage in deliberate plagiarism.

CHAPTER 4

Plagiarism in Politics

O NE WAY TO ASSESS THE IMPACT OF PLAGIARISM IS TO consider how such allegations affect the reputations of politicians. It can be difficult to assess how cribbing by novelists or musicians affects their popularity, but those who stand for public office must face the voting public in order to get elected. In some cases, a plagiarism scandal has completely derailed a political campaign, whereas in other instances, the effect has been minimal.

THE NOMINEES

Issues of plagiarism have cropped up in at least three nominations made by US presidents. During the early 1970s, two of Richard Nixon's nominees found themselves embroiled in such controversies.

The first of these was J. Richard Lucas, who was chosen in May of 1970 to serve as the Director of the Bureau of Mines. At the time, Lucas was a forty-one-year-old professor and chair of the Department of Mining Engineering at Virginia Polytechnic Institute. Lucas's nomination to the post was controversial because of the professor's ties to the coal industry, for whom he had frequently acted as a paid consultant.[1]

On May 25, the first day of the confirmation hearings before the Senate Committee on Interior and Insular Affairs, the syndicated columnist Jack Anderson published a claim that Lucas had plagiarized part of his dissertation at Columbia University, the institution that had awarded his doctorate five years earlier. Anderson alleged that Lucas had been considered by the Johnson administration for a post in the Bureau of Mines, but that a 1965 FBI background report contained the plagiarism

89

allegation.[2] Although Lucas made a "categorical denial" of the charge, the Senate's Interior Committee chose to delay its vote in order to review information provided by the FBI.[3]

On July 8, Lucas wrote to the committee chair, Henry Jackson, to withdraw his nomination. He was bowing out, he said, because the position would require him to sell off his extensive mining securities to avoid a conflict of interest. This, he asserted, would create a hardship for him and his family. In his letter to the chair, Lucas asked that the committee publicly release the results of the FBI's plagiarism investigation. Five days later, Jackson complied by inserting a press release into the *Congressional Record*. It stated that an FBI report, as well as an independent investigation, found the allegations of plagiarism were "totally without foundation, having no basis in fact."[4] Lucas continued his career at Virginia Polytechnic, and later that year, Nixon nominated Elburt Osborn to direct the Bureau of Mines. Osborn's nomination was confirmed by the Senate in October.[5]

Just a few months later, a second Nixon nomination would be shadowed by a legal determination of plagiarism. The nominee was William J. Casey, whom the president had tapped to chair the Securities and Exchange Commission (SEC). Casey had earned a law degree from St. John's University in the late 1930s and was involved in foreign intelligence gathering during the Second World War. Following the war, he specialized in business and tax law with a white shoe firm in New York City. In February and March of 1971, during the confirmation hearing with the Banking and Currency Committee, the senators asked Casey about a plagiarism lawsuit that he had settled by making a payment to the plaintiff.

The episode in question had occurred nine years earlier, in 1962. Casey served as the principal editor of a tax law publication, which included a couple of pages pirated from an article on taxation written by Henry Field. Casey blamed the appropriation on a former employee and claimed that his own role in the incident was minor.[6] He emphasized that even though the jury awarded damages to the plaintiff, the judge didn't believe that their decision was supported by the evidence. Nevertheless, Casey made a payment settlement, and the judge in the case sealed the records. In testimony before the committee, however, the judge disputed Casey's memory of the case.[7]

The Senate committee also investigated two other lawsuits; in these, Casey had been accused of violating securities laws.[8] Nevertheless, on March 10, the Senate Banking and Currency committee voted 9–3 to approve Casey's nomination, and he was approved by the Senate.[9] He would serve for two years as the SEC chairman, and then as Ronald Reagan's CIA director during the 1980s.[10] Clearly, the plagiarism episode didn't derail Casey's career.

A different outcome would befall Michael O'Neill, a forty-six-year-old professor at the George Mason School of Law. O'Neill was nominated by President George W. Bush in June of 2008 for the US District Court for the District of Columbia. O'Neill was a Yale Law School graduate and had clerked for Supreme Court Justice Clarence Thomas. He had gained some visibility – and notoriety – as the chief counsel to the Senate Judiciary Committee. In that role, O'Neill had assisted John Roberts and Samuel Alito as they navigated the treacherous confirmation process to the Supreme Court.

During his academic career, O'Neill had published a number of articles in law journals. However, in 2007 a paper he had published several years earlier was retracted by the *Supreme Court Economic Review*. The editors of the journal had discovered that O'Neill's paper incorporated text from a book review, published in 2000 by Anne Dailey in the *Virginia Law Review*.[11]

Such retractions are unusual, and in academia the appropriation of another scholar's words or ideas is viewed as an extremely serious ethical breach. When questioned about the retracted article by the press, O'Neill blamed no one but himself. The apparent plagiarism, he said, was the result of a "poor work method": he had comingled his own ideas with notes taken from other sources in the same document on his computer.[12]

Unfortunately for O'Neill, his substandard work practices were not confined to the retracted article. Two papers he had published in 2000 were found to contain text from articles published in law review articles in 1985 and 1997. An investigation by his university concluded that the duplication had not been intentional. Nevertheless, O'Neill gave up his tenure status with the understanding that he could reapply for it at a later time.[13]

As we saw in the case of William Casey, plagiarism in one's past does not, by itself, disqualify someone from being appointed to a high office. But O'Neill had been employed as a professor – a profession that often deals harshly with plagiarism when committed by students. And he was guilty of multiple instances of appropriation, making it harder for him to claim that his mistake had been a one-time aberration. Finally, an appointment as a federal judge presumes that one's probity is unimpeachable.

But the law professor had powerful friends, including his former boss, Senator Arlen Spector, who could speak on his behalf. O'Neill's mistakes, Spector argued, should not outweigh his otherwise exemplary service to the nation. O'Neill refused to withdraw his name from the nomination process, and the White House left him twisting in the wind.[14]

Undoubtedly, the administration was thinking back to October of 2005, when Bush had nominated Harriet Miers, his personal lawyer, to fill the Supreme Court vacancy created by the retirement of Sandra Day O'Connor. That decision led to widespread criticism; Miers was widely seen as unqualified, and she ended up withdrawing her name three weeks after Bush had tapped her for the court. This undoubtedly made the White House reluctant to champion a nominee with a problematic history.

In the end, O'Neill's nomination was never acted upon, and it was returned to the president six months later, with the expiration of the 110th Congress in January of 2009. This was not all that unusual – nineteen other nominees to District courts met the same fate at that time – but it does suggest that O'Neill's academic misconduct cost him a confirmation hearing. Without a hearing, there was no hope that he would get a position on the federal court.

THE SENATORS

During a 1950 Lincoln Day speech in West Virginia, Senator Joseph McCarthy made the incendiary claim that Harry Truman's State Department was overrun with Communists. As part of his remarks to the Ohio County Women's Republican Club, the politician from Wisconsin thundered that "We are not dealing with spies who get 30 pieces of silver to steal the blueprint of a new weapon. We are dealing with a far more sinister type of activity because it permits the enemy to guide and shape our policy." He went on to claim that he held in his hands a list of fifty-seven government officials who were either "card carrying members or certainly loyal to the Communist Party."[15]

McCarthy brandished his purported list during his speech and would later display it on the floor of the Senate, but he never made it public – and for good reason. As he told J. Edgar Hoover, the director of the FBI, he had gotten "carried away" during his address and pulled a laundry slip from his pocket. "There was nothing on it. I don't have any such names."[16]

Moreover, McCarthy's list wasn't the only problematic issue about his presentation; he had plagiarized his remarks from a speech about Alger Hiss that Representative Richard Nixon delivered the previous month. McCarthy repeated portions of Nixon's speech almost verbatim when he spoke in Wheeling.[17] Based on the success of his Lincoln Day speech, he would wield incredible power in Washington for the next four years, until he overreached during the Army–McCarthy hearings.

* * *

On October 28, 2013, Kentucky Senator Rand Paul gave a speech in support of the candidacy of Ken Cuccinelli, the Republican candidate in Virginia's gubernatorial election. The main topic of his remarks at Liberty University was his opposition to abortion – a position also supported by Cuccinelli. In one section of his speech, Paul compared prochoice advocates to the eugenicists depicted in the 1997 movie *Gattaca*. The film imagines a totalitarian future in which one's genetic endowment controls major aspects of one's life.

On her MSNBC program that evening, Rachel Maddow pointed out similarities between Paul's description of the movie and the film's entry in Wikipedia. She compared Paul's remarks and lines from the online encyclopedia during the broadcast and concluded that the Senator's description of the plot had been "totally ripped off."[18] But could someone have changed the Wikipedia entry after Paul's speech to make it appear he had plagiarized from the website? A check of the page's revision history, which contains time stamps, showed that no such alterations had been made.[19]

After journalists began to scour Paul's previous speeches and public writings for other instances of appropriation, an investigation by BuzzFeed News alleged that Paul had recycled content from Wikipedia's entry about *Stand and Deliver*, the 1988 film, for two speeches on immigration that he had delivered during the summer. A spokesperson for Paul claimed that the issue was "trivial" and a product of "liberal media angst."[20]

But in early November, journalist Andrew Kaczynski reported issues with a book Paul had published the previous year. *Government Bullies: How Everyday Americans are Being Harassed, Abused, and Imprisoned by the Feds* was found to have numerous attribution issues. These included over 1,300 words taken verbatim from a Heritage Foundation report issued a decade earlier. Although the report was cited as a source, the material was not set off with quotation marks to indicate that the words were not Paul's. Other similarities were found between Paul's book and the writing of a Cato Institute fellow,[21] as well as verbatim copying from articles that had appeared in *Forbes*, the Cato Institute's *Regulation*, and *Environmental Protection*.[22] In response, Center Street, the publisher of *Government Bullies*, said that the attribution problems would be corrected in later printings of the book.[23]

Paul had also been writing weekly opinion columns for the conservative *Washington Times*, and it was discovered that an article by him, about mandatory minimum prison sentences, included three paragraphs taken verbatim from one that had appeared in the news magazine *The Week*.[24] Paul and the newspaper chose to end his column, with the paper characterizing it as a mutual decision.[25]

Paul's response to these accusations varied as time went by. Initially, he was combative, saying, "This is really about information and attacks coming from haters,"[26] and even jokingly suggested that, if it were legal, he might have to challenge his detractors to a duel.[27] But a few days later, after additional allegations were made, he was more contrite. Paul acknowledged to CNN that he and his staff hadn't always cited sources properly, and admitted that "Ultimately, I'm the boss, and things go out under my name, so it is my fault."[28] He reorganized his staff and declared that "What we are going to do from here forward, if it will make people leave me the hell alone, is we're going to do them [speeches and articles] like college papers."[29]

A week after Paul's assertion, *The New York Times* noted that the script of a speech, delivered by the senator at The Citadel, contained nearly three dozen footnotes.[30] It seems that the senator and his staff had learned an important lesson from the controversy of the previous weeks.

In an ironic coda to the senator's troubles, it was discovered that content from Paul's 2010 website had been plagiarized by Greg Brannon, a Republican candidate for the 2014 senate race in North Carolina. Paul had previously endorsed Brannon, and in turn the Brannon campaign helped themselves to Paul's positions on monetary policy, education, and healthcare. The text on Brannon's site appeared to have been copied word for word from Paul's.[31] When confronted with the evidence, Brannon claimed that the web pages had been drafted by a staffer but that he approved them. He apologized for the copying and said that the website's content would be changed to "make the source clear."[32] (Brannon lost the Republican primary to Thom Tillis, who went on to notch a narrow victory over the Democratic incumbent, Kay Hagan.)

But how much damage did multiple accusations of plagiarism inflict on Paul's reputation and his political aspirations? Earlier in 2013, he had been seen as a leading contender for the Republican presidential nomination in 2016. But Paul finished fifth in the Iowa caucus that year, garnering less than 5 percent of the vote and well behind Ted Cruz and Donald Trump. Paul dropped out of the race, but was easily reelected to the Senate, defeating his Democratic challenger Jim Gray. He was elected to a third term in 2022 with an even more decisive victory over Charles Booker.

* * *

Just a few months after Rand Paul's run-in with plagiarism, his colleague in the Senate, John Walsh, was moving up in the world. After serving as the lieutenant governor of Montana for a year, Walsh was appointed to the Senate in February of 2014 by Governor Steve Bullock. The vacancy had occurred because Senator Max Baucus resigned to become the Obama administration's ambassador to China.

Walsh had been planning to run against Baucus in the 2014 Democratic primary, and with the resignation of the incumbent, he stood a good chance of prevailing over Democratic challengers in the primary, as well as his Republican opponent in November. But it was not to be. As expected, Walsh easily won his party's nomination in early June, but two months later, he dropped out of the race.

John Walsh certainly had the résumé to be a successful politician. He had risen to the rank of brigadier general in the Montana National Guard and was a decorated veteran who had commanded troops as an Army colonel in Iraq. After that year-long tour of combat duty, Walsh earned a master's degree in strategic studies in 2007 from the prestigious US Army War College. As a degree requirement, the War College asked its students to produce a document called a strategy research project. Walsh's was titled "The Case for Democracy as a Long Term National Strategy." And it was that document that was his undoing.

In a front-page article on July 23, *The New York Times* broke the story that Walsh had appropriated without attribution "about a third" of his paper from the writings of others. The *Times* called particular attention to a set of recommendations that Walsh included in his paper's concluding section. More than 800 words, the *Times* asserted, had been copied verbatim and without citation from work by scholars affiliated with the Carnegie Endowment for International Peace.

The newspaper also reported that "significant portions" had been taken from work by Sean Lynn-Jones, a scholar at the Belfer Center for Science and International Affairs at Harvard. In addition, footnoted passages throughout the paper appeared as identical or only slightly changed within Walsh's text, and they lacked the requisite quotation marks – a practice explicitly deemed as unacceptable by the War College's writing manual.[33]

The *Times*'s article was accompanied by a graphic reproducing the entire nineteen-page document, with an overlay of two colors to highlight passages in which attribution was improper or lacking entirely. Every page was stained with the highlighting, and a couple of pages were entirely filled in.[34]

The following day, the *Times* reported that the War College had begun the process of reviewing the allegations. The article emphasized that students at the Army's college receive "rigorous" and "intense" instruction on the topic of academic integrity. They are also required to sign a document asserting that the work they turn in is theirs alone. In short, there was no way that Walsh didn't understand the institution's rules about plagiarism.[35]

How had the *Times* discovered what Walsh had done? Months later, *The Hill* would report that a researcher with the National Republican Senatorial Committee (NRSC) had been the source of the plagiarism allegation, and that the NRSC had provided the *Times* with evidence of Walsh's alleged malfeasance.[36]

And how did Walsh respond to the accusation? He initially denied having intentionally engaged in plagiarism. And on the following day, he suggested he had been suffering from post-traumatic stress disorder after his year of service in Iraq. But then he backed away from that explanation, declaring that "I made a mistake and I'm going to move on."[37] The Democratic Senatorial Campaign Committee, fearing that the scandal might cost the party a Senate seat, threw its support firmly behind Walsh.[38] For their part, voters in Montana, who were not especially familiar with the senator or the significance of scholarly attribution, largely took a wait-and-see attitude.[39]

Perhaps fearing the outcome of the investigation, and only two weeks after the *Times* broke the story, Walsh decided to finish the term to which he had been appointed, but dropped out of the race that could have given him six more years in office. In a statement, he said that the accusation of plagiarism had "become a distraction from the debate you expect and deserve."[40] When in early October the War College completed its inquiry, Walsh was found guilty of plagiarizing his paper and his master's degree was revoked. As was customary in such cases, the College also removed Walsh's name from the school's bronze tablet that listed the institution's graduates.[41]

Scrambling to find a replacement candidate, the state's Democratic Central Committee settled on first-term state lawmaker Amanda Curtis.[42] And in November the former math teacher lost her bid to the Republican candidate Steve Daines. In addition to Walsh's seat, the Republicans picked up eight other seats that fall, allowing the party to regain control of the upper chamber of Congress for the first time in eight years.

It is instructive to compare what happened to Paul, who retained his seat in the Senate, and what happened to Walsh, who chose to vacate his.

Considering the public's relatively low opinion of politicians, one might argue that appropriation is simply viewed as less serious than other peccadillos, such as financial improprieties or marital infidelity. It may also be the case that Walsh, fairly or not, was held to a higher standard. As we saw in Chapter 2, academic plagiarism is considered a more serious offense than garden-variety verbal borrowing. And the revocation of one's degree is more significant than stepping away from writing an opinion column or having one's publisher revise a book's citations.

* * *

In late October of 2004, an article in *The New York Sun* alleged that the Democratic candidate for president, Senator John Kerry, had engaged in plagiarism multiple times during his political career. Evidence of this, the article claimed, had been discovered by a doctoral student who wished to remain anonymous. The graduate student was said to have identified eleven passages in works by Kerry that had been taken from others without attribution.

Half of the allegations involved a book that Kerry had published seven years earlier. Titled *The New War: The Web of Crime That Threatens America's National Security*, it addressed the dangers posed by global crime organizations. But the *Sun*'s reporting alleged that a sentence in the book had been taken verbatim from a 1993 article in *The Philadelphia Inquirer*. In addition, a three-sentence passage in Kerry's book is highly similar to one appearing in a 1996 article in *Maclean's* magazine. (This article was cited in *The New War*, but not as a source for the passage in question.)

The *Sun* also reported that a passage in *Our Plan for America*, a book released by the Kerry campaign, contained two consecutive sentences from a 2003 fact sheet put out by the Department of Energy. Finally, Kerry was said to have plagiarized from *Slate*, the online magazine, in a speech he had delivered on desegregation.[43]

Were the allegations against Kerry politically motivated? The timing of the *Sun*'s revelations – one week before the presidential election – certainly raises suspicions. The newspaper had been founded two years earlier and had established itself as a conservative voice in New York City. Perhaps the paper was trying to make a name for itself with an "October surprise" that would influence the election.[44]

The *Sun*'s story also included commentary by two plagiarism experts. Interestingly, they came to somewhat different conclusions about Kerry's culpability. Robert Harris, a professor of English, opined that the examples furnished by the paper were clear instances of plagiarism. Professor and novelist Thomas Mallon, on the other hand, argued that much of what politicians ostensibly write is prepared by their staffs, and so Kerry may not have been directly responsible for the passages in question.

It's also worth noting that the *Sun*'s reporting debunked one of the charges of plagiarism that had been leveled against Kerry. In an article published in *Foreign Policy* in 2003, the senator had provided some statistics about the shortage of translators in the US Army. Kerry's description is similar to a passage that had previously appeared in a magazine called *Government Executive*. However, a spokesperson for *Foreign Policy* told the *Sun* that Kerry's source had been a 2002 report by the Government Accountability Office (GAO). Material produced by federal agencies like the GAO are in the public domain and can be reproduced without permission.[45] (Neither Kerry nor his campaign seems to have weighed in on the *Sun*'s allegations.)

Did this controversy have any effect on the outcome of the election? Other news organizations seem not to have picked up on the paper's reporting, so its influence was probably limited. Kerry's reputation seems to have been much more affected by a group calling itself Swift Boat Veterans for Truth, which claimed that Kerry had misrepresented his record of service in Vietnam.[46] Kerry's loss to George W. Bush that fall reflected the challenge of running against a reasonably popular incumbent. And the plagiarism allegation doesn't seem to have had any long-term effect on his career: Kerry was reelected to the Senate in 2008 and then confirmed to be President Obama's Secretary of State – by a vote of 94 to 3 – in 2013.[47]

* * *

John Kerry wasn't the first presidential contender to be accused of plagiarism. Candidates and even their spouses have been criticized for their appropriations while on the campaign trail.

In the spring of 2008, Cindy McCain contributed several recipes to the campaign website of her husband, John McCain. Labeled as "McCain

Family Recipes," their provenance was called into question by New York attorney Lauren Handel, who was searching for a specific concoction created by a chef with the Food Network. However, the lawyer's web searches kept returning links to McCain's political website in addition to the expected culinary page. In this way, Handel discovered that some of the "family" recipes had been lifted from the Food Network site. At least three of Cindy McCain's ingredient lists were carbon copies.[48] And a recipe from Rachael Ray, for rosemary chicken breasts with warm spinach salad, had been altered only slightly. [49]

This culinary kerfuffle, perhaps inevitably dubbed "recipegate," was attributed by McCain to the work of an intern, who, she joked on *The View*, was "now in Betty Crocker boot camp."[50] It's worth noting that at least one of the chefs in question, instead of being upset or offended, was flattered. The creator of a purloined recipe for ahi tuna with napa cabbage slaw – a Hillary Clinton supporter – said that she would be happy to prepare her dish for the McCains.[51] Undoubtedly, the unexpected publicity was responsible for her generosity.

Later in 2008, on August 11, John McCain gave a speech about Russia's invasion of the Republic of Georgia, which had occurred four days earlier. Given that most Americans knew little about the former Soviet state, McCain's remarks included some background about Georgia's history.

McCain's address came to the attention of an editor for Wikipedia, who thought the historical introduction didn't truly fit with the rest of the speech. He checked a version of Wikipedia's entry on Georgia, one created before McCain's remarks, and found that two paragraphs – approximately one-eighth of the entire address – seemed to have been taken from the online encyclopedia.[52] The editor contacted the blogger Taegan Goddard, who publicized the alleged copying.[53]

Brian Rogers, a spokesperson for McCain's campaign, denied the charge of plagiarism. "There are only so many ways to state basic historical facts and dates," he asserted, and claimed that any similarity to the Wikipedia entry was simply a coincidence.[54] Mark Salter, McCain's primary speechwriter, released an email from the candidate that described the type of speech he wanted to give, but Salter didn't comment on the sources that were used to write it.[55]

As with his wife's purloined recipes, the press largely treated the episode as the punchline for a joke. Craig Ferguson, on *The Late Show*, was incredulous that anyone believed the seventy-one-year-old senator was guilty of theft. "McCain doesn't know how to use the internet," Ferguson deadpanned, "So how could you even accuse him of that?"[56]

Although John McCain had held off primary challenges from Mitt Romney and Mike Huckabee, he lost to Barack Obama in the general election that November. However, he was easily reelected to the Senate in 2010 and 2016. Cindy McCain, for her part, went on to serve as the US ambassador to the United Nations for Food and Agriculture during the Biden administration. Her interest in nutrition, it would seem, had been undimmed by recipegate.

VEEPS

It was John Nance Garner, vice president during Franklin Roosevelt's first three terms in office, who famously described the veep's job as "not worth a bucket of warm piss."[57] Despite such an unflattering description, the holders of this political office are often in the public eye as they campaign, give speeches, and grant interviews. And on a number of occasions, their words have led to accusations of plagiarism.

In March of 1970, for example, Spiro Agnew gave a speech to the National Alliance of Businessmen. In his address, he asserted that the country's suburbs needed to help inner-city residents to find jobs and housing. These were fine sentiments, but large portions of Agnew's remarks had been drawn verbatim from a memorandum written by two urban planners working as consultants for the NAACP. The planners, who were championing changes to the nation's zoning laws, had sent their memo to the vice president during the previous year.[58] In his speech, Agnew didn't acknowledge the memo or its authors. Nevertheless, Neil Newton Gold, who had co-authored it, told *The New York Times* that he was "delighted" by the veep's remarks, since the speech called attention to an important issue.[59]

Later that year, Agnew made his famous observation about politicians who were critical of Nixon's policies, referring to them as "nattering nabobs of negativism." Although the phrase wasn't his, it had been crafted for him by William Safire, a White House speechwriter.[60] Safire would go on to have a long career with *The New York Times*, whereas Agnew would resign three years later, after pleading no contest to a charge of tax evasion.[61]

Once chosen by their running mates, vice-presidential candidates often find their entire lives subjected to intense scrutiny by the press. And in August of 1988, it was Dan Quayle's turn under the microscope when George H. W. Bush selected him for the number two position. The forty-one-year-old senator from Indiana had received a degree in political science from DePauw University in 1969, and the *Los Angeles Times* reported on "longstanding rumors" that he engaged in plagiarism as an undergraduate.[62] Quayle's decision not to allow the university to release his academic records was criticized as "stonewalling" by the candidate.[63]

According to *The Washington Post*, these rumors were started by former staff members of Birch Bayh, who lost to Quayle in the 1980 Indiana Senate race. But when the *Post* reporters followed up with Quayle's former teachers, they found no evidence to support the allegation.[64] Bush and Quayle would win in 1988, and then lose to Bill Clinton and Al Gore in 1992. Quayle ended his own run for the presidency in September of 1999 after being outspent by his former running mate's son and by Steve Forbes.[65]

Before becoming Clinton's vice-presidential candidate in 1992, Al Gore had campaigned for the top job during the 1988 campaign. And he did himself no favors in New Hampshire by telling voters the following anecdote: "I shook hands with a group of people in a store in Manchester, and I said, 'I'm Senator Al Gore. I'm campaigning for president.' One of them said, 'Yeah we know, we were just laughing about that this morning.'"

This humorous attempt at modesty fell flat because the episode hadn't happened to him. It was claimed by its rightful owner, Morris (Mo) Udall, the Arizona senator who had campaigned in New Hampshire for the 1976 nomination. Udall wrote to his fellow Democrat, saying:

> If imitation is indeed the sincerest form of flattery, then I am flattered. You gave one of my most treasured lines as your own. I know that we politicians are often accused of thievery, but this goes beyond the bounds ... I hereby relinquish all personal claims to my stories with the exception of 'just

laughing about that this morning.' It is too personal, too meaningful for me to surrender. Good luck.[66]

Gore would finish sixth in New Hampshire the following February, well behind Michael Dukakis, the eventual nominee, and he suspended his campaign after losing in New York in April.[67] A second run for the presidency in 2000, following eight years as Clinton's veep, would end in a popular vote victory and controversial electoral vote loss to George W. Bush.

In an ironic coda to the 2000 campaign, Gore's concession speech, following the Supreme Court's ruling in *Bush v. Gore*, would itself be plagiarized. The offender was Nana Akufo-Addo, who lost his bid for the presidency of Ghana in 2012.[68] As with Gore, it was the country's Supreme Court that upheld his opponent's victory. In acknowledging his loss, Akufo-Addo's address contained verbatim sections from Gore's remarks. Four years later, when Akufo-Addo was elected president, his inauguration speech was found to be stocked with verbiage from Bill Clinton's and George W. Bush's inaugural addresses.[69]

In the annals of plagiarism, the July 2016 Republican National Convention in Cleveland looms large on the historical landscape. Melania Trump's apparent appropriation of Michelle Obama's remarks, from the Democratic convention eight years earlier, consumed a great deal of the media's attention. The episode – which will be described in full in the next chapter – may have allowed the acceptance speech by Trump's running mate, Mike Pence, to fly under the radar to some degree. But Pence's oration is worth examining because it illustrates the hazy line between theft and homage.

In his remarks, the governor of Indiana said he believed that America had "come to another rendezvous with destiny." Roosevelt had referred to a rendezvous with destiny in his 1936 acceptance speech, as had Reagan in his famous remarks in support of Barry Goldwater. Reagan's 1964 address has become known as the "A Time for Choosing" speech, and Pence made use of that line as well. But considering his convention audience and how familiar they must have been with Reagan's *oeuvre*, it is difficult to characterize Pence's quotations as anything other than tribute paid to the Great Communicator.[70]

More controversially, Pence also made use of the phrase "boundless capacity of the American people" – a line employed in 1999 by Bill Clinton, in his last State of the Union address. (It had also been used by Joe Biden in 2011 and 2013, and even by Pence himself in his address to the Conservative Political Action Conference, or CPAC, in 2015.) But it seemed like a strange quotation for Pence to include in his 2016 acceptance speech, given that he and Donald Trump were running against the wife of the man he was allegedly borrowing from.[71]

A final example of veep appropriation involves a childhood anecdote related by Kamala Harris. It was included in the preface to her 2009 book, *Smart on Crime* (at the time, Harris was the District Attorney of San Francisco):

> My early memories are of a sea of legs marching around the streets and the sounds of shouting. The conversations in our apartment in the Berkeley flatlands area on Bancroft Avenue would go late into the night, and of course, we picked up the language of the [civil rights] movement. My mother used to laugh when she told the story about a time I was fussing as a toddler: She leaned down to ask me, "Kamala, what's wrong? What do you want?" and I wailed back, "Fweedom."[72]

Harris's remembrance is charming, but the episode has a great deal in common with one related by Martin Luther King to Alex Haley, in an interview for *Playboy* magazine. Toward the end of the article, King is quoted as saying:

> I never will forget a moment in Birmingham when a white policeman accosted a little Negro girl, seven or eight years old, who was walking in a demonstration with her mother. "What do you want?" the policeman asked her gruffly, and the little girl looked him straight in the eye and answered, "Fee-dom." She couldn't even pronounce it, but she knew.[73]

The interview was published in 1965, a few months after King received the Nobel Peace Prize and three years before his assassination in Memphis.

Had Gopalan Shyamala, Kamala's mother, read Haley's interview and somehow intertwined it with her memories of Kamala's childhood? Shyamala passed away in early 2009, the year that *Smart on Crime* was published, so she was never asked about the clarity of her recollection. Harris, however, repeated the story in her 2019 book, *The Truths We Hold*[74] and also in a number of interviews. The similarity between the two accounts was noted when Harris's reminiscence appeared in a piece published in *Elle*, shortly before she was sworn into office as vice president.[75]

Both *Newsweek*[76] and Snopes, the fact-checking website,[77] investigated the striking similarity between the two stories, and both outlets concluded that, without testimony from Kamala's mother, it was impossible to draw any conclusions about appropriation. It should be noted that Harris has always made clear that the story was told by her mother and was not her own childhood memory. But as we have already seen, it can be incredibly difficult to differentiate between deliberate plagiarism and unconscious borrowing, especially given the malleability of human memory in general.

THE MECKLENBURG DECLARATION

Tourists who visit North Carolina might take advantage of its fine Atlantic beaches in the east or scenic mountains in the west. And during their visit, these visitors might catch a glimpse of the state flag, consisting of red and white bars with a blue union on the left. Within the field of blue, our tourists might note the state's initials, a star, and two dates: May 20, 1775, and April 12, 1776. The second date is easy to explain: it commemorates the Halifax Resolves, a resolution advocating for independence from Great Britain. But the first date, eleven months earlier, is mired in a controversy that has raged for more than two centuries. May 20, 1775, is the purported date of the Mecklenburg Declaration of Independence and is connected to an act of plagiarism allegedly committed by the third US president.

Every American schoolchild learns that the Declaration of Independence was ratified by delegates to the Second Continental Congress, meeting in Philadelphia, on July 4, 1776. Three weeks earlier, a committee had been appointed to draft such a declaration, and it was decided that one of its five members, Thomas Jefferson, would pen the first draft. After laboring alone for several days, he shared his handiwork with the other committee members for their input.

This revised document was then presented to the Congress. Its members spent a couple of days shortening and editing the text, and on July 2, twelve of the thirteen colonial delegations voted for independence. (The New York delegation did not have the authority to vote on the resolution.) After some additional tweaks, the declaration's wording was approved on July 4. John Hancock, in his role as president of the Congress, signed it, with most of the Congress's delegates adding their own names to a parchment copy on August 2.

What did Jefferson draw on for inspiration? The most obvious sources are the political writings of the British philosopher John Locke and the pamphleteer Thomas Paine, whose *Common Sense*, published six months earlier, had stoked the fires of colonial rebellion. Jefferson also drew on his own writings, such as drafts for Virginia's constitution.

In terms of Jefferson's choice of words, it seems clear that he borrowed from the Virginia Declaration of Rights, which was published in the *Pennsylvania Gazette* as Jefferson began drafting his own declaration. Virginia's proclamation, written principally by George Mason, includes the line "All men are by nature equally free and independent, and have certain inherent rights; ... namely, the enjoyment of life and liberty, with the means of acquiring and possessing property, and pursuing and obtaining happiness and safety."[78] This is strikingly similar to Jefferson's "We hold these truths to be self-evident, that all men are created equal, and are endowed by their Creator with certain unalienable rights, that among these are Life, Liberty and the pursuit of Happiness."

But the charge of plagiarism against Jefferson would be leveled by the second US president, John Adams. Adams was made aware of a document called the Mecklenburg Declaration in June of 1819, when a Massachusetts newspaper reprinted an article that had appeared in the *Raleigh Register*. It described a declaration that had been written and ratified in Mecklenburg County, North Carolina over a year before Jefferson's brainchild. Adams and Jefferson maintained a voluminous correspondence during their retirements from public life, and Adams sent the article about the Mecklenburg document to the Virginian, inquiring whether he had ever seen it before.[79]

The Mecklenburg Declaration was the result of a two-day meeting held in May of 1775 in Charlotte, with delegates drawn from the militia companies of the county. News had reached the village of the April battles at Lexington and Concord in Massachusetts, and emotions were running high. In an act of defiance against British rule, the delegates voted unanimously to declare independence from the crown. Five resolutions were penned by Ephraim Brevard, William Kennon, and Hezekiah Balch – a physician, a lawyer, and a Presbyterian minister who all happened to be graduates of the College of New Jersey (now Princeton University). The delegates, who were about twenty-seven in number, approved these resolutions unanimously.[80]

A few days later, so the story goes, the Declaration was dispatched to the Second Continental Congress, then meeting in Philadelphia. The 550-mile journey along the Great Wagon Road was undertaken by Captain James Jack, a tavern owner, who delivered copies of the document to the Congress's three delegates from North Carolina. These men conferred with John Hancock, John Jay, and Thomas Jefferson, but the Congress, still hoping to avoid all-out war, deemed talk of independence to be, at best, premature.[81]

Although accounts vary, after approving their Declaration, the Mecklenburg delegates drafted and endorsed a list of resolves with the goal of annulling British authority. But this is where the story becomes complicated. The original copy of the Mecklenburg Declaration was lost in a fire in 1800 and was reconstructed a few months later by John McKnitt Alexander, who had served as secretary at the Mecklenburg meeting. It is believed that he relied on his memory as well as an undated copy of the Declaration that was probably made in the early 1790s. And it was this version that had come to the attention of the *Raleigh Register* and, ultimately, to John Adams.[82]

Adams and others noted that the five Mecklenburg resolutions contained phrases echoed in the Continental Congress's declaration, such as "dissolve the political bonds which have connected us"; "absolve ourselves from all allegiance to the British Crown"; and "pledge to each other, our mutual cooperation, our lives, our fortunes, and our most sacred honor."[83] This seems much more than a coincidence, and as Adams put it in a letter to William Bentley, "Either these resolutions are a plagiarism from Mr. Jefferson's Declaration of Independence, or

Mr. Jefferson's Declaration of Independence is a plagiarism from those resolutions."[84]

A number of historians have expressed doubt about the existence of the Mecklenburg Declaration, at least in the form that appeared in the 1819 newspaper account. Some believe that there was confusion with the Mecklenburg Resolves, approved in Charlotte several days after the purported Declaration. (The Resolves themselves were lost and only rediscovered in 1838.)[85]

Nonetheless, there are many who believe that the Declaration and the Resolves were separate resolutions, and that the Mecklenburg proclamation should be recognized as the nation's first claim of independence from Britain. In 1831, a North Carolina Governor's Report, which included thirteen eyewitness accounts, concluded that the Declaration was authentic. And as we have seen, the matter has become a point of pride in North Carolina, with the date of the Declaration appearing on the state seal and flag. For many years, there were May 20 celebrations in Charlotte, and no fewer than four sitting presidents – Taft, Wilson, Eisenhower, and Ford – visited the city to join in the festivities.[86]

How did Jefferson respond to Adams's query about the Mecklenburg Declaration? In a reply to his fellow former president the following month, Jefferson stated he believed it was "spurious." Why, he wondered, had no one ever heard of it before? He also cast doubt on the purported declaration's provenance, since the article Adams had sent him mentioned that the original had been lost in a fire.[87]

During his lifetime, Jefferson provided a number of accounts about drafting the Declaration. In an 1823 letter to James Madison, he stated:

> Whether I had gathered my ideas from reading or reflection I do not know. I know only that I turned to neither book nor pamphlet while writing it. I did not consider it as any part of my charge to invent new ideas altogether, and to offer no sentiment which had ever been expressed before.[88]

And in a letter to Henry Lee in 1825, he wrote: "Neither aiming at originality of principle or sentiment, nor yet copied from any particular and previous writing, it was intended to be an expression of the American mind." In the same letter, he does mention Aristotle, Cicero, John Locke, and Algernon Sidney as sources of inspiration.[89]

If the Mecklenburg Declaration did exist, as its champions claim, then it is certainly possible that Jefferson saw one of the copies that Captain Jack delivered to the delegates from North Carolina. And he may have unconsciously plagiarized from the Mecklenburg Declaration without realizing it. However, it's also possible that he consciously helped himself to the Mecklenburg verbiage and then dissembled about never having seen it before.

On the other hand, unconscious plagiarism could have flowed in the opposite direction. It's possible that the post-1800 reconstruction of the Mecklenburg Declaration, which seems to have partly relied on McKnitt Alexander's memory, was influenced by Jefferson's eloquence. At this remove, it is simply not possible to arrive at a definitive conclusion. Jefferson may have been the first president to be accused of plagiarism, but he would not be the last.

PRESIDENTIAL PILFERING?

When Jimmy Carter died at the age of 100 in late 2024, he had been an ex-president for forty-three years – longer than any of his predecessors or successors. And after his presidency, he was a prolific author, publishing at least two dozen books, including memoirs, political tracts, and even a novel. Many of these works were well received, but a book about the Middle East, published in November of 2006, ignited a firestorm of controversy. The title of Carter's book – *Palestine: Peace Not Apartheid* – was intentionally provocative and interpreted as a comparison of the South African policy of segregation with Israel's policies toward the Palestinians living in the West Bank.[90] The book's criticism of Israel caused fourteen members of the Carter Center to resign in protest.[91]

Objections of a distinctly different nature were raised by Dennis Ross, a diplomat who served as an envoy to the Middle East during the Clinton presidency, and then as an advisor in the Obama administration. Based on those experiences, he published a 2004 memoir titled *The Missing Peace: The Inside Story of the Fight for Middle East Peace*. When Carter's book appeared two years later, Ross was working as an analyst for Fox News. On that network, he accused Carter of having appropriated, without attribution, two maps that Ross had commissioned for his memoir.[92] (He also accused the former president of mislabeling the maps in a way that misrepresented Clinton's peace proposal.[93]) Carter, for his part, claimed in a CNN interview to have never seen Ross's book.[94] And at least one media organization has concluded that the maps are "clearly not identical."[95]

* * *

Ronald Reagan, known as the Great Communicator, is well remembered for remarks that he made in front of the Brandenburg Gate in West Berlin on June 12, 1987. In the middle of his half-hour speech, Reagan addressed his words directly to the leader of the Soviet Union:

> General Secretary Gorbachev, if you seek peace, if you seek prosperity for the Soviet Union and Eastern Europe, if you seek liberalization, come here to this gate. Mr. Gorbachev, *open* this gate. [applause] Mr. Gorbachev, Mr. Gorbachev, tear *down* this wall!

At that point, the Berlin Wall had divided the eastern and western zones of the city for nearly twenty-six years. But late in the evening of November 9, 1989, East German guards began to allow the crowds thronging at the checkpoints to cross over into the West, and the wall itself was pulled down over the following days. Reagan's exhortation had seemingly been transformed from pipe dream to prescience in a mere twenty-nine months.

But Reagan wasn't the first US leader to call for the wall to come down. Two months before Reagan visited West Berlin, Democratic House Speaker Jim Wright had made similar remarks in a speech delivered in the divided city. Wright was annoyed that Reagan got the credit for "tear down this wall," but was quoted as saying, "I'm not going to sue him for plagiarism."[96]

* * *

The writing of memoirs by former presidents can be tricky affairs. Striking the right balance between justifying one's executive decisions and not appearing overly defensive or partisan is not easy. It's perhaps not a coincidence that the most highly regarded memoir penned by a former president – Ulysses Grant's *Personal Memoirs* – focuses on his military career as opposed to his time in the White House.

Except for presidents Roosevelt and Kennedy, who did not outlive their presidencies, every modern chief executive has written some sort of autobiography or memoir after his political career. It's apparently hard to resist the opportunity to control the narrative – or at least attempt to. And undoubtedly, part of the appeal is financial. It was a desire to provide for his family that motivated the terminally ill Grant. And the work is lucrative. Bill Clinton received a $15 million advance for his 2004 auto-biography, *My Life*. And in 2017, it was reported that Penguin Random House had made a joint deal for $65 million with Barack and Michelle Obama for books to be written by each of them.[97]

George W. Bush published his memoir, *Decision Points*, at the end of 2010. And soon after the 500-page book's release, a Pakistani journalist accused the former president of plagiarism. This may seem like an odd charge to level at a memoirist, but Ahmed Rashid claimed that Bush had appropriated an anecdote involving the inauguration of Hamid Karzai as president of Afghanistan in December of 2001.[98] Bush hadn't attended the event but included a direct quote from Karzai in *Decision Points*. Rashid asserted that the incident and the quote had been taken directly from an article he had written for *The New York Review of Books* in 2004.[99]

Ryan Grim, writing for *The Huffington Post*, claimed that Bush had also appropriated from books written by *The Washington Post*'s Bob Woodward, as well as *Dead Certain: The Presidency of George W. Bush*, a work published in 2007 by the journalist Robert Draper. Grim places particular emphasis on borrowings from Tommy Franks's 2004 memoir, *American Soldier*. As Grim puts it, "the similarities between the way Bush recollects his and other['s] quotes may be a case of remarkable random chance or evidence that he and his deputies were in an almost supernatural sync. If so, he essentially shares a brain with General Tommy Franks." Grim illustrated his point with passages from both books that do seem strikingly similar.[100]

A spokesperson for Crown Publishers, which had released Bush's memoir, claimed that any similarities between the ex-president's recol-lections and other books simply underscored the accuracy of Bush's account.[101] For his part, Ahmed Rashid decided not to sue the ex-president, even though his children and some of his professional colleagues encouraged him to do so.[102]

Jonathan Bailey, who created and maintains the website *Plagiarism Today*, evaluated Grim's claims and concluded that they seemed politically motivated. *The Huffington Post* undoubtedly falls on the liberal end of the political spectrum, and so similarities between the conservative ex-president's text and other published material seems to have been viewed in the least flattering light. Bailey points out that public figures find themselves in a no-win situation when writing about well-known historical events. If the quotations in their memoirs deviate significantly from what others have reported, the accuracy of their recollections will be questioned. But if the quotations match exactly, the authors open themselves up to charges of plagiarism. Bailey analyzed the fifteen passages that Grim claimed were lifted and found that only two or three of them – including the anecdote about Karzai – were problematic.[103]

The controversy over *Decision Points* wasn't the first time that charges of plagiarism had been leveled at Bush. In August of 2000, President Clinton's aides made a similar claim concerning the Texan's acceptance speech at the Republican National Convention in New York City. Specifically, they pointed to nine instances in Bush's speech that seemed to have been drawn from Clinton's own public addresses. For example, in 1997 Clinton had said, "Medicare is more than just a program; it reflects our values." And at the convention, Bush's speech included the line "Medicare does more than meet the needs of the elderly; it reflects the values of our society." (A spokesperson for the Bush campaign characterized the charge as "silly and beneath the dignity of the White House.")[104]

BIDEN'S BORROWINGS

During a debate at the Iowa State Fairgrounds on August 23, 1987, Joe Biden sparred with his fellow aspirants for the 1988 Democratic presidential nomination. The forty-four-year-old senator's profile had been raised that summer when, as Chairman of the Judiciary Committee, he had opposed President Reagan's nomination of Robert Bork to the Supreme Court. But Biden's remarks on that August day would doom his candidacy – for the 1988 contest, at any rate. Based on the amount of newsprint devoted to the episode, it must be ranked as the highest-profile example of plagiarism in US history.

Earlier in August, the senator from Delaware had given well-received remarks that included a quotation from British politician Neil Kinnock. Biden had received a videotape of a widely admired commercial that Kinnock had aired that spring during his campaign against the Conservative Party's Margaret Thatcher.[105] The senator had incorporated some of Kinnock's rhetoric into his own stump speech but had always been careful to cite the Labour Party leader when doing so. And for the debate at the fairgrounds, he and his staff decided that he would close with those same remarks.[106]

Besides Biden, the seven candidates at the two-hour debate included Jesse Jackson, Dick Gephardt, Al Gore, and the eventual nominee, Massachusetts governor Michael Dukakis. By the luck of the draw, Biden went first in making his opening statement and last in his closing remarks.

In his campaign commercial, Neil Kinnock had said:

> Why am I the first Kinnock in a thousand generations to be able to get to university? [pointing] Why is Glenys the first woman in her family in a thousand generations to be able to get to university? Was it because all our predecessors were thick? [in reference to his Welsh coal mining ancestors] Did they lack talent? Those people who could sing and play and recite and write poetry? Those people who could make wonderful, beautiful things with their hands? Those people who could dream dreams, see visions? Why didn't they get it? Was it because they were weak? Those people who could work eight hours underground and then come up and play football? Weak? Those women who could survive eleven child bearings? Were they weak? Does anybody really think that they didn't get what we had because they didn't have the talent or the strength or the endurance or the commitment? Of course not. It was because [clenching both fists] there was no platform upon which they could stand.[107]

And in his closing remarks in Des Moines, Joe Biden said:

> . . . and I started thinking as I was coming over here, why is it that Joe Biden is the first in his family ever to go to a university? [pointing] Why is it that my wife who is sitting out there in the audience is the first in her family to

ever go to college? Is it because our fathers and mothers were not bright? Is it because I'm the first Biden in a thousand generations to get a college and a graduate degree that I was smarter than the rest? Those same people who read poetry and wrote poetry and taught me how to sing verse? Is it because they didn't work hard? My ancestors, who worked in the coal mines of Northeast Pennsylvania and would [clenching one fist] come up after 12 hours and play football for four hours? No, it's not because they weren't as smart. It's not because they didn't work as hard. It's because they didn't have a platform upon which to stand . . . [108]

Biden had tried to make his remarks seem spontaneous ("I started thinking as I was coming over here"), and he did not credit his words to the British politician. It would ultimately be revealed that Michael Dukakis's campaign manager had given journalists a video comparing the Kinnock and Biden orations to call attention to Biden's borrowing.[109] And after the unattributed remarks became an issue, he would claim that he had been under time pressure, that the lack of attribution had not been wrong, and that he was not sorry for having done it.[110]

But as reporters began to burrow into Biden's past, they found other instances of cribbing. On September 18, *The New York Times* reported that twenty-two years earlier, during his first year as a law student at Syracuse University, Biden had been found guilty of plagiarism. He had taken "large chunks of heavy legal prose" – about five pages' worth – from a *Fordham Law Review* article for his own fifteen-page paper. This led to his failing a course, although he was allowed to retake the class during the following year.[111]

Biden was also found to have used the words of one of his heroes, Robert F. Kennedy, during a speech at the California State Democratic Convention, given half a year before the debate in Des Moines. RFK, during his own campaigning in Iowa in 1968, had said that "The gross national product does not allow for the health of our children, the quality of their education or the joy of their play." In California, Biden had said, "We cannot measure the health of our children, the quality of their education, the joy of their play." Kennedy, and then Biden, also talked about "the greatness to bend history."

Other speeches given by Biden were found to contain phrases that Hubert Humphrey had employed in 1976. In his defense, Biden asserted that well-known quotations are often used in speeches as a form of homage, and that their audiences understand this to be the case.[112]

A month after the Des Moines debate, Biden ended his bid for the Democratic nomination, declaring that the "exaggerated shadow" cast by the multiple accusations had served "to obscure the essence" of his candidacy.[113]

In 2007, Biden published a memoir titled *Promises to Keep: On Life and Politics*. And in a 2022 piece for *The New Yorker*, Adam Entous reported finding striking similarities between *Promises to Keep* and *What It Takes*, a book by Richard Cramer published in 1992. Entous noted that Biden "repeated many of the stories from Cramer's book, some of them almost verbatim, with similar gaps."[114]

Has Biden paid for this pattern of behavior? His cribbing from Kinnock may have put an end to his quest for the 1988 nomination, but when he was up for reelection to the Senate three years later, the people of Delaware rewarded him with 63 percent of the vote. Reelection followed in 1996 (60 percent of the vote) and in 2002 (58 percent). The voters seemed to give more weight to their familiarity with Biden and party affiliation – Delaware has been solidly blue since the Clinton era – than the fact that one politician had stolen from another.

Two decades after his first foray into presidential politics, Biden tried again in 2008. In January of that year, he finished a distant fifth in the Iowa caucus, well behind front-runners Barack Obama, Hillary Clinton, and John Edwards, earning less than 1 percent of the vote and dropping out shortly thereafter.[115] Nevertheless, Obama tapped him to run as his veep, and the two men were reelected in 2012. It seems that neither Obama nor the voting public regarded Biden's transgressions as disqualifying – even though the media dutifully resurrected the story of his 1988 run during both campaigns.

During Biden's third run for the presidency, in 2020, his education and climate plans were criticized for lifting language from the XQ Institute as well as the Carbon Capture Coalition. Once again, the appropriation was unattributed and "at times word for word." The campaign characterized the borrowing as "inadvertent" and promised that the plans would be updated with appropriate citations where necessary.[116]

And after Biden secured the Democratic nomination, the Trump campaign weaponized this aspect of Biden's history in a bid to hurt his credibility. For example, during the vice-presidential debate with Kamala Harris, Mike Pence asserted that Biden had plagiarized Trump's coronavirus response plan.[117] But it's worth noting that Neil Kinnock – the politician whom Biden had plagiarized from in 1987 – threw his support behind the Democratic candidate, declaring him to be "an honest guy."[118] It would seem that ideological compatibility was more important for Kinnock than whether Biden had shown intellectual integrity.

PMS AND MPS

The previous sections of this chapter described instances of American politicians engaging in acts of appropriation, and Chapter 2 provided examples from continental Europe. But it may also be instructive to examine charges of plagiarism against British politicians and to see how these episodes affected their later careers.

On the evening of November 15, 1852, Benjamin Disraeli, the forty-seven-year-old Chancellor of the Exchequer, rose to his feet in the House of Commons to deliver a eulogy. The subject of his oration was Arthur Wellesley, the 1st Duke of Wellington, who would receive a lavish state funeral three days later. The stirring address was interrupted multiple times by cries of "cheers!" and "hear, hear!" from the assembled members of Parliament.

Disraeli's prepared remarks appeared in several newspapers, and this allowed for close inspection of the Chancellor's sentiments. Within days, sharp-eyed readers discovered that the 1,500-word eulogy contained sections taken from remarks made by Adolphe Thiers upon the death of Laurent de Gouvion Saint-Cyr. (Thiers's oration had been published in London's *Morning Chronicle* in 1848.) To underscore the charge, British papers ran columns in which Disraeli's and Thiers's orations were displayed side by side.[119]

Disraeli, for his part, claimed to have copied some of Thiers's phrases into his commonplace book, and that he subsequently mistook them for his own.[120] But Alexander Lindley has pointed out that this explanation isn't all that tenable. Disraeli hadn't incorporated only a few thoughts by Thiers: entire paragraphs of the Saint-Cyr eulogy can be found in the Chancellor's oration. And why, in his copying, would he have failed to include the name of Thiers, who wrote the eulogy, or Saint-Cyr, its subject?[121] The irony is that Saint-Cyr had been a French general and marshal during the Napoleonic Wars, while the Duke of Wellington had commanded the allied army that carried the day at Waterloo.

Disraeli was widely ridiculed for his appropriation, but he would go on to serve twice more as Chancellor of the Exchequer, and then briefly as Prime Minister after the retirement of the Earl of Derby. And although his party lost in the general election that year, he would later serve a six-year term as Prime Minister. Today, he is frequently ranked near the top of British PMs.[122] It seems that Disraeli's praise of an English hero, using words written to honor a French general, did no significant damage to his reputation, either during his lifetime or after it.

* * *

The September 2010 release of Tony Blair's memoir *A Journey: My Political Life* also drew fire – in this case from Peter Morgan, the screenwriter for the 2006 movie *The Queen*. For the film, Morgan invented dialog for Blair's first meeting with Queen Elizabeth, having her say, "You are my 10th prime minister, Mr. Blair. My first was Winston Churchill." In his memoir, Blair recalled her saying, "You are my 10th prime minister. The first was Winston. That was before you were born." Either Morgan somehow divined what the Queen said to Blair during their private conversation, or Blair incorporated the film's dialog into his memory for the event – even though the former Prime Minister claimed he had never seen the movie.[123]

Blair wasn't the only PM accused of appropriating from the screen, although Theresa May was alleged to have borrowed from television instead of a film. As the final speaker at the annual Conservative Party Conference in Manchester on October 4, 2017, she gave an hour-long address that was marred by several glitches. She had to contend with a sore throat and fits of coughing, and at one point her speech was interrupted by a comedian who handed her a P45 form – the British equivalent of a pink slip. As a final indignity, toward the end of her remarks, a letter fell from a slogan prominently displayed next to May, transforming "Building a country that works *for* everyone" into "Building a country that works *or* everyone."[124]

What many news outlets also noted, however, was that in her closing she employed a phrase previously used by another politician – specifically, US President Josiah Bartlet. His name may not ring a bell unless you recall Martin Sheen's character on *The West Wing*, a political drama series created by Aaron Sorkin that ran from 1999 to 2006.

In an episode that aired in the fall of 2002, Bartlet delivered a speech called "Angels and Heroes." His remarks were made after a bomb attack at a (fictitious) college campus in which several dozen students were killed. Bartlet's address included the following line: "Every time we think we have measured our capacity to meet a challenge, we look up and we're reminded that that capacity may well be limitless." Several outlets, such as *The Daily Mirror*, quoted this line, as well as May's version: "It is when tested the most that we reach deep within ourselves and find that our capacity to the challenge before us may well be limitless."[125]

Are the two lines the same? One could argue that the four-word phrase "may well be limitless" is fairly generic, although Bartlet's speech became popular on the American side of the Atlantic. Even today, over twenty years after the episode aired, it is possible to go online and purchase a plaque or poster inscribed with the TV president's declaration. Its popularity may have caused it to reach the eyes or ears – and ultimately the keyboard – of May's speechwriter.

Did the appropriation affect May's political viability? In June of 2019, less than two years after the speech in Manchester, she resigned her Conservative Party leadership post. Her resignation, however, had more to do with Brexit negotiations and a vote of no confidence than a phrase borrowed from a fictional politician. May was replaced by Boris Johnson, who would have to contend with his own issues of appropriation.

On December 1, 2019, Johnson posted a sixteen-part Twitter thread on the legal background of the London Bridge terror case and the release of Usman Khan from prison. Shortly thereafter, the anonymous author of the

"Secret Barrister" blog took exception to the Prime Minister's posts. This individual claimed that Johnson had "basically copied and pasted my blog post." *The Independent*, in its reporting of the incident, noted that Johnson made the same points and in a similar sequence to those put forth by the Secret Barrister. The paper also reported that "a source close to the PM emphatically denied Mr Johnson's explanation ... was copied."[126] Eleven days later, Johnson's party triumphed in the general election, as voters provided the Conservatives with their largest parliamentary majority in decades.

And what of members of Parliament? Consider Kate Osamor's victory address after her reelection in the 2017 general election. It contained language that closely resembled a speech given by Barack Obama in 2008. Her spokesperson was quoted as saying that "Kate deliberately invoked a victory speech so famous that she thought it needed no introduction," and simply replaced mentions of "America" with "Edmonton" or "Labour" as needed.[127] Osamor left the shadow cabinet the following year, although this may have had more to do with other episodes, such as allegedly hurling profanities – as well as a bucket of water – at a reporter inquiring about her son's drug conviction.[128]

There is also the case of Rachel Reeves, whose *The Women Who Made Modern Economics* was published by Basic Books in October of 2023. The goal of its author, the Shadow Chancellor of the Exchequer, was to highlight the contributions of female economists – a group whose contributions have often been overlooked. Although criticized for its "often clunky" writing and coverage,[129] the book made news when reporters for the *Financial Times* discovered more than twenty appropriations from sources like *The Guardian* and Wikipedia.[130] Reeves admitted that she "should have done better," but also stated that "If I'm guilty of copying and pasting some facts about some amazing women and turning it into a book that gets read, then I'm really proud of that."[131]

Less than a year later, Reeves would be appointed as Chancellor of the Exchequer by Keir Starmer, following Labour's landslide victory in July of 2024 – the same position that Disraeli had occupied 172 years earlier when he delivered his borrowed eulogy. The symmetry of this development brings to mind a line attributed to Mark Twain: "History does not repeat itself, but it rhymes."

CHAPTER 5

Consequences

I N PREVIOUS CHAPTERS, WE HAVE CONSIDERED MANY INSTANCES of appropriation – both deliberate and inadvertent – and how plagiarism hunters go about identifying them. At this point, it's worth taking a step back to consider some of the issues that arise from an accusation of plagiarism.

Clearly, the most serious consequence is that an author might be falsely accused, and that what appears to be appropriation is, in truth, a case of mistaken identity. The opposite problem manifests itself as well: plagiarized texts that go unrecognized seem to be surprisingly common.

Also worth noting is how concerns about appropriation affect the creative process in general. Such allegations can, for example, blunt the creative impulses of children falsely accused of plagiarism. Furthermore, persistent and nagging fears of plagiarism seem to hover over many mature artists as they engage in their creative activities.

We will also consider how such allegations of appropriation have been weaponized in political debates or in scientific rivalries. Finally, we need to hear from the innocent bystanders – those unfortunates whose work has been appropriated – and how such experiences affect their lives and their work.

TANGLED PROVENANCE

Authors sometimes adopt someone else's story because they think it is free for the taking, and this can result in accusations of plagiarism. A good example is Mark Twain's *Tom Sawyer, Detective*, a novel serialized by *Harper's* in 1896 and then released as a stand-alone work.

Thirteen years later, a Danish schoolmaster named Valdemar Thorsen read a translation of Twain's book and noted striking similarities between the Tom Sawyer adventure and Steen Blicher's *Præsten i Vejiby* (*The Rector of Veilbye*). Blicher's story was well known in Denmark and had been published in 1829, sixty-seven years before Twain's. Thorsen made his discovery public in the pages of a Danish magazine.

The two stories are remarkably similar. In both, a clergyman is harassed by the brother of a wealthy man. The well-off brother is seeking revenge because the clergyman's daughter has rejected his advances. He hires his sibling to provoke the clergyman, who apparently kills his harasser in a fit of passion. A body is found, but it turns out not to be that of the harassing brother, who has been paid to skip town. The clergyman is ultimately cleared of the murder charge.

In addition to the plot, many details are identical: in both stories, witnesses to the "murder" can see a weapon being wielded but not the attacker, and the sighting of a green coat results in a case of mistaken identity.

Thorsen knew of no English translation of Blicher's story, although a German version was known to exist. He wrote to Twain to inquire about the remarkable resemblance and received a reply from the author's secretary. Mr. Twain, he was informed, was not familiar with Blicher's story, could not read Danish, and could not read German fluently. *Tom Sawyer, Detective*, Thorsen was assured, was an original work.[1]

The letter's assertion of true originality is a bit problematic, however, because in a footnote at the beginning of the story, Twain himself states:

> Strange as the incidents of this story are, they are not inventions, but facts – even to the public confession of the accused. I take them from an old-time Swedish criminal trial, change the actors, and transfer the scenes to America. I have added some details, but only a couple of them are important ones.[2]

It is now believed that Thorsen was mistaken, as an English translation of the story had been published in 1873. It is an almost exact retelling of Blicher's tale but presented as a true story and without any mention of the Danish author as the source.[3] If Twain made use of this version, then he must have believed the nonfiction account was fair game for adaptation into a fictional work. (As it happens, the events Blicher describes were based on a real event: the execution of Reverend Søren Jensen Quist in 1626 for a crime he did not commit.[4])

Thomas Hardy was accused of plagiarism under similar circumstances. In 1880, he published *The Trumpet-Major*, a historical novel that includes a long descriptive passage about rural British militia. Two years later, a reader named Charles Jacobs noticed striking similarities between Hardy's description and a section titled "The Militia Company Drill" in the book *Georgia Scenes*. Jacobs wrote a letter to the literary periodical *The Critic* and included side-by-side passages from the two books. He concluded that "It will need no acuteness of vision to see that there is something more than an accidental similarity between the descriptions given."[5]

Georgia Scenes had been published anonymously, although it was known to be the work of American minister Augustus Baldwin Longstreet. The scenes were originally a series of newspaper articles which were collected and published in 1840 – forty years before *The Trumpet-Major* appeared. Hardy, however, claimed he was unaware of the existence of Longstreet's *Scenes*.

The case went unresolved for more than fifty years, until Carl Weber, a professor at Colby College, managed to reconstruct what had happened.[6] Hardy had drawn on the work of English historian C. H. Gifford, who brought out *History of the Wars Occasioned by the French Revolution* in 1817. Gifford had himself copied the passage in question from an earlier source: a vignette authored by Oliver Hillhouse Prince in 1807. It first appeared in an obscure weekly publication but was then reprinted widely in the US and England. Longstreet included Prince's work in his *Georgia Scenes*, and this accounts for the similarities of the three works.[7]

This practice of using nonfiction as the starting point for fiction was common in the nineteenth century, and it played a role in a plagiarism accusation made against Jack London, an unusually prolific author. Before his death at age forty, London published nearly two dozen novels and over 200 short stories, as well as essays and poems. And he was no stranger to charges of appropriation.

After his novel *Before Adam* began to appear in serialized form in 1906, London was accused of plagiarism by Stanley Waterloo, who had brought out *The Story of Ab: A Tale of the Time of the Caveman* in 1897. Waterloo claimed that the third chapter of London's story was essentially the first chapter of his own. *The New York Times* quoted Waterloo describing London's alleged theft, which he characterized as "The most daring piece of work of the sort that I have ever seen," and that the appropriation "seems literally incredible." The *Times* also ran a patronizing letter that London had written to Waterloo, in which London asserted he had written *Before Adam* "[a]s a reply to yours [Waterloo's] because yours was unscientific."[8]

Soon thereafter, London was accused of having plagiarized for his best-known work, *The Call of the Wild.* The year before he published his book about Buck, the Alaskan sled dog, Canadian author Egerton Young had brought out *My Dogs in the North Land,* a work of nonfiction. Young alleged that London had made liberal use of his material, and London, for his part, didn't deny the charge. Instead, he claimed that drawing on factual accounts for a work of fiction was "quite legitimate."[9] London also claimed to have written a letter of thanks to Young, but the Canadian said he never received such a message, and that London never asked for permission to use his work.[10]

But it is London's short story "Moon-Face" that best demonstrates the hazards of relying on facts for one's fiction. London's story appeared in *The San Francisco Argonaut* magazine in July of 1902. Several of its readers noted that a story with the same plot had appeared only a couple of weeks earlier, in the *Century Magazine.* This was "The Passing of Cock-Eye Blacklock," authored by the novelist Frank Norris. Both stories describe a dog chasing and retrieving for its master a stick of dynamite with a lit fuse, which leads to an untimely end for both.[11]

But the similarities don't end there. The two stories also resemble Charles F. McLean's "An Exploded Theory," published in *The Black Cat* in November of 1901. But London and Norris didn't plagiarize from McLean. Apparently, all three men made use of the same newspaper account that had appeared in the *California News.* In a letter, London ruefully reflected on the episode and the "amusing consequences" that ensued.[12]

Clearly, the reworking of a true story for fictional purposes was an appealing prospect for these authors. But when two or more writers make use of the same material, the convenience of adaptation can be mistaken for the sin of appropriation.

UNDETECTED PLAGIARISM

How often does literary theft go unnoticed? This is difficult to quantify since few plagiarists make a point of calling attention to themselves. But if we cobble together the available evidence, we can start to get a sense of the issue's magnitude.

One data point comes from Kevin Kopelson, who outed himself as a serial plagiarist in 2008 in the pages of the *London Review of Books*. The professor of English at the University of Iowa confessed that his first appropriation occurred forty years earlier, when he was in the fourth grade. Asked to write an essay about a conquistador, he transcribed an encyclopedia article on Hernando Cortés. His twenty-page effort earned him an A grade and the comment "Nice work!" from his teacher.

As a music major at Yale, Kopelson submitted a paper that his older brother had written when he was a graduate student at Berkeley. It was a fifty-page analysis of a work by Mozart, studded with footnotes drawn from German, French, and Italian sources. It clearly wasn't the work of a college freshman. Nevertheless, it also earned him an A. He suspected that his teacher didn't even read it.

Kopelson made further use of his brother's paper, submitting it as a writing sample when he applied to graduate programs in English. He was accepted by two Ivy League institutions and chose to attend Brown. For a class on Henry James, Kopelson submitted an article by Eve Kosofsky Sedgwick that he found in a James anthology. This time, it was clear from the professor's comments that it had been read with some care, but once again, he received an A.[13]

It's not hard to understand Kopelson's motivation for being a serial plagiarist – he had learned that the probability of detection was low enough to be worth the risk. And it seems unlikely that his experiences are unique. If we extrapolate from this case, the world could be awash in undetected plagiarism.

One would assume that editors are fairly careful about verifying the originality of the work they publish, given that errors can be both expensive and embarrassing. But before the internet and the availability of similarity detection software, there was no easy way to perform such checking, and detection was a matter of happenstance.

In 1949, for example, an unemployed welder named Alfred J. Carter tried to earn a living by selling previously published works to magazines. He was caught when he tried to sell a Wordsworth poem to *Good Housekeeping*. Carter had already sold a prize fight story written by James Hendry to the *American Legion* magazine, and it was Hendry himself who spotted the duplication in print and alerted the editors.[14]

Other episodes involve the appropriation of entire books. In 1963, Robert E. Preyor was awarded a contract for *Position Unknown* by Little, Brown. The publisher was looking forward to bringing out his tale of a search-and-rescue operation for a military transport crew stranded in the wilds of Canada. Preyor received a $600 advance (nearly $7,000 today) for his novel. Shortly before publication, however, an alert book reviewer discovered that Preyor's book was a word-for-word copy of Ernest Gann's *Island in the Sky*, which had been published in 1944 by Viking[15] (and made into a movie, starring John Wayne, in 1953). To add to the irony of the situation, Preyor turned out to be an inmate at a prison in Columbus, Ohio.[16]

In 1956, a reviewer was perusing an advance copy of Anthony Hodgson's mystery *The Golden Ballast* when he experienced a powerful sense of *déjà vu*. Searching through his library, he found that Hodgson's book was a copy of Eliot Reed's *Tender to Danger*, published by Doubleday in 1951. Hodgson's publisher, Bouregy & Curl, was forced to recall the 2,400 copies that had already been distributed to booksellers.[17] Book reviewers, it would seem, are better at catching plagiarists than publishers are.

The same problem crops up in the academic world. In 1982, Conway Lackman, a Rutgers University professor of economics, published an article in *The Quarterly Journal of Economics*. It was, however, a paper originally written by Larry Chenault of Miami University. Lackman changed only the authorship and university affiliation from the original article. He claimed he was innocent, but to avoid a dismissal hearing, Lackman chose to resign his academic position.[18]

One could argue that these plagiarists avoided detection – for a while, anyway – because the originals they appropriated were relatively obscure. It seems unlikely that a well-known work would not be detected as a retread by editors and publishers.

To test this hypothesis, David Lassman, the director of a Jane Austen festival in England, carried out an experiment in 2007. He submitted two chapters of *Pride and Prejudice* – with only slight modifications – to eighteen different editors. Would any of them care to publish his historical novel? He made sure that his submission included the opening chapter, containing one of the most well-known lines in English literature: "It is a truth universally acknowledged, that a single man in possession of a good fortune must be in want of a wife." He received plenty of rejections, but only one editor said they identified the chapters as being the work of Austen. Lassman reported that he was "staggered" by the lack of recognition.[19]

But perhaps Austen isn't read as widely as she used to be. Surely film agents would recognize the script for *Casablanca*, the 1942 film that routinely appears on lists of the greatest films of all time. In 1982, Chuck Ross set out to determine whether "people in today's Hollywood would recognize a great film if it stared them in the face."[20] He sent the script out under the name of Erick Demos and used the title of the play the film was based on: *Everybody Comes to Rick's*. (He also changed the piano player's name from Sam to Dooley.) Ross sent it to all 217 agencies that the Writers Guild of America listed as representing film writers.

Because the submission was unsolicited, ninety of the agencies refused to look at it. Seven more didn't respond, even after he contacted them repeatedly. And another eighteen were apparently lost in the mail. But eighty-five agencies did read "his" screenplay.

Thirty-three editors recognized Ross's offering for what it was and offered amusing replies, like "Have some excellent ideas on the casting of this wonderful script, but most of the actors are dead."[21] Eight agencies noted a resemblance to *Casablanca* without realizing that it *was*, quite literally, *Casablanca*.

Other agencies raised issues with the script, the amount of dialog, the location, or its suitability to the current market. But three of them expressed interest in representing him, and one wanted to see the script turned into a novel. (Ross politely declined these offers.) Put simply, 60 percent of the film agencies were unable to recognize one of the most recognizable films of all time.

FALSELY ACCUSED

With time and practice, teachers who grade the written work of their students develop a keen eye for spotting plagiarism. In years past, this was a relatively straightforward matter of recognizing material copied directly from an encyclopedia or some other reference work. And when it came to creative writing, it was still fairly easy to spot literary productions that seemed well beyond a student's age and ability. Unfortunately, there are also cases of teachers wrongly accusing their precocious students of plagiarism, and it's worth noting the long-term consequences of these allegations. We will consider five such cases.

The first of these occurred in the late 1940s, when Barbara Chase-Riboud was a middle school student in South Philadelphia. For a class assignment, she wrote a poem titled "Autumn Leaves." Her teacher accused her of having copied it from some other source and demanded that she confess in front of the class. When she refused, she was sent to the principal's office. The principal contacted her mother and grand-mother, who said they had seen Barbara writing the poem at the kitchen table, and that the work was hers. They demanded an apology from the school but did not receive one, and the girl was suspended. Barbara's mother decided to remove her from the school and to have her tutored privately.[22] The episode affected her deeply, and she would not write poetry again for forty years.[23]

Nevertheless, Chase-Riboud went on to have a successful career, winning many awards for her visual art and her writing. But she would have to grapple with the issue of appropriation several times. In 1979, she published a novel about Sally Hemings, the enslaved woman owned by Thomas Jefferson. Three years later, Granville Burgess wrote the play "Dusky Sally," and when it was published as a book, Chase-Riboud sued for copyright infringement. A judge ruled in favor of Chase-Riboud, which effectively banned future productions of the play.[24]

In 1997, Chase-Riboud filed a $10 million suit against DreamWorks Pictures, alleging that Steven Spielberg's film *Amistad* infringed on her 1989 novel, *Echo of Lions*. Three months later, however, she dropped her suit and praised the film.[25] One issue that arose during the litigation was the claim that Chase-Riboud had herself plagiarized, from a 1936 nonfiction work, for her 1986 novel *Valide: A Novel of the Harem*. During an interview, she acknowledged making use of content from the earlier book but denied any wrongdoing.[26]

* * *

In the early 1950s, Adrienne Kennedy was an undergraduate at The Ohio State University. She had been a standout at her integrated high school in Cleveland, where she served as a class president and won academic awards. But when she attended college in Columbus, she found that the white girls in her residence hall regarded her with disdain. The young woman also felt that the faculty viewed Black students as less capable than their classmates.

Her worst fears were realized when an English professor asked her to stay after class one day. He asked her questions about an essay she had written on George Bernard Shaw. By the end of the conversation, he was accusing her of having plagiarized the paper. And the reason? According to Kennedy, "It was inconceivable to him that this tiny [Black] girl in a pink sweater could write."[27]

Soon after graduating, Kennedy moved to New York City with her husband. She became a successful playwright and one of the few women who contributed to the Black Theatre Movement of the 1960s.[28] Among many other honors, Kennedy received a lifetime Obie Award and was inducted into the Theater Hall of Fame. In 2022, at the age of ninety-one, she had her Broadway debut with *Ohio State Murders*, a one-act play she had written two decades earlier. It describes the racism experienced by a young Black woman at Ohio State in the early 1950s.[29] In many ways, her life and her art had come full circle.

* * *

In the mid 1950s, Susan Swan was a seventh grader in Midland, a town on Georgian Bay in Ontario. She wrote a short story titled "Henry B. Small" about a man trapped in a passionless marriage. After her teacher read it, he told Swan, "This is too good. You can't have done that." Shocked that he would accuse her of stealing the story, the girl protested, "No. I had made this up. This was right out of my own imagination about what married life for older people was like." Swan remembers thinking how unfair it was that her teacher would doubt her abilities.[30]

Swan would go on to write eight novels and to teach and mentor students at York University, the University of Guelph, and the University of Toronto. Together with Janice Zawerbny, she created a new annual prize for women and nonbinary people: the Carol Shields Prize for Fiction. The first award of CA$150,000 was given in 2022.[31] And in 2023, Swan became a Companion of the Order of Canada – one of her country's highest honors. Clearly, the little girl from Midland had proven her teacher wrong.

* * *

In Pittsburgh in 1960, the fifteen-year-old August Wilson felt very much out of place. He was the only Black student attending Gladstone High, a private Catholic institution.[32] And as he later told interviewers, he was confused and bored. He reached his breaking point, however, when his history teacher accused him of plagiarism. The man had asked the class to write a paper about a historical figure, and the assignment piqued his interest. Wilson chose Napoleon because he was a self-made man. After researching and writing the paper, Wilson rented a typewriter with money he had earned from doing odd jobs and paid his sister to type it.[33]

The teacher, however, didn't believe the work was his, even though Wilson had included a complete bibliography and footnotes. The man suspected that one of the boy's older sisters was the author instead. When he asked Wilson to explain the paper to him, he refused because he didn't feel that he needed to. As a result, Wilson was given a failing grade. As he later recalled, "I tore the paper up and threw it in his wastebasket and walked out of the school."[34]

He didn't return, but he also didn't want his mother to know that he had dropped out. Instead, Wilson spent large amounts of time during the day reading at Oakland's Main Carnegie Library. It was there that, as he put it, "The world opened up" to him via the hundreds of books he read.[35]

Wilson tried his hand at poetry, then turned to writing plays. In the late 1970s he decamped to Minnesota and continued to develop as a dramatist. He also began to find success, most notably with *Fences*, which premiered in 1985. It would earn him both a Pulitzer Prize for Drama and a Tony Award for Best Play.[36] And Wilson did finally receive a high school degree. It was awarded in 1989 by the Carnegie Library of Pittsburgh to recognize him for his literary achievements.[37]

* * *

Nely Galán, who would become Telemundo's first Latina president of entertainment, also faced down a childhood accusation of plagiarism. In 1978, when she was fifteen, she wrote a story for an assignment at her Catholic high school in Demarest, New Jersey. The story concerned "[a] wealthy woman who left her heirs nothing but a long letter in which she revealed her philosophy of life."[38] Her teacher initially praised the work but later decided that a young girl couldn't have produced such a polished piece of writing. Her parents, who were Cuban immigrants with limited English, were called to the school, and they urged their daughter to apologize. Like Chase-Riboud, she refused, and like her, she was suspended.[39] Her teacher later relented and gave Galán an A, but the high schooler found the whole episode humiliating.

In Galán's case, however, the effect of the accusation was empowering. During her suspension, she was motivated to write a humorous article about "why you should never send your kids to an all-girl Catholic school" and submitted it to *Seventeen*. It wasn't published, but the magazine's editors thought she had real talent, and they asked her to become a guest editor. As she reflected on the incident, Galán told a reporter for *The New York Times* that it turned out to be "the best thing that ever happened to me." She ended up graduating early and taking "total revenge on the nuns."[40]

It's worth noting that four of these five writers are people of color: Chase-Riboud, Wilson, and Kennedy are Black, and Galán is Latina. In addition, four of the five are female. Undoubtedly, many white children and boys have also been falsely accused of plagiarism, but the fact that these accomplished authors made a point of retelling their stories, often decades later, underscores how significant these early episodes were for them. And if there is a predilection for teachers to accuse minority children and girls of appropriation, then it also speaks to the hidden – and maybe not so hidden – biases we have about who is capable of originality at a young age.

FEAR OF PLAGIARIZING

Do concerns about appropriation hang over the heads of writers, musicians, and other creative types? Given how often the topic comes up, the answer would seem to be yes. Clearly, no one wants to be perceived as merely imitating the work of others. And in some cases, the desire for originality can drive artists to extremes as they try to avoid befouling the purity of their own muses.

Some artists take proactive measures to protect their bona fides. For example, when the German playwright Gerhart Hauptmann announced in 1908 that he was producing a play about Charlemagne, his countryman Hermann Sudermann made a public statement that he too had been working on a drama about the Frankish king for many years. His goal was to preemptively block any accusation of plagiarism that might be levied against him later.[41]

In a similar vein, Julian Green began writing a novel in 1933 about the American South. But when he learned of the impending release of *Gone with the Wind,* he also feared being labeled a plagiarist and put the project in mothballs.[42] It took the prodding of his son for him to revisit the manuscript he had set in antebellum Georgia, and *The Distant Lands* finally saw the light of day over a half-century later, in 1987.[43]

In the fall of 1929, *The Nation* estimated that almost half of successful theatrical productions – defined as those running for 200 performances or more – made payments to individuals who claimed infringement of their intellectual property. A few of these cases were tried in court, but about 90 percent were settled privately. It appears that producers were anxious to avoid the bad publicity that a whiff of scandal could generate. Some of these suits were undoubtedly legitimate, but the majority were, according to the magazine, "little more than simple blackmail."[44]

In some cases, a setting can be so evocative that others choose to avoid using it, lest they be accused of appropriating the iconic locale. John

Ford, for example, shot nine of his Westerns in Monument Valley, on the Arizona–Utah border. The sandstone buttes are distinctive and so closely linked to Ford's *oeuvre* that other directors have chosen to film their Westerns elsewhere.[45]

A fear of plagiarism can be so great that some writers largely cut themselves off from the works that have given them so much pleasure. Margit Sandemo, the prolific author of historical fantasy novels, was quoted by a Norwegian publication as saying that, in a deliberate attempt to avoid inadvertent plagiarism, she read much less in adulthood than she had when she was younger.[46]

Such fears can loom large and interfere with enjoyable activities. Perri Klass, the award-winning author and pediatrician, once described sending off a book review and then treating herself to a night at the opera. As the performance began, she managed to convince herself that her review's seven-word opening had been appropriated from someone else. Instead of enjoying the production, she found herself anxiously rehearsing an apology to her editor. Later that night, when she was able to type the accursed phrase into a search engine, no matches popped up, and her evening of worry had been for naught.[47] Klass's paranoia probably stemmed from having been accused – anonymously and falsely – of plagiarizing an article about medical ethics when she was an intern, many years earlier.[48]

The writer Donna Leon, known for her series of crime novels set in Venice, told an interviewer that she typically does her reading while reclining on a sofa. "Late morning is a good time, as is late afternoon. I need a pencil. No paper: that smells of plagiarism."[49] It seems that by avoiding the temptation of making notes, she lessens the likelihood that a particularly fine turn of phrase will burrow its way into her brain and then into her writing.

While Stephen King was a student at the University of Maine in the late 1960s, his friend George McLeod told him about a story he was composing. Recalling an episode from his childhood, McLeod described how he and some friends went searching for a dead dog rumored to be near a set of train tracks. Although McLeod had worked out the entire plot, he never got around to completing it. In 1982, King published a novella titled "The Body" in the collection *Different Seasons*. It tells the story of four boys who go looking for the corpse of a dead twelve-year-old, rumored to be near a set of train tracks. King made the connection to his friend's tale explicit by dedicating the story to him.

When McLeod read "The Body" he accused King of having stolen his plot, and according to him, King admitted to the appropriation. Four years later, a coming-of-age film based on King's novella was released. Directed by Rob Reiner, *Stand by Me* was a success at the box office. McLeod asked King for a writing credit and a share of the film's profits, but King refused. The two men's friendship ended when McLeod filed suit against King. Having learned his lesson, King has been careful not to read the many unsolicited manuscripts he receives from aspiring writers.[50] For the same reason, most authors routinely refuse such requests for feedback or encouragement.

A fear of plagiarism plays a central role in one of the most popular songs recorded by the Beatles. It also provides a good example of the near-paranoia that artists live with as they struggle to create something that is truly original.

On a late morning in November of 1963, Paul McCartney awoke from a dream. At the time, he was living with the family of his girlfriend, Jane Asher, at a residence on Wimpole Street in London. In a half-conscious state, McCartney realized that he dreamt a melody. Still half asleep, he stumbled to a piano and started pecking out the notes.[51]

His first thought was that it must be one of the songs his father used to play, and he was simply having trouble remembering which one. As he later described it, "Well, this is very nice, but it's a nick [from another song]. I don't know what it is."[52] McCartney and his bandmate John Lennon "were always very careful. The great danger with writing is that you write someone else's song without realizing. You spend three hours ... and you've written a Bob Dylan classic."[53]

McCartney was also suspicious of the tune's provenance because of the unusual way it had come to him. As he would tell others, "Well, it can't be mine. I just woke up *dreaming* it! There was no logic to it at all. And I'd never had that. And I've never had it since ... it was the only song I ever dreamed."[54]

Had McCartney's epiphany occurred in 2023 instead of 1963, determining whether the tune was plagiarized would have been as easy as humming it into a smartphone running an app like Shazam. Instead, he recalled, "For about a month, I went round to people in the music business and asked them whether they had ever heard it before. Eventually it became like handing something in to the police. I thought if no one claimed it after a few weeks, then I could have it."[55]

The Beatle kept tinkering with his brainchild when he found the time, such as during breaks while the band was filming *Help!* He spent so much time noodling on a piano that Richard Lester, the movie's director, threatened to have the instrument removed from the premises of the shoot.

One of the reasons McCartney was so fixated on the composition was that he hadn't yet figured out the lyrics. For a long time, he referred to it as "Scrambled Eggs." It would take a year and a half, but during a long road trip in Portugal, the words finally came, "quickly and naturally."[56] "Yesterday" finally had both its melody and its lyrics. George Martin proposed the arrangement for string quartet, and the song was recorded in two takes in mid June of 1965.[57]

Are there any traces of the song's DNA in the work of other musicians? Ian Hammond, while maintaining that "Yesterday" is truly original, suggested that McCartney was influenced by Ray Charles, and more specifically, the singer's rendition of "Georgia on My Mind," originally composed by Hoagy Carmichael in 1930. Hammond points to the similar melodic content and chord progressions in both songs. Neither attribute is unique, and so it might be more accurate to say that McCartney was influenced by "the generic *style* rather than the actual *song*."[58]

WEAPONIZING PLAGIARISM

In July of 1991, President George H. W. Bush nominated Clarence Thomas to serve as an associate justice on the US Supreme Court, to fill the vacancy created by the retiring Thurgood Marshall. Accordingly, the nominee appeared before the Senate Judiciary Committee in September. Following his testimony, the committee deadlocked on issuing a favorable recommendation but still sent the nomination forward to the full Senate. Before a vote could be held, however, a journalist for National Public Radio broke a story that upended the entire process.

Citing a leaked FBI report, legal affairs correspondent Nina Totenberg revealed that Anita Hill, a law school professor, had accused Thomas of sexual harassment. Hill alleged this had occurred when the two worked together at the Department of Education a decade earlier, and also at the Equal Employment Opportunity Commission. Joe Biden, the Judiciary Committee chair, chose to reopen the hearings to allow Hill to testify, as well as to let Thomas and other witnesses rebut her allegations. For three days that October, the public witnessed the ultimate "he said, she said" spectacle, and tempers flared on both sides of a growing partisan divide.

Even before Hill's testimony, conservative groups supporting Thomas were airing a television ad that called into question the ethics of the Democrats on the Judiciary Committee. In the case of Biden, viewers were reminded that he had plagiarized from Neil Kinnock four years earlier.[59] That episode, which ended his presidential campaign, was discussed in Chapter 4. But Totenberg was also taken to task – and for the same offense.

Albert Hunt, the Washington bureau chief for *The Wall Street Journal*, ran a column accusing Totenberg of having committed plagiarism in 1972, when she was a reporter for the *National Observer*. "Purposeful plagiarism," Hunt thundered, "is one of the cardinal sins of journalism from which reporters can never recover their credibility."[60] The charge was true: in a profile of Senator Tip O'Neill, Totenberg had included five quotations that originally appeared in *The Washington Post* but provided no attribution as to their source. She was fired shortly thereafter – although she claimed this was the result of her own experience with harassment, and not only for the attribution errors.[61]

Hunt's claim about Totenberg's plagiarism needs to be considered in light of the journalistic standards of the times. In 1972, "quoting quotes" without attribution was a routine practice at many newspapers, although it would be considered problematic today.[62] This is yet another example of how the concept of plagiarism has changed and broadened over time.

As in the Clarence Thomas hearings, accusations of plagiarism are often ideologically driven. A good example of this occurred in 2010, when Jane Mayer, *The New Yorker*'s chief Washington correspondent, published a lengthy article about David and Charles Koch's financial support of conservative causes.[63] Over the next few years, Mayer discovered she was being investigated by an outfit called Vigilant Resources International. She also learned that *The New York Post* and *The Daily Caller* had received documents accusing her of plagiarism.[64] But when these conservative outlets checked with the authors that Mayer had purportedly stolen from, they discovered that the accusations were baseless.[65]

In 2011, progressive Democrat Elizabeth Warren began her campaign against Republican Scott Brown, who had been appointed as a Massachusetts senator two years earlier. In May of 2012, political reporter Katrina Trinko, writing for the conservative *National Review*, accused Warren and her daughter, Amelia Tyagi, of plagiarizing material for their 2006 book *All Your Worth: The Ultimate Money Lifetime Plan.* Trinko reported that two paragraphs were virtually identical to those found in Rob Black's *Getting on the Money Track*, which had been published a year earlier.

The problem with Trinko's accusation was that the 2006 version of Warren and Tyagi's work was the paperback edition of their book. It had first appeared in hardcover in March of 2005, with Black's tome following in October.[66] To her credit, Trinko quickly deleted her piece from the *National Review*'s website and replaced it with a correction and an apology.[67] The false accusation was posted for only about an hour, and probably had little effect on the election outcome that November, in which Warren defeated Brown, receiving 54 percent of the vote.

The practice of attacking one's opponents by accusing them of plagiarism has a long history in disputes over scientific discoveries. Galileo, for example, in a dispute over who first sighted the moons of Jupiter in 1610, accused the German astronomer Simon Marius of plagiarism. Marius's reputation suffered as a result, and it was not until the early twentieth century that his reputation was rehabilitated.[68] In another case, which we will explore in Chapter 7, supporters of Isaac Newton claimed that the German mathematician Gottfried Leibniz plagiarized the principles of calculus from his British rival.

Disputes about initial discovery continued into the nineteenth century, when there were several disputes regarding the genesis of Charles Darwin's ideas. The engine at the heart of evolutionary theory – the concept of natural selection – was appropriated, according to Scottish grain merchant Patrick Matthew, from his own book on naval timber. His work had been published in 1831, a full twenty-eight years before *On the Origin of Species*. (In later editions of his book, Darwin did acknowledge Matthew's priority but said he had been unaware of the work when writing his own.)[69]

And in the twentieth century, Einstein was accused of plagiarism by Theodor Vahlen, a German mathematician. Vahlen was an early supporter of National Socialism, and the idea that a Jew could be responsible for the breakthrough theory of relativity was anathema to him. To resolve his cognitive dissonance, Vahlen claimed that Einstein had somehow appropriated his ideas from the work of "Aryan" scientists.[70]

Social media has made it easy for virtually anyone to be accused of plagiarism. During the spring of 2022, for example, the Fairfax County Virginia Circuit Court heard a defamation complaint filed by Johnny Depp against his ex-wife Amber Heard. Depp's suit was the result of an op-ed published by *The Washington Post* in 2018, in which Heard asserted she was a victim of domestic abuse.[71] Given the prominence of the two actors, the nature of the charges, and the fact that the trial was live-streamed, public interest in the case was unusually high.

After Heard began her testimony, a rumor began to spread that she was plagiarizing movie dialog in her statements to the court. Postings on social media compared her opening statement to lines from the 1999 film *The Talented Mr. Ripley*. Specifically, it was claimed that Heard said: "The thing with Johnny, it's like the sun shines on you, and it's glorious. And then he forgets you and it's very, very cold ... When you have his attention, you feel like you're the only person in the world. That's why everybody loves him."

These lines do appear in the film – Gwyneth Paltrow's character makes her observations about "Dickie" (played by Jude Law) when speaking to Matt Damon's Tom Ripley. The implication was that Heard was only acting and trying to play on the sympathies of the jury, and this innuendo was apparently spread by supporters of Depp. However, Heard made no opening statement at the trial: her attorney did so. And according to an investigation by fact-checkers at Snopes, she never quoted the lines during her time on the witness stand.[72]

(UN)CONVENTIONAL WISDOM?

On the evening of July 18, 2016, Melania Trump stood before the 2,500 delegates at the Republican National Convention in Cleveland. Born Melanija Knavs, the forty-six-year-old Slovenian immigrant and former model had become candidate Donald Trump's third wife eleven years earlier. And although she had played a minor role in her husband's primary campaign, she was a headliner on the first night of the convention. Breaking with tradition, she was introduced to the audience by the candidate himself. She appeared calm and composed during her televised address to an audience of about 23 million people.[73]

One of those viewers was journalist Jarrett Hill, who was watching a live stream of the speech at a Starbucks in California. He reported experiencing *déjà vu* when Trump uttered the phrase "Their [children's] willingness to work hard for them [their dreams]," and remembered that Michelle Obama had used the same wording during her 2008 Democratic convention address. Hill immediately took to Twitter to point out this and other striking similarities between the two women's remarks.[74] Jon Favreau, who had been an Obama administration speechwriter, saw Hill's posts and then watched the speech himself. He tweeted, "They're nearly identical. Someone is seriously fired."[75]

How similar were the two women's orations? Michelle Obama's seventeen-minute address in Denver consisted of 2,162 words. The fifteen-minute speech given by Melania Trump eight years later contained 1,366 words. When the transcripts are compared, some duplication is to be expected: both women, for example, employed the phrase "President of the United States" in their addresses.

But there are three or four other stretches of text, totaling about fifty words, that are also identical. At one point during her speech, Melania's remarks matched Michelle's for twenty-three consecutive words: " ... values that you work hard for what you want in life, that your word is your bond and you do what you say ... ." (Michelle Obama had been referring to the values that she and Barack had been raised with, and Melania Trump was recalling her parents.)

Could the similarities between the two speeches be chalked up to coincidence? There are, after all, a set of common talking points that candidates' spouses typically include in such addresses, and the values instilled by one's parents fit this script well. However, the document similarity checking firm Turnitin estimates the odds of sixteen consecutive words matching, purely by chance, at less than one in a trillion. And the chance that twenty-three consecutive words would be identical is astronomically lower still.[76]

Once the press had picked up on the claims of Hill and Favreau, the controversy threatened to overshadow the entire convention. The purloined verbiage was seen as an unforced error that exemplified the undisciplined and improvisational nature of Trump's candidacy. The campaign went into damage control mode, although this effort was also disorganized. Paul Manafort, the campaign's chairman, tried to deflect criticism of the speech. He flatly declared on CNN that there had been "no cribbing of Michelle Obama's speech."[77] However, Sam Clovis, a campaign co-chairman, admitted on MSNBC that there had been "unfortunate oversight" in vetting the speech.[78]

Others took a "yes, but so what?" approach. Chris Christie, on the *Today* show, pointed out that "93 percent of the speech is completely different."[79] However, this was also a tacit admission that 7 percent had been appropriated.

So how had Michelle Obama's words ended up in Melania Trump's speech that night?

At the request of Trump's son-in-law, Jared Kushner, veteran political speechwriters Matthew Scully and John McConnell prepared a draft of Mrs. Trump's remarks. However, she chose to work instead with Meredith McIver, a Trump Organization staff writer and co-author or ghostwriter on several of her employer's business books.[80]

On the third day of the convention, a letter by McIver was released to the public. In it, she related that Melania was an admirer of Michelle, and that the candidate's wife "read me some passages from Mrs. Obama's speech as examples. I wrote them down and later included some of the phrasing in the draft that ultimately became the final speech. I did not check Mrs. Obama's speeches. This was my mistake." She concluded by apologizing to the Trumps and to Michelle Obama. "No harm was meant," she emphasized.[81] McIver offered to resign from the Trump

Organization, but the candidate refused to accept her offer. The campaign characterized the transgression as an "innocent mistake."[82]

What made this story catnip for the press wasn't only the appropriation – it was the source of Mrs. Trump's inspiration. Donald Trump had been harshly attacking Michelle's husband during Obama's entire presidency, via his Twitter account and on the campaign trail. For Melania Trump to have plagiarized from the Obamas would have been like Richard Nixon cribbing from Joseph Stalin. Had she quoted Ronald Reagan instead, her words would probably have been perceived as homage.

After the convention, Melania Trump remained a marked woman. In October, her statement concerning her husband's "Access Hollywood" remarks was said to have been lifted from a 1998 statement by Hillary Clinton about her own husband's behavior, although this was false.[83]

Not surprisingly, once she became the First Lady, Mrs. Trump's public activities and announcements continued to be scrutinized for instances of appropriation. Many such claims were made, and they often circulated as memes on social media. All of them were thoroughly investigated and debunked by Snopes.

In August of 2017, for example, Melania Trump's denunciation of the violence at the Unite the Right rally in Charlottesville was falsely attributed to remarks made by Michelle Obama during the previous year.[84] A month later, a speech she gave at the United Nations was said to have come from an address given by Mrs. Obama in 2014.[85] In January of 2018, she was accused of recycling a 2016 statement by – who else? – Mrs. Obama to commemorate Martin Luther King Jr. and MLK Day.[86] And a statement on Women's History month in March of 2018 was wrongly attributed to Mrs. Obama's remarks from 2012.[87]

A couple of months after that, Mrs. Trump's signature "Be Best" campaign was said to have been based on an Obama-era Federal Trade Commission booklet.[88] This was followed a couple of weeks later by the false claim that a 2018 Memorial Day tweet plagiarized Mrs. Obama's own post commemorating the day in 2014.[89]

The case of Melania Trump illustrates important truths about plagiarism. One is that a single episode of appropriation can permanently alter one's public persona. And another is that accusations of cribbing are now simply another cudgel to be wielded against one's political opponents.

THE EFFECT ON THE VICTIMS

When we think about plagiarism, our attention is invariably drawn to the actor – that is, the person who commits the appropriation. It is rare that we stop to consider the plight of the victim, who has their words, music, design, or other work taken from them. But the effects can be devastating. As we have already seen, well-known authors have been accused of making extensive use of someone else's work without giving that person appropriate credit – or any credit at all. Three particularly poignant examples of this phenomenon will be described in this section.

In 1939, John Steinbeck published *The Grapes of Wrath*, his novel about the Joad family and their migration from Oklahoma's Dust Bowl to California. It was based, in part, on a series of articles that he wrote for *The San Francisco News*. But Steinbeck also made use of reports and field notes compiled by Sanora Babb, a volunteer with the Farm Security Administration (FSA). Babb assisted Tom Collins, the manager of a migrant camp in the Central Valley. Collins shared Babb's material without her knowledge as part of a quid pro quo arrangement with Steinbeck, who promised to edit Collins's future work.

Like Steinbeck, Babb was seeking to publish a novel based on her experiences in the migrant camps. In early 1939, she sent several chapters to the co-founder of Random House, who enthusiastically agreed to bring out her work. But after the release of Steinbeck's novel by Viking Press and its instant bestseller status, Random House chose to withdraw its offer. Dumbfounded by this turn of events, Babb approached other publishers, but her story was now perceived as a mere echo of *The Grapes of Wrath*, and the work was rejected by all of them.[90] It would be nearly twenty years before she published her first book, an autobiographical work about her father's career as a gambler.

Babb's novel about the migrant crisis, titled *Whose Names Are Unknown*, was finally released in 2004, sixty-five years after she had written it.[91] By then, the author was ninety-seven and she died the following year. Reviewers of the book noted a number of similarities with *The Grapes of Wrath*,[92] which supports the idea that Steinbeck made extensive use of her research and notes.

In the dedication to his novel, Steinbeck expressed his gratitude to Collins ("To Tom, who lived it"), but he never acknowledged his debt to Sanora Babb. Did he experience any regret or guilt over this? It's interesting to note that in Steinbeck's last novel, *The Winter of Our Discontent*, the protagonist's son plagiarizes his entry for an essay contest on the topic of "I love America." When the misdeed is discovered and his father confronts him, the boy replies, "Who cares? Everybody does it . . . everybody right up to the top . . . I bet you took some in your time, because they all do."[93]

* * *

From her perch at *The New Yorker*, film critic Pauline Kael wielded enormous influence in the cinematic world for more than two decades. Her reviews were outspoken and often contrarian, but they were always read. In February of 1971, early in her tenure at the magazine, she published a lengthy, two-part article titled "Raising Kane." In it, she advanced the thesis – now discredited – that Herman Mankiewicz, Orson Welles's co-writer for *Citizen Kane*, was the true creative force behind the cinematic masterpiece.[94] The articles cemented Kael's role at the forefront of American film criticism.

The research supporting Kael's articles had been conducted by Howard Suber, a young assistant professor of film at UCLA. He was flattered when Kael called, asking if he would share his voluminous research on the iconic film with her. In return, she promised him co-authorship on the project she was contemplating, as well as half of the profits. In his excitement and naïveté, Suber failed to request a written contract. When Kael's articles were published, they ran below a single byline: her own. And Suber received a payment of only $375 (about $2,800 today). He felt powerless to object and chose not to go public concerning his treatment by the famous critic.

In a rejoinder to Kael's thesis about *Citizen Kane*, director Peter Bogdanovich penned an article for *Esquire* exposing the flaws that he saw in her arguments. He had also heard about her shabby treatment of Suber and mentioned that as well.[95] Bogdanovich's claim was later supported by the work of Brian Kellow, who published a biography of Kael in 2011. In going through the papers that Kael had donated to the Indiana

University Library, he found that her research for the *Citizen Kane* articles consisted almost entirely of Suber's work.[96]

* * *

Perhaps the most extensive – and disturbing – account of the vicissitudes of plagiarism was written by Neal Bowers. In 1992, he was a professor at the University of Iowa, enjoying a successful career as a teacher, poet, and critic. But then he received a phone call from a colleague who suspected that one of Bowers's poems had been republished under a different person's name. The colleague sent him the evidence, and he was shocked to see verses he had published two years earlier under a different title and attributed to someone named "David Sumner."

Over the next two years, Bowers discovered that two of his poems had been accepted by no fewer than nineteen different literary magazines. He was able to intervene and stop half of this number from reaching print, but in eleven cases he saw his work – always appearing under a different title and with minor changes – attributed to his plagiarist.

In 1997, Bowers published an account of how he, his wife, and a private investigator pursued their quarry and how the thievery finally came to an end.[97] *Words for the Taking* is a fascinating story, but for present purposes our focus is on how the episode affected him and how others reacted to his plight.

To combat his doppelgänger, Bowers sent letters of warning to the editors of poetry outlets who might receive submissions from Sumner. Many of these letters went unanswered. Some editors replied they would need clear proof of plagiarism before considering taking any action. Others even published Sumner's counterfeits after Bowers had sent them evidence of the duplicated works. And some seemed to find the whole thing amusing. Bowers eventually realized that being a whistleblower was also making him into a pariah:

> More than a few friends advised me not to alienate editors by pushing my case too hard. Others cautioned me not to link my name too closely with plagiarism, even as a champion of right, because in the long-term people might not remember which side of the theft I was on.[98]

Others criticized him for pursuing someone who was clearly mentally ill and not responsible for his actions.

Bowers first wrote about his experiences in a 1994 article for *The American Scholar*,[99] which led to a feature in *The New York Times*.[100] Other stories soon appeared in a variety of venues. While they served the purpose of highlighting Bowers's travails, they essentially negated his twenty-five-year career as a successful poet and transmogrified him into a crime victim.

Bowers also became a foil for those who believe that artists don't truly own what they create. Michael Martone, for example, became aware of Bowers's predicament and responded by publishing some of his own work under Bowers's name.[101] This served Martone's goal of subverting the concepts of authorship, authenticity, and originality, but it reduced Bowers to a pawn in the service of his colleague's pet theories.

The experience with his plagiarist left Bowers unable to craft new poems for several years. He turned instead to writing fiction – that is, when he wasn't being interviewed as an "expert on plagiarism."

It's not unusual for the victims of plagiarism to compare the sense of personal violation they feel to a physical assault. Nora Roberts, whose *Sweet Revenge* was extensively pilfered by Janet Daily, was quoted as saying, "It's like mind rape. To think how far along it's been going ... it's like being stalked."[102] And Howard Suber, the UCLA film professor, told Kellow that "It may be excessively dramatic to describe it as rape, but that's what it felt like." Suber, who later became an expert on copyright law, added that "If I'd only known what I know about copyright now, I would have sued her [Kael's] ass, but I didn't."[103]

CHAPTER 6

Copyrights and Contexts

HARRY POTTER AND THE FAIR USE LOOPHOLE

In the wildly successful *Harry Potter* series, published between 1997 and 2007, J. K. Rowling constructed an intricately detailed world of magical spells, potions, locales, and fantastic creatures. In an attempt to bring some order to her sprawling fictional universe, a children's librarian in Michigan created a website – "The Harry Potter Lexicon" – to keep track of it all.[1] Steve Vander Ark established his online encyclopedia in 2000, after the publication of the first three books in the series, and it soon became a popular destination for fans of Rowling's books. The author herself admitted to consulting it from time to time.[2]

In August of 2007, after the final work in the series was released, RDR Books announced its plan to bring out a print version of Vander Ark's project: a 400-page tome with 2,437 entries.[3] Soon thereafter, Rowling and Warner Brothers, the film studio behind the Harry Potter movies, brought a suit against Vander Ark's publisher. A print version of the lexicon, the plaintiffs claimed, would be an infringement of Rowling's copyright. The author hadn't objected to the lexicon when it was freely available online, but RDR's plans to monetize it, she asserted, would compete with her own plans to create a definitive guide to the Harry Potter universe.[4]

Testifying in a Manhattan courtroom during a four-day trial in April of 2008, Rowling indicated that her opinion of the lexicon had changed considerably. She now characterized it as "sloppy," "riddled with errors," and "derivative."[5] Vander Ark, for his part, was moved to tears after an emotional three-hour stint on the witness stand.[6]

145

Five months later, Judge Robert Patterson ruled against the defendant, finding "substantial similarity" between RDR's lexicon and the Harry Potter novels. The plaintiffs received $6,750 in damages (about $9,600 today).[7] But after some negotiation, Rowling allowed a modified version of the lexicon to be published in early 2009. The revised work eliminated plot spoilers and provided commentary in addition to the inventory of Rowling's creations.[8]

So why was the first version of Vander Ark's lexicon problematic, while the revised version passed muster? Welcome to another magical land, the world of fair use, where creators can freely use works still protected by copyright – provided that the resulting work meets certain requirements. The problem is that the necessary conditions for fair use are somewhat vague, poorly understood by the public, and not consistently applied.

Section 107 of the US Copyright Act of 1976 specifies a four-factor test to be employed when deciding whether a particular work meets the standard of fair use. The first of these factors is its purpose. For example, is the derivative work something that will be sold, or is it noncommercial? Rowling didn't object to the web-based version of the lexicon – Vander Ark made a little money from ads that ran on the site, but users could freely access its content. It was only when RDR Books made plans to sell copies of the lexicon that Rowling objected. If a derivative work has a commercial purpose, it may fail to meet the standard of fair use.

Another aspect of the purpose factor is whether the derived work is transformative in some way. The judge ruled that Vander Ark's lexicon passed this test, since it recast the people, places, and things described in Rowling's seven novels into an alphabetical list.

A second factor is the nature of the copyrighted work. For example, is it a fictional creation that required considerable ingenuity to produce? In this case, millions of fans of the boy wizard would say yes. And in general, the courts have provided greater copyright protection to works of imagination than to factual works.

A third factor is how much of the original is used. If it is only a little, then it's easier to argue that the derivative work is fair use. This factor is clearly problematic for Vander Ark's lexicon, because he made use of material appearing on almost every page of Rowling's books.

The final factor addresses how the derivative work would affect the market for the original. At first blush, one might conclude that the effect should be minimal. It's difficult to imagine anyone choosing to read Vander Ark's lexicon *before* diving into the Harry Potter series. On the other hand, this factor pertains to potential markets as well, and Rowling was on record as saying that she intended to produce her own Harry Potter encyclopedia at some point.

It's fairly easy to see why Patterson ruled as he did: the lexicon was problematic in terms of three factors related to the standard of fair use. It did meet one factor in that it was transformative. With the addition of commentary, the directory could be viewed as a form of literary criticism.

The Rowling case provides a relatively simple example of how the four-factor test might be employed to determine fair use. But the verbiage in Section 107 includes concepts that can be difficult to quantify or to forecast. How much must a work be transformed before it is considered fair use? Is it possible to accurately forecast the effect of a derivative work on demand for the original? Nor is it true that all four factors receive equal weighting by the courts: an analysis of case law showed that the first factor (purpose/transformativeness) and the fourth (market effects) are the best predictors of judicial opinions.[9]

Copyright law in the US allows for fair use in other contexts, such as educational purposes. This corresponds to the noncommercial use case mentioned earlier – the first factor of the four-factor test. Another exception for fair use is parody, and here things become even murkier. A parody is a work that uses imitation and exaggeration for comic effect, and in theory, the four-factor test can be applied to such works. In practice, making such a determination is not easy, and different courts have come to different conclusions.

In September of 1953, NBC aired "From Here to Obscurity," an episode of Sid Caesar's *Your Show of Shows*. The twenty-minute skit is a send-up of *From Here to Eternity*, the drama that Columbia Pictures had released the previous month. Columbia sued NBC, claiming that the skit infringed on their copyright and that it "libeled and maligned" their film.[10] In this case, the judge ruled in favor of the defendant: clearly, the parody wasn't intended to compete with the movie. And for a parody to work, the parodist must, the judge declared, "make a sufficient use of the original to recall or conjure up the subject matter being burlesqued." Fair use permits this, the judge continued, "so long as the taking is not substantial."[11] This seems like a perfectly reasonable decision, but what constitutes substantial taking? In other words, where should the line be drawn between parody and outright plagiarism?

The difficulty in making such judgments was on full display when 2 Live Crew released the song "Pretty Woman" in 1989. The rap group's intent was to lampoon "Oh, Pretty Woman," Roy Orbison's 1964 ballad, but with the song's titular character transformed into "a hairy, pregnant hooker."[12] 2 Live Crew approached Acuff-Rose Music about licensing the song, but they were rebuffed. Undeterred, the group released their version without the copyright holder's permission, and Acuff-Rose filed suit. The rappers argued that their version was a parody and that the use of Orbison's song constituted fair use. Several years of litigation ensued.

A Federal District Court in Nashville issued a ruling in favor of the rappers, but this was overturned by the Court of Appeals for the Sixth Circuit. The appellate court ruled that since the parody was created for a "blatantly commercial purpose," it failed the first factor of the four-factor test and was not protected by fair use. The case ended up before the Supreme Court in 1994, with the judges ruling unanimously to overturn the ruling by the Sixth Circuit. It was not a blanket ruling in favor of parody, however; writing for the court, Justice David Souter stated that a "case-by-case determination" would need to be made regarding parody and fair use.[13]

During the forty-year period that separates "From Here to Obscurity" and the Supreme Court's ruling on "Pretty Woman," it could be argued that the public's attitudes about parody became more liberal. It's certainly difficult to imagine a film studio suing a television network over a parody today: if anything, the studio would be grateful for the free publicity. Starting with *Mad* magazine and running through the work of "Weird Al" Yankovic and *Saturday Night Live*, parody has gone mainstream. This provides yet another example of how views of appropriation can shift as the culture itself shifts.

THE LONG ARM OF THE (COPYRIGHT) LAW

Does Sherlock Holmes have emotions? This may seem like a peculiar or even an inane question, but it was a central issue in a New Mexico court case in 2020, and one that is intimately tied to the concepts of copyright and intellectual property.

Copyright is essentially an entitlement granted to creators to reap the benefits of their ingenuity for a specified period of time. This privilege is enshrined in Article I of the US Constitution, and Congress was granted the power to create and modify the legal framework for this protection. It first did so in 1790 by stipulating a copyright length of fourteen years. If the rights holder were still alive after that time, the copyright could be renewed for an additional fourteen-year period. Otherwise, the work in question would become part of the public domain and be available to everyone to freely copy or modify.

Why should any sort of limit be placed on the length of copyright? The underlying logic is that a balance must be struck between the rights of creators, who are granted a period of exclusivity in order to profit from their work, and the rights of the public, who might benefit from being able to make use of it.

A series of revisions to copyright law has been passed over the past two centuries. The changes were made to take into account the impact of new technologies on intellectual property rights, and also to bring US copyright law into conformity with international agreements, such as the Berne Convention.[14] One consequence of these changes, however, has been that the period of exclusivity granted to creators has steadily crept upwards.

In 1831, in the first major revision of copyright law, Congress approved a term of twenty-eight years with the possibility of a fourteen-year extension. And in 1909, the legislators extended copyright to a term of twenty-eight years with a possible extension of twenty-eight more years. In 1976, the duration was changed to the lifetime of the author plus fifty years, which would allow the creators' heirs to benefit from copyright exclusivity. And in 1998, the Copyright Term Extension Act changed this to the life of the creator plus seventy years. This law also decreed that works published between 1923 and 1978 would retroactively receive ninety-five years of copyright protection.

If the purpose of copyright is to provide creators with a limited window of exclusivity, it would seem that the 1976 and 1998 extensions decisively shifted the balance of power away from the public and toward the creators. Why did this happen? Many well-known composers or their estates advocated for a longer period of exclusivity, although the 1998 extension has come to be known – somewhat unfairly and inaccurately – as the Mickey Mouse Protection Act.[15] Everyone's favorite rodent first appeared in *Steamboat Willie*, an animated short released in 1928 by Walt Disney Studios. Before the 1998 extension, the character would have entered the public domain in 2003. But as a result of the legislative update, Disney's grip on its iconic mouse – or at least the Steamboat Willie version – was moved out to January 1, 2024, a full ninety-five years after Mickey's debut as a riverboat captain.[16]

As it happens, there are other ways to circumvent the problem of expiring copyrights. Edgar Rice Burroughs was one of the first to set up a corporation to regulate the use of his literary creations, such as Tarzan and John Carter of Mars.[17] He also trademarked his characters as a way of controlling his intellectual property, and other companies have followed suit. A trademark is a distinctive symbol, design, or character that a corporation can register with an entity like the US Patent and Trademark Office. Trademarks have a distinct advantage over copyrights: as long as the required paperwork is kept up to date, trademarks never expire. This can allow corporations like Disney to maintain a degree of control over their characters even after their copyrights lapse.[18]

So what does any of this have to do with Sherlock Holmes and his emotions? Well, almost everything, as it happens. Arthur Conan Doyle published his first story about the fictional detective in 1887. After tiring of and then apparently killing off his creation in 1893, he yielded to public pressure and wrote more stories between 1901 and 1927. By applying the ninety-five-year rule, we can see that Sherlock Holmes stories began to enter the public domain in 1981.

Following the author's death, the lucrative rights to the Sherlock Holmes and Dr. Watson characters passed to his heirs.[19] Over the next several decades, the Conan Doyle Estate Ltd. charged writers, filmmakers, and others a licensing fee to make use of their intellectual property. And since the final stories in the Sherlock Holmes *oeuvre* wouldn't enter the public domain until January 1, 2023 (that is, 1927 plus ninety-five years), adaptors played it safe, even after the first stories entered the public domain in 1981, by making payments to the author's estate.

But in 2013, the American writer Leslie Klinger tried to publish an edited volume of new Holmes stories with Pegasus Books. Not so fast, the estate declared: Klinger was told that he had to pay up, or the book's distribution would be blocked. The editor, who was a lawyer in addition to being a fan of the fictional detective, chose to sue the estate, arguing that Sherlock Holmes had already made the leap into the public domain.[20] The estate argued that the Holmes character was protected until 2023, when the entirety of his character arc would be complete, but this argument was rejected by a district court in 2013. The ruling was affirmed by the Seventh Circuit court the following year.[21] Finally, the estate appealed for an emergency stay to the Supreme Court, but the justices declined to hear the case.

The story of Sherlock Holmes and copyright challenges doesn't end there, however. In 2020, Legendary Pictures and Netflix produced the film *Enola Holmes*, depicting the exploits of the teenaged sister of Sherlock. The movie drew on a young adult series called "The Enola Holmes Mysteries" which Nancy Springer began publishing in 2006. The Enola character doesn't appear in the Conan Doyle fictional universe, however: she was purely the product of Springer's imagination. Even though Enola's older brother makes an appearance in the stories, the Conan Doyle estate took no action against Springer.[22]

But the Netflix film project roused the heirs to action: they sued Netflix, Springer, and Penguin Random House – Springer's publisher – for infringement. Essentially, the estate claimed that there were two different versions of Sherlock Holmes. The detective described in Conan Doyle's first forty-eight stories, they asserted, was unemotional and arrogant. In contrast, the character depicted in the author's final set of stories, published between 1923 and 1927, was sensitive and empathic. As lawyers for the estate put it, "He could express emotion. He began to respect women."[23] The Netflix depiction of Holmes, they argued, portrayed the sensitive, later version of the detective. And as luck would have it, some of these stories were still protected by copyright.

The court found the estate's reasoning to be somewhat tortuous. A major obstacle for the Conan Doyle estate was that there are clear examples of Holmes displaying emotion in plots that had already entered the public domain. In 1890's *The Sign of the Four*, for example, Holmes is depicted as showing "kindness and respect" to a female character.[24] The court dismissed the suit with prejudice, and the parties involved arrived at a settlement.[25] All of this became moot a few years later, when – on New Year's Day of 2023 – the final Holmes stories, emotions and all, entered the public domain.

THE FAN FICTION CONUNDRUM

Every author wants an audience, and if they are talented and persevere at their craft, they may be fortunate enough to attract one. And if the stars align just right, they may even win over a coterie of devoted fans, eager to devour every word they publish. A subset of these fans may go a step further and create their own stories based on their favorite author's work. Some writers welcome this, but many strongly oppose the practice, viewing it as a form of infringement of their intellectual property. It's ironic that an author's greatest fans can also become the cause of one of their biggest headaches.

The appropriation of fictional characters is not a new phenomenon. We saw this in Chapter 1 in the case of the serialized novels of Dickens. And two centuries before Nicholas Nickleby was commandeered, Cervantes was compelled to write the second part of *Don Quixote*, following the publication of an unauthorized sequel.[26] The motivation in both cases was financial, as others sought to profit from the original author's success. But what is the harm in appropriation when the goal is to simply luxuriate in the author's fictional world by extending it? This is the dilemma created by fan fiction, more commonly referred to as fanfic.

The modern incarnation of fanfic can be traced to devotees of *Star Trek* in the late 1960s. The Original Series, as it is now known, lasted for only three televised seasons before being cancelled, and it would not be resurrected for a decade. To fill the void, thousands of fans – many of them female – continued the adventures of the crew of the "Enterprise" in fanzines sent through the mail or circulated at conventions.[27]

In theory, the writing of fan fiction has several attractive aspects. Chief among these is that it provides a creative outlet for budding authors. In addition, it lowers the cost of entry by providing a scaffolding for one's first literary productions. Instead of building a world and a cast of characters from scratch, the aspiring writer is provided literary training wheels by an existing property and is free to focus largely on plot and dialog. The fan fiction community has also shown itself to be a generous place, with contributors providing supportive feedback on each other's work in a kind of "distributed mentorship."[28]

In practice, however, fanfic has developed a somewhat tawdry reputation. Part of this is due to the subject matter of many stories. It's not uncommon for fans to write about romantic pairings that deviate significantly from the creator's intentions. A story set in the *Star Trek* universe, for example, might feature a love affair between Captain Kirk and his Vulcan science officer. Stories based on "shipping" two characters, such as Kirk/Spock, Holmes/Watson, or even Harry Potter/Dumbledore, are referred to as slash fiction.[29]

One of the truly amazing things about fanfic is how much of it has been written. The largest online repository for such works is FanFiction.net. Established in 1998, as of 2022 it had over twelve million registered users, who had contributed over fourteen million stories.[30] Another site, Archive of Our Own (AO3), launched ten years later. At the time of this writing, it has nearly 60,000 fandoms – specific categories, such as "Twilight" – and over six million users. It is home to more than eleven million works.[31] And there are also several other sites that feature fan fiction, such as Wattpad and Tumblr.

The stories on fan sites include crossovers that blend two (or more) fictional worlds. Want to read a story that combines the characters from *Lost* and *The Walking Dead*, perhaps with a little *World War Z* thrown in? FanFiction.net has you covered.[32] Such a mash-up, or almost any other conceivable permutation, is only a few mouse clicks away. The quality of the writing, as one might imagine, varies considerably from story to story.

It should be noted that some successful commercial fiction has its origins in fanfic. By far the best-known example is E. L. James's "Fifty Shades of Grey" series, which began life as a "Twilight" fanfic titled "Master of the Universe.' James (as "Snowqeens Icedragon") initially posted her story to FanFiction.net in 2009. After a positive response, James decided to try to publish it. This involved reworking her story so that Edward Cullen became Christian Grey and Bella Swan was transformed into Anastasia Steele.[33] The first volume of the "Fifty Shades" trilogy was published in 2011, and books in the series went on to become the bestselling books of the 2010s, with a combined 35 million copies in print.[34]

The attitude of the original authors toward fan-generated content varies considerably. Anne Rice, creator of the "Vampire Chronicles" universe, was well known for her opposition to stories involving her characters. She tried to purge as much of it from the online world as she could.[35] George R. R. Martin, the author of *A Game of Thrones*, says that he is extremely possessive and thinks of his characters as his children. Diana Gabaldon, who writes the "Outlander" series of novels, is on record as saying, "I think it's immoral, I *know* it's illegal, and it makes me want to barf whenever I've inadvertently encountered some of it involving my characters."[36]

At the other extreme, some writers have encouraged readers to make up their own stories based on the worlds they created. C. S. Lewis, for example, wrote seven novels in the "Chronicles of Narnia" series between 1950 and 1956. A letter that he wrote to a young Narnia fan in 1961 provides an example of his largesse: Lewis informs him that "There will be no more of these stories," but adds, "Why don't *you* try writing some Narnian tales? I began to write when I was about your age, and it was the greatest fun. Do try!" (emphasis in the original).[37] And H. P. Lovecraft, who created the Cthulu Mythos in the late 1920s, "freely gave every writer around him permission to write fanfiction of his works, be they remixes of his stories or new stories with crossover elements."[38]

Some authors have staked out a middle-ground position with regard to fan fiction. J. K. Rowling, for example, has assumed a relatively benign attitude toward much of the fanfic written about her wizarding world. However, she draws the line at works that feature adult content: in those cases, it's not uncommon for writers to receive a cease-and-desist letter from her legal team.[39] And Stephenie Meyer, of "Twilight" fame, reports conflicted feelings on the subject. While she doesn't have an issue with others making use of her characters, she would prefer to see fans expending their energy on creating worlds that are completely their own.[40]

It's worth noting that many authors dabble in writing fanfic themselves, which undoubtedly influences their views on the subject. Neil Gaiman's relaxed attitude toward the practice, for example, is probably the result of him writing fanfic about Narnia, Cthulu, and Sherlock Holmes. And the first novel written by Naomi Novik – an outspoken supporter of fanfic – was a story set in the "Master and Commander" universe created by Patrick O'Brian. Others, such as Orson Scott Card, advise aspiring writers to "not waste their time or talent in trying to tell stories in someone else's universe," even though he has produced fanfic based on the works of Shakespeare and Isaac Asimov.[41] This makes his stance appear somewhat hypocritical.

Many authors, however, scrupulously avoid reading fanfic based on their own work because doing so would limit the scope of what they can write about in the future. They may be aware of what happened to fantasy author Marion Zimmer Bradley ("The Mists of Avalon" and the "Darkover" series). She read the fanzines devoted to "Darkover" and decided to develop an idea from a fanfic novella into a novel in her series. She offered the fanfic author an acknowledgement in exchange for using their concept, but the fan wanted co-authorship and half the royalties. When she said no, the fan threatened to take her to court. Bradley ended up abandoning the project she had been working on for two years.[42]

Is fan fiction legal? This is a gray area that has yet to be explored by the courts. It could be argued that fanfic is protected by the fair use exceptions provided by Section 107 of the US Copyright Law. And if the fan fiction deviates significantly from the original, the infringing author could claim their work was parody – another exception in copyright law. It's worth noting that, as of late 2022, no fanfic writer has ever been sued by an author.[43] But even if fan fiction is legal, the question of whether it is ethical remains. Do fans have a moral obligation to respect an author's wishes if that author has made known their opposition to the practice?

COOKING THE BOOKS

As we saw in the discussion of copyright traps, a list of facts, such as a directory of telephone numbers, can't be copyrighted. For a work to be afforded such protection, a bare listing of elements requires a certain degree of transformation. The amount of modification required, however, is a matter of some debate.

Most published recipes fall into this legal gray area, since they consist of an inventory of ingredients and instructions for their preparation. No matter how delicious the result, an unadorned recipe is simply a culinary prescription that exists in the public domain – just like a list of phone numbers. Nevertheless, borrowing them creates a bad look – as Cindy McCain found out in 2008 when she was accused of appropriating "family recipes" for her husband's campaign, an event described in Chapter 4.

Fifty years ago, *The New York Times* noted that "There is no branch of American publishing today where the lifting of uncredited material has become such a standard procedure as in cuisine."[44] Unlike most other written material, the content of recipes can't be easily paraphrased: the details, such as ingredients, their amounts, and the time for cooking or baking need to be specified with some degree of precision.

This is one reason why modern cookbooks often contain elaborate photographic spreads or extended stories about the recipes themselves: the addenda are intended to be transformational and may afford the author a degree of protection of their intellectual property. But nothing prevents a plagiarist from stripping out this narrative and absconding with the chef's blueprint for a given dish.

Bartolomeo Platina, an Italian gastronomist, authored the first printed cookbook in 1475. Platina gave his collection the charming title *On Honest Indulgence and Good Health*, but he seems to have drawn heavily from Martino da Como's manuscript *Book on the Art of Cooking*, which had been compiled some twenty-five years earlier.[45] The culinary arts and the art of cribbing, therefore, seem to have been joined together from the beginning.

Hannah Glasse is responsible for one of the first popular cookbooks in English. *The Art of Cookery Made Plain and Easy*, published in 1747, consisted of nearly a thousand recipes. However, at least a quarter of these were "ruthlessly plagiarized" from earlier compilations.[46] A century later, many of the recipes in *Mrs. Beeton's Book of Household Management* were "brazenly copied" from previously published compilations, including Glasse's.[47]

In the early 1980s, two cases of culinary appropriation received journalistic attention. Martha Stewart, the doyen of all things domestic, was accused of borrowing three Chinese recipes for inclusion in her first cookbook, *Entertaining*. (The book, published in 1982, had been ghost-written by Elizabeth Hawes.)[48] The recipes in question had appeared in Barbara Tropp's *The Modern Art of Chinese Cooking*, published the year before. After some unflattering coverage in the media, Stewart acknowledged Tropp for her "inspiration" starting with the third printing of the book.[49]

And in 1983, culinary instructor Richard Nelson was accused of cribbing recipes from several other cookbook authors. Specifically, journalists at the *New York Daily News* and *Washingtonian* magazine found that *Richard Nelson's American Cooking* contained recipes developed by Richard Olney, the author of *Simple French Food*, and Francesco Ghedini's *Northern Italian Cooking*. To add insult to injury, Nelson even appropriated recipes from his mentor, James Beard, who wrote the foreword for Nelson's collection. Nelson denied that he had stolen anyone's recipes.[50]

Richard Olney, however, chose to file suit against Nelson and his publisher, New American Library, claiming that thirty-nine of his recipes appeared in Nelson's book. The case was ultimately settled via a consent judgment, with the publisher agreeing to remainder unsold copies of *American Cooking*. In addition, Nelson and his publisher paid for Olney's court costs as well as a confidential amount in damages.[51] The out-of-court settlement set no legal precedent, however, leaving the issue of recipe ownership in legal limbo.[52]

In October of 2007, Jessica Seinfeld – wife of comedian Jerry – published *Deceptively Delicious: Simple Secrets to Get Your Kids Eating Good Food*. To publicize her book, she made an appearance on *The Oprah Winfrey Show*, thus propelling the title to the top of the bestseller lists. The book's popularity, however, meant that its contents were scrutinized by many readers. And some of them began making online posts about similarities between Seinfeld's book and another recently published cookbook – *The Sneaky Chef* by Missy Chase Lapine.

Both books describe "stealth" methods for adding pureed vegetables and fruits into foods that kids like. And at least three recipes featuring unlikely combinations, such as hiding spinach in brownies, appear in both. Lapine's book had been twice rejected by HarperCollins before being acquired by the Perseus Books Group in June of 2006. This was the same month that Jessica Seinfeld signed a contract – with HarperCollins – for her own book. Lapine's cookbook appeared six months before Seinfeld's.[53]

Three weeks after his wife's appearance on *Oprah,* Jerry Seinfeld went on the *Late Show with David Letterman* and stated that Lapine had accused Jessica of "vegetable plagiarism," even though Lapine hadn't done so. He also denigrated the author by saying that she thought this could be her "wacko moment."[54] He described Lapine as "angry and hysterical" and compared her to assassins Mark David Chapman and James Earl Ray, simply because she had three names.[55]

Two months after the Letterman appearance, Lapine sued the couple for copyright infringement – because of the book – and for "malicious defamation" – because of Jerry Seinfeld's remarks.[56] A year and a half later, in September of 2009, a federal judge ruled for the defendant. "No reasonable fact finder could conclude," the judge stated, that the two books "have the same aesthetic appeal."[57] Lapine appealed the ruling, but the Second Circuit Court of Appeals concurred with the lower court's decision in April of 2010.[58] The defamation suit against Jerry Seinfeld was dismissed by the courts in February of 2011.[59]

And in 2021, British chef Elizabeth Haigh faced allegations of plagiarism after publishing *Makan: Recipes from the Heart of Singapore.* Sharon Wee, who nine years earlier had published the memoir *Growing Up in a Nonya Kitchen,* took to social media to announce that "certain recipes and other content from my book had been copied or paraphrased without my consent." Wee alerted Haigh's publisher, and although the author did not issue a public response, her book was withdrawn due to "rights issues." Wee said she was gratified that the publisher chose to take that step.[60]

The upshot is that the issue of recipe ownership remains unclear. Current US law states that to be protected by copyright, a recipe must be "accompanied by substantial literary expression in the form of an explanation or directions."[61] Exactly how much literary expression is required, however, will need to be decided by courts in the future.

DEAR GRADUATES

If there is a circumstance seemingly tailor-made to bring out one's inner plagiarist, it must be the venerable commencement address. Each spring, colleges and universities, as well as high schools and elementary schools, honor their graduates with a ceremony of some sort. These events typically include remarks given by school officials or guests as well as the students themselves. Many schools also have convocations at the beginning of the academic year to welcome new students. Given that tens of thousands of educational institutions hold such events annually, it shouldn't come as a surprise that some become newsworthy for all the wrong reasons.

Being chosen to speak at a commencement ceremony can be a distinct honor. However, it can also be incredibly stressful. Most people aren't naturally gifted orators, and the requirements of the form – the heartfelt delivery of remarks that are eloquent, inspirational, and pithy – are extremely challenging. Given the plethora of truly exceptional commencement speeches readily available online, it's not surprising that would-be speakers seek inspiration there. Unfortunately, it is all too easy to cross over the ill-defined boundary between inspiration and homage and into outright appropriation.

People who give speeches for a living are generally careful about acknowledging their sources. The pros know that this can be accomplished quickly and easily. A simple introductory statement, like "As [famous person] once said," or "In the words of [famous person]," is all that is needed to provide the necessary credit. But given the premium that our culture places on originality, nonprofessional speakers often craft remarks that are a tangled admixture of their own ideas and those drawn from others. They may also be unsure of the best way to give credit – or even lack the awareness that such a tip of the hat is required.

To raise the stakes even further, an enduring record of the performance is often available. Most speakers make use of prepared remarks, and it wasn't uncommon, in days gone by, for transcripts to appear in local newspapers. More recently, videos of these speeches, either recorded professionally or captured by mobile phones, can be uploaded to YouTube, allowing anyone to compare a given speech to similar addresses. Memorable turns of phrase can be typed into search engines to determine whether the speaker's eloquence was authentic or simply the recycled musings of an actor or a tech billionaire. It's a wonder that anyone agrees to subject themselves to such scrutiny.

School officials, such as superintendents and teachers, are perhaps most at risk when they appropriate without attribution. It is they who are responsible for teaching their charges about plagiarism, and they also mete out penalties for any such transgressions. These individuals are also expected to uphold the standards they seek to instill, so any failing on their own part is perceived as the rankest hypocrisy. Despite these obvious dangers, such incidents do happen.

In 2005, for example, the principal of Springstead High School in Florida gave an inspiring address to her graduating class. However, her remarks consisted of a word-for-word recitation of the well-known "wear sunscreen" essay written by Mary Schmich. Her advice was originally published in the *Chicago Tribune* in 1997 and has become widely available online.[62] However, the principal chose to preface her remarks by stating that what followed were her personal thoughts. And at other points during her speech, she used the phrase "my advice" to reinforce the perception that the ideas were her own.

To make things worse, the principal wasn't a first-time offender. In a commencement speech delivered the previous year, she appropriated from a collection of inspirational thoughts titled "All I Need to Know I Learned from Noah's Ark." Although the provenance of these sayings is murky, she left her audience under the impression that the ideas were her own.

In an apology for both episodes, the principal admitted to "unintentional errors." The school district put a letter of reprimand in her personnel file and gave her a one-day suspension, although it was with pay.[63] A state inquiry in 2007 resulted in a $1,500 fine, although she was allowed to retain her state certifications as an educator.[64]

The Springstead case isn't unique: a principal at West Boca Raton High also achieved the dubious distinction of being a two-time offender. In 2015, the principal pilfered from an address given by teacher David McCullough Jr., and in the previous year had helped himself to the words of Professor Marc Lewis. The principal denied the charges of plagiarism, stating that "I take things off the Internet and change things around and clean them up."[65] His school district moved him to a charter school office, and he was fined $750 by the state of Florida in 2018. He was also required to take a college-level creative writing class, presumably to learn about techniques for proper source attribution.[66]

A commencement address given at Kenyon College in 2005 by author David Foster Wallace has been appropriated by at least two school principals. The first was in 2011, at the Clinton School for Writers and Artists in New York City. The principal said he had intended to provide an attribution but forgot to do so.[67] Three years later, the principal of Garden Spot High School in Pennsylvania also channeled his inner Wallace. "I found it [Wallace's address] to be very moving and inspirational," he explained. "Looking back on it, in hindsight, I should probably have cited [Wallace] in my speech."[68]

A highly ironic example of appropriation was committed by the Dean of the College of Communication at Boston University in 1991. The subject of his commencement speech was the decline of morality in society. Unfortunately, the dean's speech contained nearly fifteen paragraphs, repeated virtually word for word and without attribution, from an article written by PBS film critic Michael Medved. The dean resigned his administrative position but remained on the university's faculty.[69]

School officials account for the lion's share of such episodes, but students also succumb to the siren's song of appropriation. In the US, students who graduate with the highest class rank are often called upon to give valedictorian and salutatorian addresses, and they may feel as much pressure as school officials do to make witty and memorable remarks.

In 2010, the valedictorian for Columbia University lifted a bit from Patton Oswalt's 2006 stand-up routine. The graduate in question made liberal use of the comedian's "physics for poets" gag. In a tweet, Oswalt sarcastically praised the student's speech and provided a link to the graduate's remarks. Columbia issued a statement acknowledging the incident and provided assurances that the student had apologized to his classmates and to Oswalt.[70]

Also in 2010, the valedictorian at Walpole High in Massachusetts recycled facetious remarks about Chipotle that had been posted to

YouTube by another graduate nine years earlier. She apologized for her mistake via Twitter, explaining, in part, that she was "genuinely not a creative person." The principal said the school would start screening the students' speeches beforehand to prevent such episodes in the future.[71]

There is no guarantee, however, that plagiarism will be detected when speeches are reviewed in advance. The remarks given by the 2008 high school valedictorian in Circleville, Ohio had been vetted beforehand, but some members of the audience thought they sounded familiar.[72] The student admitted to cribbing two-thirds of his address from an online medley of song lyrics titled "The Perfect Beatles Graduation Speech." (After a legal dispute with the school, the student was granted co-valedictorian status.)[73]

Late-night talk show hosts are not above using bad commencement addresses to entertain their audiences. Jimmy Fallon, in a 2017 segment for *The Tonight Show,* played a montage of clips from then-President Donald Trump's commencement speech at Liberty University, intercut with the graduation address given by Elle Woods (Reese Witherspoon) in the 2001 movie "Legally Blonde." Viewers were invited to draw the conclusion that Trump had plagiarized from Witherspoon's character.

An investigation by Snopes, however, revealed that the two videos were tightly edited – down to short phrases – to make it appear that the speeches contained identical content. In truth, commencement addresses are extremely formulaic; most of them probably contain words and phrases like "into the world," "most importantly," and "passion."[74]

THE EUROVISION HOTHOUSE

Some types of public performance almost seem to have been designed to encourage appropriation. Commencement addresses are one example, as we have seen, and the annual music competition known as the Eurovision Song Contest is another. The contest began in 1956 with seven countries participating, but by the 2010s about forty nations were competing each year, and it had become a true cultural phenomenon.

Although it tends to receive less attention from Americans – many of whom associate it with cheesy performances and even cheesier wardrobe choices – the event has helped to create pop superstars. Famously, it served as the launchpad for the Swedish supergroup ABBA in 1974 (their entry was "Waterloo"). And in 2003, a Junior Eurovision Song Contest was added. This competition allows youth between the ages of nine and fourteen to participate. In a typical year, about fifteen nations take part in the Junior competition.

There have been a dizzying number of changes to the contest's rules, format, and voting procedures over the years, but in its current incarnation, up to forty-four countries are allowed to participate each year, with no more than twenty-six competing in the finals. Each participating nation is represented by one song, which must be a new composition – defined as not publicly released before September 1 of the previous year – and no more than three minutes in length. For many years, the song had to be performed in one of the country's national languages, but this requirement was dropped in 1999.[75]

The song that will represent each nation is chosen according to a selection process determined by local television broadcasters, under rules that vary from country to country. In the Eurovision competition, each entry must be performed live on stage by no more than six performers, although a recorded backing track is permitted.

Three live shows – two semi-finals and one final – are broadcast annually during a one-week period in May. Audience members can vote for their favorite acts via text or online, although they aren't permitted to vote for the song representing their own country. There are also national juries, and they operate under the same restriction. The votes from the audiences and the juries are combined, and points are allocated according to overall rankings.[76] The winning country is given the honor of hosting the following year's competition.

Although Eurovision is supposed to be apolitical, emotions tend to run high among the supporters for each country taking part, and accusations of rule violations are common. As Eurovision has grown, it has become a hotbed for plagiarism allegations. Wikipedians have chronicled over fifty such cases, with the majority occurring since the mid 1990s. Many of these disputes occur at the national competition stage, but some have also involved songs that make it to the final round.

Every country that participates gains an advantage by making accusations against, and potentially disqualifying, a competing nation's entry. In this way, the contest resembles a musical demolition derby. Fans and journalists scrutinize the entries to determine whether each song is truly original, and claims of song plagiarism are investigated by the contest's governing board. Given the sheer number of songs involved – several hundred each year, if one includes the national contests – it's almost inevitable that controversies will erupt. As an exasperated spokesperson for a German broadcaster put it, "Each year there are attempts to create scandals."[77]

One problem with determining whether appropriation has taken place is that many pop songs sound very much alike. And as we have seen throughout this book, determining what constitutes plagiarism in music is an enterprise fraught with difficulties.

It's hard to say what effect these allegations of plagiarism have had on the voting and on which songs have won the contest. Many such claims are ultimately found to be without merit. In 2007, for example, the Swedish singer Pandora claimed that "Flying the Flag," Britain's entry in that year's contest, had appropriated the chorus from her 1999 song "No Regrets."[78] In response, the BBC confirmed that the song was an original creation and that the songwriters were unfamiliar with Pandora's work.[79] "Flying the Flag," as performed by Scooch, finished in twenty-second place at Helsinki that year – although this may have had as much to do with the group's decision to dress as flight attendants as with the attributes of the song, or the concerns raised by Pandora.

The following year, another Swedish singer, this time fifteen-year-old Amy Diamond, accused Paolo Meneguizzi of stealing from her song "It Can Only Get Better." Meneguizzi, whose pop ballad "Era Stupendo" (It Was Gorgeous) was the 2008 entry for Switzerland, was candid when asked about the resemblance. "I've listened to the song and yes there are similarities," he said. However, he added, "I think a lot of songs nowadays have bits that sound similar ... if you come up with a melody, you can be sure that it sounds like one that has already been written somewhere in the world!" [80] "Era Stupendo" was not disqualified, and the song went on to a seventh-place finish during the second semi-final round in Belgrade.

Self-plagiarism has also arisen as an issue in the Eurovision contest. Starting in the mid 1970s, the prolific German songwriter Ralph Siegel composed several songs for the competition and co-wrote the contest's winning entry – "Ein bisschen Frieden" (A Bit of Peace) – in 1982. In 1999, he co-wrote "Reise nach Jerusalem" (Journey to Jerusalem) which finished second in the national competition. After the top vote-getter was disqualified – the song had been previously recorded – Siegel's effort became the German entry for that year.

Some critics, however, claimed that Siegel's handiwork bore a striking similarity to "Wo geht die Reise hin?" (Where Does the Journey Go?), a song he had written fifteen years earlier. The European Broadcasting Union, which oversees the competition, conducted an investigation and determined that the purported similarities were insufficient to trigger disqualification. At the competition held in Jerusalem that year, the song was performed by the German-Turkish group Sürpriz and finished in third place.[81]

If a songwriter's primary goal is to win the competition, then one strategy might be to reverse-engineer a song with demonstrably broad appeal. And what better place to start than with a Eurovision entry from yesteryear? This seems to have been the approach taken by songwriters in creating "Listen to Your Heartbeat." It emerged victorious from the Swedish national competition in 2001 and was performed by the pop band Friends at the competition. However, it came under fire as being too similar to "Liefde is een kaartspel" (Love is a Card Game), the 1996 Belgian entry performed by Lisa del Bo. The alleged copying was blatant enough that 70 percent of the Swedes themselves thought it had been plagiarized.[82]

A lawsuit was threatened by SABAM – the Belgian songwriter's association – against composers Thomas G:son and Henrik Sethsson. In the end, the Swedes reached a financial settlement with the Belgian songwriters who had written the 1996 entry.[83] Ironically, the imitation performed better than the original on the Eurovision stage: "Listen to Your Heartbeat" finished fifth in Copenhagen, whereas "Liefde is een kaartspel" had finished in sixteenth place at the competition in Oslo five years earlier.

At the time of this writing, only one of Eurovision's winning songs has been involved in a plagiarism dispute. In 2018, Israel won the competition with "Toy," in a performance by Netta Barzilai in Lisbon. After the competition, the songwriters received a pre-suit notice from the Universal Music Group, noting resemblances between "Toy" and the White Stripes' "Seven Nation Army," which had been released in 2003. A confidential settlement was reached by the parties involved, but it is known that Jack White, the White Stripes' former frontman, received a retroactive songwriting credit for "Toy."[84]

MUSIC AND SAMPLING

Allegations of plagiarism and appropriation in the music industry occur on a regular basis, and some of these episodes have been described in earlier chapters. It's not hard to understand why. There may be an infinity of ways to string together a sequence of musical notes, but only a tiny fraction of these are pleasing to the ear. Some composers, such as Schoenberg and Webern, experimented with compositions outside this fairly restrictive melodic envelope, but the resulting works have never been popular. Atonal or serial works may be of intellectual interest, but for the most part they have not been embraced by music lovers.

Given these constraints, it is almost inevitable that portions of popular songs will sound alike to some degree. The real question is whether these similarities occur by chance or whether they are the result of deliberate appropriation.

Ed Sheeran, who is no stranger to such allegations, believes that unintentional resemblance is almost inevitable. After successfully defending himself in a suit alleging that part of his "Shape of You" was taken from Sami Switch's "Oh Why," the singer/songwriter observed that "It's really damaging to the songwriting industry. There's only so many notes and very few chords used in pop music. Coincidence is bound to happen if 60,000 songs are being released every day on Spotify. That's 22 million songs a year, and there's only 12 notes that are available."[85]

Just as with cases of literary plagiarism, litigation involving music can drag on for years. A good example is Michael Skidmore's suit against Led Zeppelin. Skidmore, a trustee for Randy California, claimed that Led

Zeppelin had lifted the opening riff of "Stairway to Heaven" – one of the most iconic of all rock songs – from California's band Spirit and their song "Taurus." Led Zeppelin had once toured with Spirit, and Skidmore claimed that part of Spirit's track, released in 1968, was incorporated into Led Zeppelin's megahit three years later.[86]

Skidmore's suit was filed in 2014 against Jimmy Page and Robert Plant, and a trial took place two years later. A jury found in favor of the defendants, but Skidmore appealed the verdict, and the Ninth Circuit overturned the original decision. Ultimately the appeals court upheld the jury's original verdict.[87] An appeal to the Supreme Court in 2020 was unsuccessful, and this brought *Skidmore v. Led Zeppelin* to an end, six years after it was filed.[88] Far from being uncommon, expensive multiyear suits are the norm, and this state of affairs dissuades many artists from pursuing their own claims of copyright infringement. More commonly, such disputes are settled out of court.

When successful, however, the payday for an infringement claim can be large indeed. In 2013, the heirs of Marvin Gaye brought suit against Robin Thicke and Pharrell Williams, alleging striking similarities between Gaye's "Got to Give It Up," released in 1977, and the defendant's "Blurred Lines." A trial found in favor of the Gaye estate and the jurors awarded the heirs more than $7.3 million (nearly $9.5 million at present),[89] although the judge later reduced the damages to $5.3 million.[90] Both the verdict and the size of the award were significant and were seen as having a "chilling effect" on the music industry. One result was that songwriters began to take out insurance policies to protect themselves against future claims of infringement.[91]

In some cases, however the copying is overt and deliberate. Many pioneers of hip-hop, such as The Sugarhill Gang, Grandmaster Flash, and Kurtis Blow, intentionally included snippets from earlier recordings in their own creations. These samples often function as breaks or provide an accompaniment to the artist's rap. When hip-hop became a world-wide – and extremely lucrative – phenomenon, the musicians and composers whose work had been used in this way began to sue for copyright infringement.

During 1990, two musicians became infamous for having sampled, without permission, well-known tracks from other artists. In February,

MC Hammer (Stanley Kirk Burrell) released "U Can't Touch This" on his album "Please Hammer Don't Hurt 'Em." It was quickly noted that the song made repeated use of a riff from Rick James's "Super Freak," which had dropped in 1981. James threatened a lawsuit but the dispute was settled out of court, with Burrell agreeing to a songwriting credit for James – a concession that provided James with a share of the track's royalties.[92]

Six months later, Vanilla Ice (Robert Van Winkle), K. Kennedy and DJ Earthquake released "Ice Ice Baby," which used the distinctive bass line from the 1981 hit "Under Pressure," recorded by Queen and David Bowie. Van Winkle asserted that the two melodies were similar but not identical, because the rapper had added an extra note in his version.[93] When representatives for the artists threatened an infringement suit, Van Winkle added Bowie and three members of Queen as songwriters.

Although the reputations of both MC Hammer and Vanilla Ice took a hit because of these episodes, neither of the disputes had been litigated, and this left the legal status of sampling up in the air.

That issue was addressed in the following year, in the case of *Grand Upright Music, Ltd. v. Warner Bros. Records Inc.* The plaintiff, Gilbert O'Sullivan, claimed that the first eight bars from his 1972 song "Alone Again (Naturally)" were sampled by rapper Biz Markie for his track "Alone Again" on his *I Need a Haircut* album. Judge Kevin Duffy ruled in favor of the plaintiff. Even though the sampling of other artists' work was widespread at the time, Duffy ruled that the ubiquity of the practice was not an adequate defense. The issue, he believed, was simple, and could be summarized by the biblical admonition that "Thou shalt not steal."[94]

Duffy's ruling was reaffirmed by another landmark ruling in 2005. In *Bridgeport Music v. Dimension Films*, the issue was sampling of Funkadelic's 1975 track "Get Off Your Ass and Jam" for N.W.A.'s 1990 cut "100 Miles and Runnin'." In this case, the sample is only two seconds long – much shorter than the measures that Biz Markie had appropriated – and a federal judge initially ruled that Bridgeport's copyright had not been violated. The decision, however, was appealed and overturned by the Sixth Circuit. The appeals court, in its ruling, provided unambiguous guidance: "Get a license or do not sample. We do not see this as stifling creativity in any significant way."[95]

These decisions, and others like them, have changed the face of hip-hop. Following these verdicts, artists had no choice but to seek permission and license excerpts through a process called sample clearance. This has proved to be an onerous requirement for unknown or unsigned musicians. Hank Shocklee, who made a documentary about sampling, observed that "Jay-Z and Kanye can afford to pay the sample rates, but not the kids starting out in their own little home studio in their house, and that, to me, is what's holding back creativity."[96] In addition, sample clearance can take a significant amount of time.

Sample clearance can also create confusion for an artist's fans. In the days when music was primarily distributed on physical media, such as record albums and compact discs, the clearance of samples would be listed in the recording's liner notes. But those who only listen to music via streaming services have no simple way of verifying that any samples have been licensed from the original artists or their rights holders.

It seems reasonable that artists should be compensated when their work is deliberately appropriated, as in the case of sampling. But does a musician truly own the "feel" or the "sound" of a song? As I mentioned in Chapter 1, it can be difficult to determine whether one musician was influenced by another, or paying homage, or whether both were influenced by the same musical milieu. Judges and juries continue to struggle with these issues. Robin Thicke may have sung "I hate these blurred lines," but that sentiment could also serve as the refrain for those who must adjudicate musical appropriation.

CHAPTER 7

Plagiarism Past, Present, and Future

PROJECTIVE PLAGIARISM

In November of 2014, music producer Mark Ronson brought out "Uptown Funk," a single released ahead of his *Uptown Special* album, which dropped three months later. The funk-inspired single, featuring Bruno Mars, was a huge hit, spending fourteen weeks perched atop Billboard's Hot 100 list.[1] It would also earn Ronson a Grammy Award for Record of the Year in 2016.

Reviewers, however, were divided on whether the song was paying homage to other artists or ripping them off. A reviewer for *Forbes* opined that "Mars doesn't just wear his influences on his sleeve – his sleeves tend to be sewn entirely from the material of his influences."[2]

Soon after the single's release, members of The Gap Band charged Ronson and Mars with infringement of their 1979 single "Oops Up Side Your Head." It was claimed that the two songs "shared overwhelming similarities," particularly with regard to the cadence of the choruses.[3] In an out-of-court settlement, five writers for The Gap Band were added as co-songwriters and awarded a total of 17 percent of the publishing royalties.[4]

In 2016, the Minneapolis-based funk group Collage filed suit, claiming that Ronson and Mars made heavy use of their 1983 single "Young Girls." Specifically, the complaint alleged that "Many of the main instrumental attributes and themes of 'Uptown Funk' are deliberately and clearly copied from 'Young Girls.'"[5] In this case, the suit was dropped, and it remains unclear whether there was a financial settlement.[6]

The following year, Lastrada Entertainment sought redress, alleging that Ronson and Mars's hit infringed on their rights to the 1980 single "More Bounce to the Ounce" recorded by the funk band Zapp. The charge was that Mars's repetition of the syllable "doh" during the song's first forty-eight seconds constituted infringement.[7] The case was settled the following year, but its terms were not made public.[8]

Also in 2017, the rap group The Sequence brought suit against Ronson and Mars for infringing on their 1979 single "Funk You Up." Specifically, they claimed that "Uptown Funk" made use of "significant and substantially similar compositional elements" from their hip-hop recording.[9] The outcome of this case is unknown.

Musician Charly García complained to Billboard Argentina that the "Uptown Funk" artists had "copped the bassline and horns" from "Franky." The song had appeared on his *Cómo conseguir chicas* ("How to Get Girls") album in 1989. García claimed that Mars owed him $2 million.[10] And Serbian singer Viktorija claimed that "Uptown Funk" "contains 80 percent" of her 1984 single "Ulice Mračne Nisu Za Devojke" (Dark Streets Are Not for Girls).[11] There is no evidence that either García or Viktorija sought legal remedy, however.

Not to be outdone, fans of the BBC's *The Really Wild Show* claimed that "Uptown Funk" sounded suspiciously like the theme song for the children's nature program.[12] In an interview, Ronson was asked about this, but claimed he wasn't familiar with the long-running show. When the theme was played for him, however, he did note a resemblance in the horns. Ronson suggested that both works had been "influenced by Quincy Jones."[13]

In case you've lost count, a total of seven claims of appropriation were made concerning "Uptown Funk." But so far, it appears that only one of these claims – brought by The Gap Band – resulted in financial compensation. And although this case is extreme, multiple claims of appropriation are not uncommon. In 1927, four infringement suits were brought within five months against the authors and producers of *The Spider*, a Broadway play.[14] Why do artists so often see or hear their work in the creations of others?

Over the past half-century, psychologists have documented a variety of cognitive biases that affect how we think about and make sense of the world. These biases can help us understand a phenomenon that might be called projective plagiarism – a belief in appropriation that isn't justified or recognized by others.

One of these biases is egocentrism. When we encounter something new, we tend to think about it in terms of how it applies to ourselves. This might be especially true if it relates to our profession or avocation. Perhaps without even realizing it, an architect will evaluate a design by comparing it to plans they themselves have executed. A chef will appraise a recipe with an eye to how they would have prepared the dish. And an actor might consider whether a fellow thespian's performance has the same emotional impact as their own. Artists, performers, and other creatives will focus on the fine details of design, structure, and execution that might not even be discernible to others.

In addition, we tend to think of ourselves as unique, and this extends to the things that we create.[15] When we encounter a work that is similar to our own efforts, we might perceive this as a potential threat and carefully evaluate the elements that appear to be shared. If we discover there are several common elements, or even if only one detail possesses a striking similarity to our own work, it's easy to imagine jumping to a conclusion of appropriation – even if others fail to see the resemblance.

As mentioned earlier, in the section on coincidence, people excel at finding what they think are meaningful patterns in ambiguous stimuli, even if there is no underlying pattern to be found. The visual form of this phenomenon is called pareidolia. For example, we see the shapes of animals in clouds or the face of a man in the moon. This concept is also the basis for projective instruments like the Rorschach inkblot test. But perhaps the concept can be extended to cases of suspected plagiarism, which helps to explain why people who suspect appropriation reject coincidence as a reason for the resemblance.

Accepting that similarity can occur by chance might be a bitter pill to swallow. It can be hard for us to believe that our stroke of genius could have occurred to someone else – except that the historical record is replete with episodes of such independent creative acts. According to the *Zeitgeist* (spirit of the times) theory of history, a new idea can be said to be "in the air" at a particular moment in time. As a result, several people working on the cutting edge of a discipline might all be able to perceive it. The actual identity of the person who makes the discovery, or who has the critical insight, is essentially a matter of luck and circumstance.[16]

A famous example of this is the discovery of calculus. The notebooks of Gottfried Wilhelm Leibniz show that he was making use of differentials as early as 1675, and he published his work on calculus in 1684. The English polymath Isaac Newton began developing his "method of fluxions" in 1666 but didn't publish anything on the topic until 1693 – nine years after Leibniz. This fact, however, didn't stop members of the British Royal Society from accusing the German mathematician of intellectual thievery. Many historians of science, having examined the affair in detail, now argue that both Newton and Leibniz contributed to the development of calculus, and that neither man can truly be said to have "discovered" it.[17]

It is also the case that one's beliefs can grow even stronger when they are challenged. Psychologists refer to this bias as the backfire effect. Experiments have shown that, at least in some cases, the following of misleading political claims with corrections can *increase* belief in the incorrect information. One study, for example, showed that politically conservative participants were *more* likely to believe that Iraq possessed weapons of mass destruction after reading a news account that no such weapons had been found.[18]

Extrapolating this result to claims of plagiarism can help explain why some accusers become even more certain that others have appropriated their work, even as judges and juries repeatedly rule against them. We've already seen this in the case of Florence Deeks in Chapter 1, and there are similar examples in the world of music as well.

Consider the case of Jesse Graham, an R&B artist who released "Haters Gonna Hate" in 2013. After Taylor Swift dropped "Shake It Off" the following year, Graham filed a $42 million lawsuit, claiming that Swift made use of his hook "more than 70 times" in her song and that 92 percent of her track was taken from his.[19] Over the next few years, Graham sued Swift three times. The third suit was dismissed with prejudice, which should have meant that he was out of options, but he sued her a fourth time, this time through his company, in 2019. He lost that case as well, chose to appeal, and then lost again.[20]

TEFLON PLAGIARISTS

As we have seen, some plagiarists pay a high price for their transgressions. They may lose their jobs or see their books pulped by their publisher. For many, the blow to their reputations is both serious and lasting.

In other cases, however, an episode of plagiarism seems to have little effect on a person's career or their public standing. These individuals might be thought of as Teflon plagiarists. (This is an adaptation of the term "Teflon president" – a moniker bestowed on Ronald Reagan because "no matter what happens, no blame sticks to him").[21] How is it that a lucky few escape the opprobrium that is heaped upon others?

In some cases, the public's image of an individual has become so fixed that it is resistant to any sort of revisionism. A good example is the reputation of John James Audubon. Most people, upon hearing his name, think of the National Audubon Society, the nonprofit conservationist group established in the early twentieth century. The organization was indeed named in honor of the acclaimed nineteenth-century ornithologist. But in 2023, the Society held a vote on changing its name.[22] Why did the organization consider doing such a thing?

Audubon was a gifted artist, but he was also a slaveholder who held racial attitudes that are a poor fit with his namesake society. It has also become clear that Audubon engaged in fabrication and plagiarism during his career. Most significantly for our purposes, he made extensive use of Alexander Wilson's work for the illustrations in his acclaimed *Birds of America*, published in 1827. This went beyond mere inspiration or homage: some of Audubon's work, such as his illustration of the male yellow-shafted flicker, were tracings from Wilson's *American Ornithology*, published over a decade earlier.[23] Ironically, after Wilson's death at an early age, Audubon accused Wilson of having plagiarized from *him*.[24]

A resistance to revisionism may also explain why Jane Goodall's plagiarism did not affect her public image. In the spring of 2013, Goodall was nearly eighty years old and had been engaged in fieldwork with the chimpanzees of Tanzania for more than fifty years. She and her co-author, Gail Hudson, were set to release the book *Seeds of Hope: Wisdom and Wonder from the World of Plants*. Shortly before its publication, however, *The Washington Post* identified "at least a dozen passages" in the book that had been taken from Wikipedia entries and a variety of other websites. Although the book included an extensive acknowledgements section, it lacked footnotes or any sort of referencing for its contents.[25]

Goodall, when confronted with the copying from online sources, issued a prompt apology, and her publisher, Grand Central, recalled copies of the volume from bookstores. A year later, the book was reissued with nearly sixty pages of endnotes. In an interview at that time, she lamented her poor note taking. "In some cases," she said, "you look at my notebooks, there's no way you can tell whether this is from talking to somebody or whether it was something I read on the internet."[26]

Should Goodall have known better? It clearly wasn't a rookie mistake: before *Seeds of Hope*, she had authored or co-authored more than two dozen books for adults and children. But this body of work, along with her decades of appearances in films and on television, had cemented the image of a patient and careful scientist in the collective minds of the public. Six years after the plagiarism episode, she was included in *Time* magazine's list of the 100 most influential people in the world.[27] And her next book, 2021's *The Book of Hope: A Survival Guide for Trying Times* – also written with Gail Hudson – debuted at number thirteen on *The New York Times* bestseller list.[28]

Perhaps the reputations of Teflon plagiarists remain unsullied because of the relative obscurity of the charges levied against them. The appropriations of Audubon were discovered in his lifetime, but until the Society's vote in 2023, most discussions of his borrowings were to be found only in ornithological journals – not exactly mainstream reading. And Goodall's reputation seems to have benefited from the ephemeral nature of appropriation journalism, since stories about plagiarism rarely last longer than one news cycle.

But what happens when a story about plagiarism has legs, as in the case of Doris Kearns Goodwin? In early 2002, *The Weekly Standard* accused the Pulitzer Prize-winning historian of having appropriated without sufficient attribution for her 1987 book *The Fitzgeralds and the Kennedys*. The magazine's story was sparked by a letter claiming that Goodwin had cribbed from three earlier books about the Kennedys, and especially from Lynne McTaggart's *Kathleen Kennedy: Her Life and Times*, published in 1983.[29]

Unlike most plagiarism episodes, this story remained in the news for an extended period: over the next five months, Goodwin was mentioned no fewer than eleven times in articles appearing in *The New York Times*. (Unfortunately for her, this was the same period during which the appropriations of fellow historian Stephen Ambrose were being uncovered, and she was often mentioned in stories about him.) And in August, the *Los Angeles Times* raised questions about Goodwin's *No Ordinary Time*, her 1994 book about the Roosevelts. The paper pointed out instances of "parallel language" between her book and Joseph Lash's *Eleanor and Franklin*, published in 1971.[30]

Goodwin did admit to attribution issues in her book about the Kennedys, and the publisher, Simon & Schuster, reached a financial settlement with Lynne McTaggart.[31] Goodwin also paid a public price: she lost her role as a commentator on PBS's *NewsHour with Jim Lehrer*,[32] and she resigned from the Pulitzer Prize Board.[33]

Three and a half years later, Goodwin released *Team of Rivals*, her book about Abraham Lincoln and the fractious members of his cabinet. And how did the book-buying public respond to her new 944-page offering? Ten weeks after its release, *Team of Rivals* moved up to the number one spot for nonfiction on *The New York Times* list.[34] In November of 2008, president-elect Obama claimed that the work was his "desert island" book.[35] Goodwin's previous transgressions were common knowledge, but they didn't affect the reception of an expertly crafted book on a popular subject.

Finally, accusations of plagiarism don't seem to stick when institutions have a vested interest in not pursuing them. This seems to explain the case of William Meehan, a long-serving president at Jacksonville State University in Alabama. Meehan completed his doctorate in June of 1999, only four days before becoming president of the institution. A decade later, questions were raised about his dissertation and its resemblance to a thesis written by Carl Boening three years before Meehan's, and under the direction of the same advisor.

The two dissertations were case studies of faculty sabbaticals, with Meehan's project being a replication of Boening's research at a different university. In 2009, concerns were raised that Meehan's thesis borrowed more than Boening's methodology: an outside examiner found that approximately 3ᵇ percent of the second chapter of Meehan's dissertation was taken from Boening's.[36] Meehan was also accused of plagiarizing a newspaper column in 2007, although this was attributed to a university publicist who served as the president's ghostwriter.[37] However, this pattern fits with Sheenagh Pugh's observation that plagiarists never do it just once.

Certainly, Jacksonville State would have had no desire to see its image besmirched by pursuing allegations of plagiarism by the institution's president. The same was true for the University of Alabama at Tuscaloosa, the school that had awarded Meehan's doctorate. Officials at Tuscaloosa claimed to have conducted an investigation, but Meehan's dissertation advisor, who had by then relocated to the University of Arkansas, reported that no one from Alabama had contacted him.[38]

Meehan continued to serve as the school's president for another six years after the allegations. When he retired in 2015, his tenure in office had outlasted the concerns raised about his academic work.[39] In 2023, he was inducted into the University of Alabama's Education Hall of Fame.[40] Questions about the originality of Meehan's dissertation remain unanswered, illustrating what happens when no one benefits from looking for answers.

UNREPENTANT PLAGIARISTS

As we have seen throughout this book, responses to charges of appropriation vary considerably. Some plagiarists confess and apologize – either immediately or after some period of denial. Those belonging to a second group maintain that they never saw or heard the work they are charged with copying. (Some of these individuals ultimately wind up in the first group.) But there is a smaller, third group of appropriators who maintain that what they're doing isn't plagiarism at all. They can be thought of as unrepentant appropriators. Let's consider two such individuals in detail: one from the realm of literature, and one from the world of music.

In 1999, author and social critic Susan Sontag published her fourth novel, *In America*. Loosely based on the story of Helena Modjeska, the nineteenth-century Polish actress who emigrated to the US,[41] it won the National Book Award for Fiction the following year.[42]

One of *In America*'s readers was Ellen Lee, a museum docent who discovered that Sontag's 400-page novel included a dozen unattributed passages from several books about the Polish-American actress. These included the memoirs of Modjeska herself as well as Nobel laureate Henryk Sienkiewicz, novelist Willa Cather, and Modjeska biographer Marion Moore Coleman. Sontag's verbatim borrowings include a few sentences and several lines of verse from these earlier authors.

Sontag's response to Lee's discoveries was published by *The New York Times* and deserves to be quoted in full:

> "All of us who deal with real characters in history transcribe and adopt original sources in the original domain" said Ms. Sontag, who noted that the passages in dispute amounted to fewer than three pages in total. "I've used these sources and I've completely transformed them. I have these books. I've looked at these books. There's a larger argument to be made that all of literature is a series of references and allusions."[43]

Sontag also claimed that borrowing from sources was different than borrowing from other writers. Modjeska wasn't a writer, and "You can use a sentence that's exactly the same because it is from her [Modjeska's] words." Cather, on the other hand, was a writer, and Sontag claimed to have included a toast given by Majewski – from Cather's *My Mortal Enemy* – as a "literary joke."[44]

Are there episodes in Sontag's past that might suggest she had a tendency to appropriate? She is thought to have ghostwritten *Freud: The Mind of a Moralist*, a work ostensibly authored by her then-husband, the sociologist Philip Rieff.[45] And Len Gutkin, writing in 2019, found that the work contains passages taken from M. H. Abrams's *The Mirror and the Lamp: Romantic Theory and the Critical Condition*, which had been published six years before the book on Freud.[46] Sontag, who died in 2004, could not respond to Gutkin's charges. But if she plagiarized Abrams, then her criterion – that it is acceptable to borrow from "sources" but not from "writers" – is one that she didn't always follow: Abrams authored many distinguished works of literary criticism.

Joining Sontag in this unrepentant group is the singer and songwriter Bob Dylan. From the beginning of his career in the early 1960s, Dylan made extensive use of traditional and classic folk tunes.[47] Over the next forty years, he released thirty records and developed a passionate fan base. But it was his thirty-first album, 2001's *Love and Theft*, that led to an explicit charge of appropriation.

Chris Johnson, an English teacher visiting Japan, read a book by Dr. Junichi Saga and noticed resemblances between wording in that text and Dylan's lyrics. Saga's 1991 book, *Confessions of a Yakuza*, told stories about one of his patients, and Johnson found that about a dozen lines from these stories were similar to lyrics in Dylan's song "Floater." Johnson's discovery was reported on the front page of *The Wall Street Journal*.[48] Saga, for his part, claimed he would be "honored" if Dylan acknowledged him on future pressings of *Love and Theft*.[49] (This did not happen.)

In late 2004, Dylan published *Chronicles: Volume One*. It was a memoir that focused on three points in his long career: 1961, 1970, and 1989. The book was well received and became a bestseller. But Scott Warmuth, a New Mexico disc jockey, discovered that it contained unattributed passages from a variety of authors, such as Jack London, H. G. Wells, F. Scott Fitzgerald, and Ernest Hemingway.[50]

Two years after his memoir appeared, Dylan released the album *Modern Times*. Once again, it was deejay Scott Warmuth who found instances of unattributed copying. A little web surfing revealed that at least ten phrases in the lyrics of "When the Deal Goes Down" and "Spirit of the Water" match up with verse composed by Henry Timrod, a Civil War-era writer sometimes called the Poet Laureate of the Confederacy. There are no indications of this in the album's liner notes, which state "All songs written by Bob Dylan."[51]

It was Dylan's reaction to these discoveries, however, that raised a few eyebrows. When Mikael Wood interviewed Dylan for *Rolling Stone* in 2012, he asked him about the claims of appropriation regarding *Love and Theft* and *Modern Times*. In response, Dylan claimed that "All my stuff comes out of the folk tradition" and that "You make everything yours." He added that it was only "wussies and pussies [that] complain about that stuff." Noting that some of his critics had compared him to Judas, he told Wood that "All those evil motherfuckers can rot in hell."[52]

Clearly, there is no love lost between Dylan and other performers. In a 2010 interview with the *Los Angeles Times*, Matt Diehl pointed out to Joni

Mitchell that both she and Bob Dylan had taken different names when they became performers. In response, Mitchell acidly remarked, "Bob is not authentic at all. He's a plagiarist, and his name and voice are fake. Everything about Bob is a deception. We are like night and day, he and I."[53]

On October 13, 2016, Dylan was awarded the Nobel Prize in Literature "for having created new poetic expressions within the great American song tradition."[54] Although he chose not to attend the December ceremony in Stockholm, he did record a Nobel lecture the following June. In his twenty-six-minute speech, Dylan talked about three works of literature that had greatly affected him as a child. One of these was *Moby-Dick*.

Andrea Pitzer, writing for *Slate*, discovered that Dylan had relied heavily on the summary of Melville's masterwork that appears on the SparkNotes website. Specifically, she found that, of the seventy-eight sentences in Dylan's speech that mention the book, "more than a dozen of them appear to closely resemble lines from the SparkNotes site."[55] Pitzer noted that Dylan submitted his lecture right before the deadline for receiving his $923,000 prize ($1.16 million today), so it may be that time pressure was responsible for his cribbing from the online synopsis.

But Dylan also has plenty of defenders. Scott Warmuth, who discovered the borrowings in *Chronicles*, maintains that Dylan's cribbing is both strategic and intentional.[56] David Kinney, who wrote a book about Dylan's fans, suggests that the allusions in his memoir form a sort of palimpsest, and that what appears to be plagiarism might be best described as inside jokes and word play masquerading as appropriation.[57]

Some would argue that Sontag's and Dylan's appropriations constitute a return to the Dionysian concept of *imitatio* discussed in Chapter 1 – the virtuous reframing and reshaping of the work of others.[58] Respected intellectuals like Sontag or beloved artists like Dylan might be accorded this privilege, but it's not clear whether lesser lights are eligible for such a dispensation.

EXCUSES, EXCUSES

In May of 1952, New York attorney Alexander Lindey published *Plagiarism and Originality*. It was the first book-length treatment of the topic and included a discussion of the psychology of plagiarism. In a section titled "Why do people plagiarize?" he proposes five motivating factors in response to his query. At a remove of over seventy years, some of these reasons seem as true as ever, whereas others are perhaps less true than they once were. It also seems that several additional motivations could be added to his list.

The first reason Lindey provides is remarkably direct and succinct: "They steal for money."[59] This certainly rings true today, and earlier chapters included several examples in which the primary motivator appears to have been financial gain. In some cases, the effect can even be quantified. Until 2017, recipients of doctoral degrees in Romania received a 15 percent bump in their pay if they worked in certain professions. And as we saw in Chapter 2, many countries in the Balkans, including Romania, struggled with dissertation plagiarism. Soon after the salary adjustment rule was revoked, the number of doctorates awarded in the country fell by two-thirds.[60]

Lindey's second reason, "They steal because they admire," remains a common motivator as well. As he puts it, "Admiration induces imitation; the closer the imitation, the narrower the dividing line between it and outright copying."[61] The earlier chapters of this book reviewed several examples of inspiration or homage turning into something more akin to theft.

A third rationale provided by Lindey is that plagiarists steal for "praise and prestige." His example is the schoolboy who appropriates from Nathaniel Hawthorne or Herman Melville, although it's a bit hard to imagine either author being cribbed from by students today. And the desire to be perceived as a sage imparting wisdom might explain why commencement speakers steal from YouTube videos, as discussed in Chapter 6.

Another explanation Lindey provides for why people plagiarize is that they are unaware of the relevant statutes, such as the concept of fair use or the length of copyright. It makes sense that Lindey would include this reason because his specialty was literary property. Ignorance about what constitutes plagiarism is clearly a factor in many cases, such as the high school student in Chapter 1 who plagiarized an essay for Eddie Cantor's contest, or the jury member who required instruction on the concept of appropriation during a plagiarism trial.

Lindey's final reason is that people plagiarize because they're mentally ill. This explanation is echoed in *Stolen Words*, Thomas Mallon's book-length treatment of plagiarism published nearly forty years after Lindey's. Specifically, Mallon writes that plagiarism and kleptomania are alike in that "neither crime is something that one commits just once." [62] This is the same claim made by Sheenagh Pugh, the poet we encountered in Chapter 2. Poor impulse control – a diagnostic characteristic of kleptomania[63] – may also be common to both conditions.

However, there also seem to be important differences between kleptomania and plagiarism. Contrary to popular belief, kleptomaniacs don't want to be apprehended: they seek the thrill of the act of stealing and the freedom to continue doing so.[64] We would assume that plagiarists don't want to be caught either, since this could result in termination from one's job or the end of one's political career. But this might not always be the case. Mallon speculates that some plagiarists may have a "death wish": they must want to be discovered, he suggests, because their appropriation is so extensive or so brazen.

Consider the case of Kaavya Viswanathan, the Harvard sophomore who published *How Opal Mehta Got Kissed, Got Wild, and Got a Life* in 2006. It was discovered that she cribbed more than forty passages from two books written by Megan McCafferty, the popular author of young adult (YA) literature. Whereas Viswanathan characterized her plagiarism as "unintentional and unconscious," a representative for McCafferty's publisher replied that it was "inconceivable that this was a display of youthful innocence or an unconscious or unintentional act."[65] (Little, Brown, Viswanathan's publisher, had to recall and destroy 55,000 copies of the novel that were already in bookstores.)[66]

Kleptomania seems unlike plagiarism in other ways as well. The former is rare – it is diagnosed in only 0.3 to 0.6 percent of the population – whereas a majority of students claim to have plagiarized.[67] It's also the case that kleptomaniacs typically steal things they have no need for and which are not especially valuable. Finally, there is no evidence that plagiarists feel what kleptomaniacs report experiencing, which is pleasure or relief when they steal.[68]

Another difference is that plagiarists often try to find a scapegoat for their misdeeds. For example, it was discovered during the 2014

Tennessee senate race that Gordon Ball, the Democratic candidate, appeared to have "plagiarized nearly every word on his [website's] issues pages" from other politicians. An intern was blamed for the copying.[69] (Ball was decisively defeated, although he was running against a popular Republican incumbent in a red state.) And as we saw in Chapter 4, Cindy McCain blamed "recipegate" on the work of an intern.

Another excuse, and one that crops up over and over again, is that what appeared to be plagiarism was the result of sloppy record-keeping. Historians seem to be particularly vulnerable to this failing: Doris Kearns Goodwin and Stephen Ambrose, discussed earlier in this chapter, both cited this as the reason for the attribution errors in their books.[70] It does require an almost fanatical devotion to one's sources to keep track of what is a quote and what is a paraphrase, but readers deserve to know whose ideas they are encountering.

Some researchers have speculated there might be personality traits reliably associated with plagiarism. Work on this topic is sparse but suggestive. In 2013, Ide Siaputra published the results of a study of undergraduate psychology students in Indonesia. Those who self-reported having plagiarized more were also more likely to be frequent procrastinators. In addition, plagiarism was related to low conscientious-ness – a trait associated with a lack of care or diligence. Students with higher levels of self-reported plagiarism also had lower achievement motivation scores.

It should be noted, however, that all these correlations were modest and so their explanatory power is limited. In other words, a predilection for appropriation isn't simply a function of one's personality. Interestingly, Siaputra's study found no relationship between plagiarism and academic achievement, as measured by the students' grade point averages.[71] This form of cheating, then, isn't simply the last resort of less able students.

Although Lindey doesn't include it on his list, time pressure is another reason why people plagiarize. Reporters, journalists, and even bloggers need to produce content on a regular basis, and their assignments must often be completed within a specified period. If one is experiencing writer's block while staring down a deadline, the temptation to cheat can be enormous. Mark Hornung, an editorial page editor for the *Chicago*

Sun-Times, succumbed to this pressure in 1995 when he appropriated "a substantial portion" of an editorial that had appeared the previous day in *The Washington Post.*[72] (Hornung resigned from his editorial position but remained with the *Sun-Times*.)

The composer James Horner worked under immense time pressure on the music for the 2004 movie *Troy*. Gabriel Yared had labored to score the film for nearly a year, but his efforts were poorly received by preview audiences, and Horner was brought on to the project at the last minute. He was given only two weeks to compose material for the nearly three-hour film and accomplished this feat by recycling works by Britten, Shostakovich, Prokofiev, and Vaughan Williams. Many filmgoers may not have noticed or cared, but some critics were less than impressed by Horner's apparent lack of originality.[73]

The "publish or perish" ethos in higher education undoubtedly contributes to many of the acts of plagiarism seen within the academy. The extremely tight job market and competition for full-time positions is one hurdle, and tenure is another. Assistant professors are reviewed for tenure at a specific point in their careers, typically five to seven years after beginning their employment. If the faculty member's publication record is judged insufficient at that point, their contract is not renewed and they receive an additional year to find a position elsewhere. As a result, the pressure to churn out journal articles or essays can be immense.

Shifts in cultural attitudes may play a role as well. Soon after seventeen-year-old author Helene Hegemann published her novel *Axolotl Roadkill* in 2010, her novel became a bestseller in Germany. And shortly after that, it was discovered that the wunderkind had made liberal use of a novel titled *Strobo*. This included copying an entire page with minimal changes. Hegemann claimed that she was part of a new generation that saw mash-ups not as appropriation but as a new form of creation. She was quoted as saying, "There's no such thing as originality anyway, just authenticity."[74]

A final motivation for plagiarists is a simple one: the odds are stacked in their favor. For example, no one seems to have noticed the cribbing in Laurence Sterne's *Tristram Shandy* – from Robert Burton's *Anatomy of Melancholy*, as well as other authors – until many years after Sterne's death.[75] Undetected plagiarism, as noted in Chapter 5, is a real issue. After all, if literary and film agents can't recognize *Pride and Prejudice* or *Casablanca* when it's sent their way, what are the chances that someone will spot a duplicated poem in a limited-edition chapbook? Although our tools to ferret out plagiarism have improved greatly, the number of books, articles, songs, and films that are released increases each year. The task of detection would be enormous even if many people were on the lookout for plagiarism, but few are.

PLAGIARISM RECONSIDERED

The digitization of the analog world, which began in earnest in the 1990s, fundamentally changed people's conception of creative works. Until that time, the acquisition of a song or a film involved purchasing physical media from a retailer at a bricks-and-mortar store. But once these works were converted into digital files, it was inevitable that they would be shared via the internet, often in violation of copyright. At first this was accomplished through peer-to-peer file sharing via applications such as Napster, and then by BitTorrent services like The Pirate Bay, and finally through the Dark Web.[76]

None of this is plagiarism, but file sharing has profoundly altered many people's views regarding the sanctity of copyright. After all, why buy the cow (in this case, a physical copy of a book or song) when the milk (a digital copy) is available for free? People who otherwise scrupulously obey the law nevertheless download copyrighted material without paying for it. It's easy to rationalize such behavior: everybody else is doing it, so spending money on content seems like something that only suckers do.

But once this line has been crossed, the actual appropriation of another person's work becomes much easier. If a student can download a term paper for free, doesn't that imply that the words themselves are also free for the taking?

Long before the world went digital, the line between sharing and taking was becoming blurred. The development of appropriation art in the nineteenth century continued through the twentieth, as in the work of Pop artists like Roy Lichtenstein and Andy Warhol. Lichtenstein was especially controversial in his appropriation of panels from comic books, such as 1963's *Okay Hot-Shot, Okay!* In this painting Lichtenstein combined panels from the work of graphic artists Russ Heath and Irv Novick into a six-foot-tall portrait of a jet fighter pilot.[77]

The critics were unimpressed – *The New York Times* referred to Lichtenstein as "one of the worst artists in America" who was "making a sow's ear out of a sow's ear"[78] – but his work was popular and made Lichtenstein a fortune. The same could not be said of the comic strip artists from whom he appropriated. One of them, Hy Eisman, was quoted as saying, "It's called stealing. I worked like a dog on this stupid [comics] page and this guy has $20 million to show for it. If it wasn't so tragic, it would be [funny]."[79]

The combining of the work of others into something new continues in the present, most notably with the rise of remix and mash-up culture. This is especially true in music, but it can be found in other pursuits as well. As we saw in the last section, some plagiarists, like novelist Helene Hegemann, explicitly referred to this influence in explaining her literary appropriation.

Some of these appropriations can be explained as a reaction against the strictures of copyright law, which, as we have seen, has shifted decisively in favor of the large corporations that hold the rights to creative works. This viewpoint was vividly expressed by David Shields. In his 2010 manifesto, *Reality Hunger*, he claimed that copyright has "obstructed the natural evolution of human creativity, which has always possessed cannibalistic tendencies."[80] It's worth noting that Shields's original manuscript included many quotations that were unreferenced. However, as he explained in the book, the lawyers at Random House required him to provide citations – although Shields encouraged his readers to excise those pages from their copies "to restore the book to the form in which I intended it to be read."[81]

The novelist Jonathan Lethem makes a similar argument in a 2007 article in *Harper's Magazine*. "Contemporary copyright, trademark, and patent law," he claims, "is presently corrupted. The case for perpetual copyright is a denial of the essential gift-aspect of the creative act." He closes his essay with the following exhortations: "You, reader, are welcome to my stories. They were never mine in the first place, but I gave them to you. If you have the inclination to pick them up, take them with my blessing." [82] An echo of these ideas can be found in a 2019 article by philosopher Agnes Callard: "Give with an open hand, and stop thinking about the tokens with which you will be repaid. Be happy to be worth stealing from."[83]

All of this is a throwback to the time before copyright, when appropriation was considered acceptable as long as the appropriator improved upon the original. It was T. S. Eliot who, in 1920, famously observed that "Immature poets imitate; mature poets steal; bad poets deface what they take, and good poets make it into something better, or at least something different. The good poet welds his theft into a whole of feeling which is unique, utterly different from that from which it was torn."[84]

Nearly a century after Eliot, we find Malcolm Gladwell expressing similar sentiments. In writing about the appropriation of his words by Bryony Lavery in the play *Frozen*, he reports how he was initially unhappy that his prose had been used without his permission, going so far as to send Lavery a letter accusing her of theft. With time, however, he came to a different conclusion, realizing that no "writer's words have a virgin birth and an eternal life. I suppose that I could get upset about what happened to my words. I could also simply acknowledge that I had a good, long ride with that line – and let it go."[85]

The literary theorist and academic gadfly Stanley Fish made waves when he published an editorial in *The New York Times* titled "Plagiarism Is Not a Big Moral Deal." Students, he claimed, are taught a set of rules about proper citation that are as arcane as those that govern the sport of golf. "It follows," he asserted, that "students who never quite get the concept right are by and large not committing a crime; they are just failing to become acclimated to the conventions of the little insular world they have, often through no choice of their own, wandered into."[86] Many readers interpreted Fish's argument as a defense of student plagiarism – a mistaken conclusion that he took pains to counter in a follow-up editorial.[87]

Others have argued that penalizing students for committing plagiarism is ultimately counterproductive. If the goal is to teach students to write clearly and persuasively, then a little borrowing can materially assist students in honing their skills. The wholesale plundering of texts is clearly problematic, but many students are faulted for simply attempting to mimic the authors that they read and admire. As Jennifer Mott-Smith, a professor of English at Towson University, puts it, "Writers who are learning a new field often 'try out' ideas and phrases from other writers in order to master the field. That process, which allows them to learn, involves little or no deceit."[88]

Just as there are different motivations for committing plagiarism, there are also many voices calling for a reevaluation of traditional notions of appropriation. Plagiarism is viewed as both legally and morally wrong in contemporary culture, but this is a reflection of a highly individualistic society – one that is both capitalistic and extremely litigious. It is possible to imagine an alternate universe in which readers are, as Jonathan Lethem puts it, welcome to an author's stories. But this would require a fundamental shift in our economic system and our notions of intellectual property. We learn in the biblical book of Ecclesiastes that "What has been done will be done again; there is nothing new under the sun,"[89] but such ancient wisdom tends to be ignored when there are reputations to be burnished and profits to be made.

THE RISE OF THE CHATBOTS

On November 30, 2022, the technology company OpenAI released ChatGPT 3.5 to the world. It was an evolutionary step – other chatbots based on large language models had existed before it – but it was a historic moment: it was the first time that the power of these models impressed itself on the public consciousness. OpenAI's chatbot could be used by anyone for free, and many who did so were dumbfounded by its sophisticated linguistic abilities. Other tech companies rushed to build their own large language models and bots, and ChatGPT was soon joined by efforts from Google (Gemini), Microsoft (Copilot), Meta (LLaMA), and others. The generative AI boom had begun.

These models require vast amounts of high-quality linguistic input for their training, and the tech firms scraped billions of web pages for the raw material needed to feed their fledgling bots. Much of this content was in the public domain – think of the millions of pages that constitute Wikipedia – but a great deal of it was copyrighted material. One training dataset, created by AI researcher Shawn Presser, consists of pirated ebooks that can be found online. This file – dubbed "Books3" – comprises over 190,000 texts in total.[90]

Alex Reisner, in a series of articles for *The Atlantic*, obtained and wrote about the dataset,[91] then provided curious readers with a query tool so that it could be searched by author.[92] When I heard about this, I did what any published writer might do – I typed in my name to see whether this corpus contained anything of mine.

I wasn't surprised by what I found. My first book, co-authored with a former student and published by MIT Press in 2015,[93] is widely available online as a pirated ebook. This development is something that I have mixed feelings about. On the one hand, I'm glad that people have an easy way to access what I wrote. But I'm also aware that this piracy has cost my publisher in terms of unrealized profits and me in terms of royalties. I am fortunate in that I don't depend on the income from my writing to make a living, but previous sales are taken into account when authors try to interest agents and publishers in new book projects.

The discovery of my work in the Books3 dataset, however, engendered different feelings. For a while, I joked to friends who were impressed by ChatGPT that I had helped to train it, and that this explained the high quality of its output. But I'm also aware that generative AI is a gold mine for the tech firms that developed the bots. As far as I know, no one is selling pirated copies of my book on street corners. But companies like Meta and OpenAI stand to earn vast sums made possible by training sets like Books3.

Some authors whose books were scraped from the web have chosen to take a litigious stance. In July of 2023, a class-action lawsuit was filed against OpenAI and Meta by a group of authors, including comedian Sarah Silverman, whose copyrighted works had been used to train their large language models "without consent, without credit, and without compensation."[94]

Other suits quickly followed. Two months later, a group of well-known writers, including George R. R. Martin and John Grisham, also filed an infringement suit against OpenAI. The suit alleged that the company was guilty of "flagrant and harmful" infringement of the authors' copyrights, and "systematic theft on a mass scale."[95] And three months after that, *The New York Times* sued Microsoft and OpenAI, alleging that millions of its published articles had been used for training purposes. The newspaper had tried to reach a settlement with the two tech companies, but the negotiations broke down and the question of compensation ended up in court.[96]

Some of this litigation is ongoing as of this writing, but the suit brought by the group including Silverman was largely dismissed in federal court in February of 2024. The rationale provided by Judge Martinez-Olguin was that the chatbot's output is not "substantially similar – or similar at all – to [the authors'] books."[97]

The tech companies have argued that their bots are transformative by their very nature and that the training is protected under the doctrine of fair use – a topic discussed in the last chapter. They also have legal precedents on their side, such as a 2005 suit brought by the Authors Guild against Google Books. In that case, the courts decided that providing "snippets" of information from original sources was not a violation of the work's copyright.[98]

In other words, a large language model trained using Silverman's 2010 memoir *The Bedwetter* will not spit out the complete transcript of the comedian's book. When I tried to coax ChatGPT into doing so, it generated the following response: "I'm unable to provide the entire text of Sarah Silverman's book 'The Bedwetter' as it is a [sic] copyrighted material. However, I can give you a summary or discuss specific sections or themes from the book if that would be helpful. Let me know how you'd like to proceed!"

Perhaps seeing the writing on the wall, some media outlets have chosen to license their content. News Corp, which includes *The Wall Street Journal* and *The New York Post*, reached an agreement with OpenAI in May of 2024 to allow the company to train its models using their archived material.[99] Vox Media and *The Atlantic* followed suit a week later.[100]

The sudden appearance of ChatGPT 3.5 also disrupted higher education. Only weeks after its introduction, a survey found that 30 percent of college students had made use of the chatbot for their written assignments, and three-quarters of them did so despite believing that this was cheating.[101] Predictably, there was much hand-wringing during the spring 2023 semester, before instructors had a chance to revise their assignments, or to add prohibitions against using bots to their course syllabi.[102]

But should students be barred from using chatbots? One school of thought argues that since generative AI isn't going away, educators would be better off teaching students how to use them effectively. For example, educators could teach students how to craft prompts that allow for efficient brainstorming. To do anything less would handicap students when they enter the job market. According to this way of thinking, doing anything less would be as short-sighted as telling accountants that they can't use spreadsheets in their calculations.

For instructors who prefer taking a more punitive approach, similarity detection services like Turnitin have begun to provide checks for AI-generated content to their wares. An evaluation of such tools in 2023, however, found them to be "neither accurate nor reliable," and biased towards identifying AI content as written by people instead of the bots.[103] And as large language models are improved, the detection of artificially generated text will become even more difficult.

Is there any reason to believe that academicians themselves are using chatbots to help them write their papers? It has been noted that ChatGPT shows a predilection for using certain low-frequency words, such as "elevate," "delve," and "tapestry."[104] Philip Shapira, who studies science and technology, has documented an enormous spike in the use of "delve" in papers appearing in the PubMed database starting in 2023, when ChatGPT first became widely used.[105] Such a correlation isn't necessarily causal – perhaps "delve" is becoming more popular even without assistance from AI – but the abrupt change in its frequency of use is suspicious.

But is the use of a chatbot's output akin to plagiarism? I would argue that such a practice has more in common with ghostwriting, since there is no "original" that is being copied. The *training* of large language models with copyrighted text may or may not be deemed problematic. But stretching the already tattered definition of plagiarism to include AI-generated *output* only muddies the already murky distinction between plagiarism and originality.

Epilogue

I T SHOULD BE CLEAR FROM THE CASES APPEARING IN THIS BOOK
that plagiarism, as a concept, lacks an agreed-upon definition. And
plagiarism isn't unique in this regard: the same is true for many of the
more abstract notions that people routinely make use of. Cognitive
scientists refer to these abstractions as fuzzy concepts. They can be
thought of as mental groupings consisting of items that clearly exemplify
a category, as well as others that are less typical. And at the indistinct
borders of the category, people might disagree about whether
a particular example even belongs in that grouping.

A good example of a fuzzy concept is the term "emotion." Everyone
knows what an emotion is, but most people will struggle if asked to
delineate what is – and is not – an emotion. Fuzzy concepts typically
have well-defined central members that everyone agrees on, such as
"happiness" or "anger," while the status of other members is less clear.
For example, some people might believe that "loyalty" or "stubbornness"
are emotions, whereas others might think of them as belonging to
a neighboring concept, such as states or traits.[1]

If we reconceptualize plagiarism as a fuzzy concept, we can begin to
make some headway in understanding why people think about it in
different ways. Virtually everyone would agree that the copying of dozens
of consecutive words constitutes so-called "copy and paste" plagiarism.
This seems to be a core part of the concept. But what about insufficient
attribution? A failure to enclose word-for-word borrowing within quotation marks is considered impermissible appropriation by schools,

publishers, and the courts. But it's not clear that such a definition is universally shared or understood.

Consider the case of Carlos Decotelli, a Brazilian economist accused in 2020 of academic plagiarism. His 2008 thesis contains excerpts from sources cited in the document's bibliography, but he failed to offset the adopted words within quotation marks. When questioned by journalists, Decotelli said, "There was no plagiarism, because plagiarism is when someone does 'control + c, control + v' ["copy" and "paste" keystrokes] and that's not it."[2]

A similar episode was reported in 2007 in connection with Yale Law School professor Ian Ayres. The *Yale Daily News* identified nine passages in his book, *Super Number Crunchers*, that had been taken from various newspaper articles. As with Decotelli, Ayers cited his sources but failed to employ quotation marks to specify direct quotes. Ayers claimed that "The endnotes represent proper citation for a book intended for a popular audience," although he did apologize and said that future printings of the book would provide clearer attribution.[3]

If we can extrapolate from examples like these, it would seem that wholesale copying is a central part of the plagiarism concept: everyone agrees that such behavior qualifies. On the other hand, insufficient attribution may be part of the concept's fuzzy boundary – it constitutes plagiarism according to some people's understanding of the concept, but that opinion may not be shared by everyone. Having only one term to refer to both types of appropriation is not an ideal state of affairs. As things currently stand, "plagiarism" is the scarlet letter applied equally to all transgressors, without taking into account the seriousness of the offense. The label equates sloppy citations with cases of extensive cribbing from another person's work.

But other fields of human endeavor are more discriminating. In US jurisprudence, we have the legal term "murder" for the taking of a human life. But the law also recognizes varying degrees – first, second, and third – based on factors like premeditation, intent, and extenuating circumstances. Catholic doctrine differentiates between sins that are mortal and those that are venial. Soccer players are disciplined with yellow or red cards.

The linguist John McWhorter has suggested that something similar is needed to designate second- and third-degree plagiarism. Such a term could be used for lesser offenses, such as a failure to cite a source for so-called "boilerplate statements" – those that are commonly accepted within a given field of study.[4] It's not a perfect solution, but it's a good start.

Another point of disagreement concerns the *amount* of copying. How many consecutive words can be borrowed from a source before a citation is required? As discussed in Chapter 1, even professional organizations and editors don't agree, with the permissible number ranging from two or three words to as many as seven. This lack of consensus provides another example of the fuzziness of the plagiarism concept.

The role of cultural norms serves to muddy the waters even further. As we have seen, appropriation was viewed as thievery in the ancient world, but what came to be called *imitatio* was perceived positively during the Middle Ages. If Chaucer and Shakespeare were writing today instead of in the fourteenth and sixteenth centuries respectively, they might well have been dragged into court for appropriating the intellectual property of others. Plagiarism only became a problem with the rise of concerns about intellectual property and copyright infringement during the eighteenth century. If today's hip-hop artists were to time-travel to medieval England, they would undoubtedly revel in an ethos of artistic freedom that has become impossible in the twenty-first century.

A similar dynamic played out in Asia. In feudal Japan, poets employed *honkadori* in their compositions. This was the deliberate appropriation of well-known works by earlier poets. It was assumed that readers would recognize such quotations and view their use as intended – as a form of homage.[5] Such a shared understanding is a hallmark of high-context cultures, in which members of a society share a great deal of context and common ground.[6] In relatively heterogenous and individualistic cultures like the twenty-first-century US, however, a lack of shared understanding and context may prime individuals to perceive appropriation as plagiarism instead of as homage or tribute. And the dividing lines between parody and satire, on the one hand, and infringement on the other remain blurry at best.

It is disturbing to note that plagiarism seems to turn up almost everywhere that one goes looking for it. A high-profile example is the case of Claudine Gay, the former president of Harvard. Those who sought to discredit her went looking and found attribution issues in her dissertation.[7] In turn, the wife of one of Gay's primary critics, Neri Oxman, was found to have committed plagiarism in her own dissertation.[8] The weaponization of plagiarism, as described in Chapter 5, will undoubtedly continue to play a significant role in bringing such cases to light.

But even if appropriation can be found almost anywhere that one chooses to hunt for it, the fact remains that not many people are hunting. Publishers and institutions of higher education, for example, have little to gain – and much to lose – by trying to uncover and root out appropriation by their authors and faculty. A presumption of innocence has long been the default stance, but this undoubtedly allows many, many instances of appropriation to remain undetected, unless someone with an agenda rolls up their sleeves and starts poking around in an author's backlist or a professor's theses.

Allegations of plagiarism are typically ephemeral, with many such episodes being quickly forgotten. Unless the accusation winds up in court as a copyright infringement suit, the coverage of a given episode may last for only one news cycle or go unreported entirely. Many, and perhaps most, are settled out of court. The parties involved – such as celebrities, publishers, universities, and governments – are usually keen to avoid negative publicity and the expense of legal representation. The details of such settlements are typically not made public. For all these reasons, such episodes typically vanish from public consciousness in the blink of an eye.

In addition, the consequences for plagiarists vary greatly. In some cases, as we have seen, the repercussions are severe: a failing grade or even expulsion in the case of students, and the loss of employment for educators or research scientists. Verdicts of copyright infringement against authors or musicians can result in substantial costs and damages. And as we saw in Chapter 4, some politicians have seen their political careers end when episodes of plagiarism have come to light.

But in Chapter 7, we also saw how some individuals – or their legacies – have emerged largely unscathed from appropriation scandals. Why are some plagiarists sanctioned while others are not? At least part of the answer can be found in our expectations concerning the person who commits such acts. Senator John Walsh, for example, was a politician, but he was also a decorated combat veteran. Members of the military are held in higher esteem in the US than are politicians – but that also means we hold them to a higher ethical standard as well. This may be the reason that Walsh felt compelled to drop out of his political campaign.

But this can't be the whole story. We also hold men and women of the cloth to high standards. And when Martin Luther King's academic plagiarism came to light in 1990, there was no wholesale reassessment of his legacy.[9] It seems that King's efforts to secure civil rights for Black Americans – and ultimately his martyrdom for that cause – serves to offset any potential downward revision of his reputation. And while Joe Biden's plagiarism scandal ended his 1988 presidential campaign, he would ultimately become vice president twenty years later, and then ascend to the presidency. In Biden's case, a long career in the US Senate and the cultivation of a "folksy demeanor"[10] may have been enough to cause the public to view his plagiarism as a mere peccadillo as opposed to a career-ending transgression.

New venues for distributing one's creative work have led to new opportunities for appropriators. Plagiarism has become rampant, for example, in the world of self-publishing. A 2019 report by *The Guardian* found that genres like romance were being flooded with books containing plagiarized content.[11] But less than five years later, and one year after the public release of ChatGPT, the focus shifted to the scourge of AI-generated content.[12] After all, why bother with all that pesky copying and pasting when a chatbot can churn out large quantities of text instantly?

Underscoring how many books were being generated with AI assistance, Amazon's Kindle Direct Publishing platform chose to prohibit authors from uploading more than three titles per day.[13] In this domain, at least, concerns about plagiarism may fade into the woodwork as generative AI becomes ubiquitous.

Video is another lucrative platform for content creation. Anyone with a smartphone and a TikTok or YouTube account can become an auteur, and a lucky few, supported by advertising and endorsement deals, have turned this into a full-time occupation. If the algorithm gods smile upon your work, you too can become an influencer or a thought leader. But even here, appropriators have spoiled the party. Harry Brewis, under the moniker "Hbomberguy," has documented how video essayists churn out large amounts of content by stealing from books, articles, and other videographers.[14]

We have also seen how shifts in copyright law have lengthened the time that works remain as the exclusive property of their creators. This trend, combined with zealous challenges by rights holders, has undoubtedly contributed to the increase in cease-and-desist warnings and infringement cases that have flooded the courts.[15] As we saw in Chapter 6, this tilt in favor of organizations that control rights has been lamented by those who are unable to make use of creative works until they have entered into the public domain.

That doesn't mean that the public always makes the best use of such works when they do become available, however. Winnie-the-Pooh, A. A. Milne's character beloved by children, crossed over into the public domain in 2022, and became the central figure in the 2023 horror movie *Winnie-the-Pooh: Blood and Honey*.[16] It's not clear that much was gained by turning the beloved talking bear into a murderous psychopath, and the film was not a critical success: it currently has a 3 percent score on the Rotten Tomatoes website. So the expiration of copyright and resultant derivative works aren't always an unalloyed good.

Throughout this book, I've made the argument that plagiarism must be understood in its social and historical context, and the current context is one undergoing significant change. In the last chapter, I described how the digitization of the world's creative work has made infringement a trivially easy act to engage in. It would be hard to find anyone who doesn't have a song, movie, or book that they didn't pay for on their computer, phone, or tablet. The sharing of passwords for streaming services, such as Netflix or Hulu, is another manifestation of the same attitude. While the ethics of this can be debated,[17] the consumption of intellectual property without paying for it may function as a gateway drug that normalizes the act of appropriation.

The explicitly stated view of some Millennial and Gen Z artists, such as Helene Hegemann, is that appropriation is simply a new form of creation. This same spirit seems to animate the companies developing large language models, which make use of hundreds of thousands of copyrighted works to create chatbots like ChatGPT, Perplexity, Gemini, Copilot, and their ilk.[18]

But as the public has become increasingly comfortable – or at least accepting – of infringement and appropriation, rights holders have become increasingly litigious. Plagiarism has also become easier to detect due to the growing sophistication of similarity detection services like iThenticate and Turnitin. It will be interesting to see whether these conflicting trends can be reconciled, and whether our attitudes concerning plagiarism and appropriation may be shifting yet again.

Notes

PREFACE

1. S. McGill. (2012). *Plagiarism in Latin Literature*. Cambridge University Press.
2. R. McFarlane. (2007). *Original Copy: Plagiarism and Originality in Nineteenth-Century Literature*. Oxford University Press; R. Terry. (2010). *The Plagiarism Allegation in English Literature from Butler to Sterne*. Palgrave Macmillan.
3. A. Abraham. (2019). *Plagiarizing the Victorian Novel: Imitation, Parody, Aftertext*. Cambridge University Press.
4. H. M. Paull. (1928). *Literary Ethics: A Study in the Growth of the Literary Conscience*. Kennikat Press.
5. A. Lindey. (1952). *Plagiarism and Originality*. Harper & Brothers.
6. T. Mallon. (1989). *Stolen Words*. Harvest Books.
7. R. A. Posner. (2007). *The Little Book of Plagiarism*. Pantheon Books.
8. I. Zack. (1998, September 23). Universities finding a sharp rise in computer-aided cheating. *The New York Times*.

CHAPTER 1 SETTING THE STAGE

1. Eddie Cantor offers peace essay prize. (1936, January 6). *The New York Times*.
2. 212,000 seek peace prize. (1936, February 23). *The New York Times*.
3. Missouri youth, 17, wins Cantor prize. (1936, April 6). *The New York Times*.
4. Prize essay a copy, farm boy admits. (1936, April 14). *The New York Times*.
5. Education: Peace piece. (1936, April 20). *Time*.
6. Cantor scholarship goes to Oregon boy. (1936, April 20). *The New York Times*.
7. Say picture was copied. (1922, November 28). *The New York Times*.
8. I. Masic. (2012). Plagiarism in scientific publishing. *Acta Informatica Medica*, *20*(4), p. 209.
9. M. Bouville. (2008). Plagiarism: Words and ideas. *Science and Engineering Ethics*, *14*, p. 318.
10. A. Takrimi & S. E. Eaton. (2021). Exploring Rogeting: Implications for academic integrity. *Canadian Perspectives on Academic Integrity*, *4*(1), pp. 110–117.
11. Mark Twain Tonight! Hal Holbrook this morning! (1966, April 23). *The New Yorker*.

12. C. Dagan. (2010, February 2). Hal Holbrook, Emmy and Tony-winning actor who portrayed Mark Twain, died at 95. *The Chicago Tribune*.

13. K. Mac Donnell. (2019). The voice of Mark Twain, 1872–2017. *Mark Twain Journal, 57* (2), pp. 55–112.

14. R. Dyer. (2007). *Pastiche*. Routledge.

15. Notes on people. (1976, January 23). *The New York Times*.

16. Mac Donnell. The voice of Mark Twain.

17. S. Schillaci. (2011, October 11). Beyoncé's "Countdown" video: Ann Teresa De Keersmaeker reacts to plagiarism allegations. *The Hollywood Reporter*.

18. L. Schmidt & J. de Kloet. (2017). Bricolage: Role of media. In P. Rössler (Ed.), *The International Encyclopedia of Media Effects, Volume 2*. Wiley, pp. 99–107.

19. A. Sternbergh. (2011, November 3). When is a homage more than a homage? *The New York Times*.

20. J. Pareles. (1994, March 2). Top Grammy to Houston; 5 for "Aladdin." *The New York Times*.

21. R. Aniftos. (2022, January 13). Whitney Houston's "I Will Always Love You" is certified diamond by RIAA. *Billboard*.

22. S. Goodman. (2019, May 1). "Avengers: Endgame" has taken over the world: Let's talk about fan service and Marvel's legacy. *The New York Times*.

23. J. A. Fuller-Maitland. (1933). Brahms's orchestral music. *The Musical Times, 74*(1083), pp. 401–406.

24. S. McClatchie. (2000). Hans Rott, Gustav Mahler and the "New Symphony": New evidence for a pressing question. *Music & Letters, 81*(3), pp. 392–401.

25. A. Clements. (2022, October 27). Hans Rott, Symphony No 1/Mahler review – friends but not equals. *The Guardian*.

26. M. M. Brunsday. (2016). *Encyclopedia of Nordic Crime Fiction*. McFarland & Co.

27. S. Lyall. (2006, April 7). "Da Vinci Code" author cleared of stealing idea. *The New York Times*.

28. T. Egeland. (2010, February). Interview: Star Wars. http://starwarsinterviews1.blog spot.com/2010/02/tom-egeland-interview-star-wars.html

29. Novels alike in plot. (1909, July 10). *The New York Times*.

30. A. Waugh. (1983, December 10). Another voice: Tale of two authors. *The Spectator*.

31. J. Trewin. (1984, January 6). Auberon Waugh: Subliminal plagiarism for "Lord of the Flies?" *Publishers Weekly*.

32. E. C. Bufkin. (1985). The Nobel Prize and the paper men: The fixing of William Golding. *The Georgia Review, 39*(1), pp. 55–65.

33. J. Brice. (2007, August 7). Sentinels, not senators: Hungry, hungry hippos. *Silver Bullet Comics*.

34. D. Kreps. (2015, January 26). Sam Smith on Tom Petty settlement: "Similarities" but "complete coincidence." *Rolling Stone*.

35. D. Kreps. (2015, January 29). Tom Petty on Sam Smith settlement: "No hard feelings. These things happen." *Rolling Stone*.

36. M. Locker. (2015, January 25). Sam Smith to pay Tom Petty songwriting royalties for "Stay with Me." *Time.*

37. A.-H. Chroust. (1961). Charges of philosophical plagiarism in Greek antiquity. *The Modern Schoolman, 38*(3), p. 126.

38. D. M. Murdock. (2014). *Did Moses Exist? The Myth of the Israelite Lawgiver.* Stellar House Publishing.

39. J. C. Paget & S. Gathercole (Eds). (2012). *Celsus in His World: Philosophy, Polemic and Religion in the Second Century.* Cambridge University Press.

40. S. McGill. (2012). *Plagiarism in Latin Literature.* Cambridge University Press, p. 27.

41. J. M. Seo. (2009). Plagiarism and poetic identity in Martial. *American Journal of Philology, 130*(4), pp. 567–593.

42. Martial. *Epigrams, Volume I: Spectacles, Books 1–5* (1993). D. R. Shackleton Bailey (Ed. & trans.). Loeb Classical Library 94. Harvard University Press, p. 79.

43. G. Nisbet. (2020). Martial's poetics of plagiarism. *American Journal of Philology, 141*(1), pp. 55–81.

44. Seo. Plagiarism and poetic identity in Martial.

45. S. L. Reams. (1978). The sources of Chaucer's "Second Nun's Tale." *Modern Philology, 76*(2), pp. 111–135.

46. R. P. Miller (Ed.). (1977). *Chaucer Sources and Backgrounds.* Oxford University Press.

47. R. M. Correale & M. Hamel (Eds.). (2002). *Sources and Analogues of The Canterbury Tales, Volumes I and II.* D. S. Brewer.

48. B. Millett. (1984). Chaucer Lollius, and the medieval theory of authorship. *Studies in the Age of Chaucer, Proceedings,* No. 1, p. 97.

49. S. L. Wing. (1984). The Two Noble Kinsmen: Shakespeare and Fletcher's reinterpretation of Chaucer's "The Knight's Tale." Unpublished dissertation, The University of California Los Angeles.

50. R. A. Posner. (2007). *The Little Book of Plagiarism.* Pantheon Books, p. 53.

51. B. Franklin. (1810). *The Way to Wealth; or, "Poor Richard Improved."* W. & T. Darton.

52. C. Van Doren. (1938). *Benjamin Franklin.* Viking Press.

53. R. Newcomb. (1957). The sources of Benjamin Franklin's sayings of Poor Richard. Unpublished doctoral dissertation, The University of Maryland.

54. J. A. L. Lemay. (2006). *The Life of Benjamin Franklin, Volume 2: Printer and Publisher, 1730–1747.* University of Pennsylvania Press.

55. P. J. Karol. (2021). Albrecht Dürer's enforcement actions: A trademark origin story. *Vanderbilt Journal of Entertainment & Technology Law, 25*(3), pp. 421–482.

56. C. Hirsch. (2010, December 14). Frames from fiction: Renaissance erotica. *The New Yorker.*

57. S. Isomaa, S. Kivistö, P. Lyytikäinen, S. Nyqvist, M. Polvinen & R. Rossi (Eds.). (2012). *Rethinking Mimesis: Concepts and Practices of Literary Representation.* Cambridge Scholars Publishing.

58. K. Pask. (2002). Plagiarism and the originality of national literature: Gerard Langbaine. *English Literary History, 69*(3), pp. 727–747.

59. R. Terry. (2007, Spring). "Plagiarism": A literary concept in England to 1775. *English, 56*, pp. 1–16.

60. A. Abraham. (2015). Plagiarizing Pickwick: Imitations of immortality. *Dickens Quarterly, 32*(1), pp. 5–20.

61. A. Burke. (2010). Purloined pleasures: Dickens, currency, and copyright. *Dickens Studies Annual, 41*, pp. 61–79.

62. The Encyclopædia Britannica suits. (1880, January 10). *The Publisher's Weekly, 17*(417), p. 27.

63. R. G. Cohen. (2022, March 28). Will Smith, Chris Rock, and the slap heard round the world. *The Boston Globe.*

64. Theodore Dreiser dies at age of 74. (1945, December 29). *The New York Times.*

65. E. Sorel. (2020, December 31). That time when Theodore Dreiser slapped Sinclair Lewis in the face. *The New York Times.*

66. R. Lundén. (1978). Theodore Dreiser and the Nobel Prize. *American Literature, 50*(2), pp. 216–229.

67. Lewis is slapped by Dreiser in club. (1931, March 21). *The New York Times.*

68. Lewis calls witness to challenge Dreiser. (1931, March 25). *The New York Times.*

69. J. M. Hutchisson & S. R. Pastore. (1999). Sinclair Lewis and Theodore Dreiser: New letters and a reexamination of their relationship. *American Literary Realism, 32*(1), pp. 69–81.

70. J. D. Adams. (1963, April 14). Speaking of books. *The New York Times.*

71. J. Salzman. (1969). Dreiser and Ade: A note on the text of Sister Carrie. *American Literature, 40*(4), pp. 544–548.

72. Biography/History, Theodore Dreiser papers. Kislak Center for Special Collections, Rare Books and Manuscripts, University of Pennsylvania.

73. Professors assail history by Wells: Consensus of about 100 college educators is that author is no historian. (1922, May 9). *The New York Times.*

74. Oppose Wells in schools. (1922, October 14). *The New York Times.*

75. 1925: H. G. Wells ban. (2000, June 22). *International Herald Tribune.*

76. A. B. McKillop. (2000). *The Spinster and the Prophet: Florence Deeks, H. G. Wells, and the Case of the Plagiarized Text.* Four Walls Eight Windows.

77. H. G. Wells. (1920). *The Outline of History: Being a Plain History of Life and Mankind.* Macmillan Co.

78. M. Skelton. (2001). The paratext of everything: Constructing and marketing H. G. Wells's "The Outline of History." *Book History, 4*, pp. 237–275.

79. Writer sues H. G. Wells. (1925, October 15). *The New York Times.*

80. Writer sues H. G. Wells. (1930, June 3). *The New York Times.*

81. McKillop. *The Spinster and the Prophet.*

82. McKillop. *The Spinster and the Prophet.*

83. D. Y. Hughes. (1966). H. G. Wells and the charge of plagiarism. *Nineteenth-Century Fiction, 21*(1), pp. 85–90.

84. R. Chamberlain-King. (2018). Robert Cromie (1856–1907). *The Green Book, 12*, p. 45.

85. Plagiarism suit ends on Outline of History. (1930, September 28). *The New York Times.*

86. McKillop. *The Spinster and the Prophet.*

87. Florence Deeks loses appeal against Wells for plagiarism. (1932, November 4). *The New York Times.*

88. Wells's defense costly. (1932, April 7). *The New York Times.*

89. D. N. Magnusson. (2004). Hell hath no fury: Copyright lawyers' lessons from *Deeks v. Wells. Queens Law Journal. 29*(2), pp. 680–738.

90. Suit over "Gone with the Wind." (1937, April 29). *The New York Times.*

91. A. Price Davis. (2013). *The Margaret Mitchell Encyclopedia.* McFarland & Co., p. 57.

92. Price Davis. *The Margaret Mitchell Encyclopedia*, p. 91.

93. Plagiarism suit dropped. (1937, July 31). *The New York Times.*

94. "Gone with the Wind" suit. (1937, September 9). *The New York Times.*

95. Ends "Gone with the Wind" suit. (1938, March 25). *The New York Times.*

96. S. B. Conroy. (1991, September 25). Riding the wind: Scarlett revisited. *The Washington Post.*

97. M. Oliver. (2004, January 27). Alexandra Ripley, 71: Wrote "Gone with the Wind" sequel. *Los Angeles Times.*

98. J. Maslin. (1991, September 27). In "Scarlett," only the names are the same. *The New York Times.*

99. S. L. Carter. (2007, November 4). Almost a gentleman. *The New York Times.*

100. Metro-Goldwyn-Mayer v. Showcase Atlanta Co-Op. Prod., 479 F. Supp. 351 (N.D. Ga 1979).

101. A. Riding. (1989, December 7). Court finds French author plagiarized "Gone with Wind." *The New York Times*

102. Reuters. (1990, November 22). An author is cleared of plagiarism charges. *The New York Times.*

103. D. Kirkpatrick. (2001, March 28). Court asked to stop "Gone with the Wind" rewrite. *The New York Times.*

104. D. Kirkpatrick. (2001, April 21). Court halts book based on "Gone with the Wind." *The New York Times.*

105. D. Kirkpatrick. (2002, May 10). Mitchell estate settles "Gone with the Wind" suit. *The New York Times.*

106. D. Kirkpatrick. (2001, June 11). Legal battle increases interest in book sequel. *The New York Times.*

107. V. Shannon. (2004, November 8). One internet, many copyright laws. *The New York Times.*

108. C. Thompson. (1991, September 24). Real-life cowboy wins decades-old battle with television industry. *AP News.*

109. W. T. Jaeger. (1968). Copyright: Misappropriation of a character. A careful thief doesn't have to pay. *California Law Review, 56*(6), pp. 1780–1789.

110. First "Paladin" now has justice, will travel. (1991, September 25). *Tampa Bay Times.*

111. G. Studlar. (2015). *Have Gun – Will Travel.* Wayne State University Press.

112. R. Severo. (1974, April 17). Court rules CBS pirated Paladin from a cowboy. *The New York Times.*

113. B. Hope. (1954). *Have Tux, Will Travel: Bob Hope's Own Story, as Told to Pete Martin.* Simon & Schuster.

114. K. E. Spahn. (1992). The legal protection of fictional characters. *University of Miami Entertainment and Sports Law Review, 9*(2), pp. 331–348.

115. T. Lewin. (1983, March 27). When does a creative idea become intellectual property? *The New York Times.*

116. Justices decline to hear Paladin. (1967, December 12). *The New York Times.*

117. Severo, Court rules CBS pirated Paladin from a cowboy.

118. CBS-TV is upheld in suit disputing Paladin's creation. (1975, June 26). *The New York Times.*

119. Night, Knight. (1991, September 29). *The New York Times.*

120. "Paladin" creator dead at 84. (1993, February 1). *UPI.*

121. Thompson. Real-life cowboy wins decades-old battle.

CHAPTER 2 THE PLAGIARISM HUNTERS

1. W. H. Harris & J. S. Levy (Eds.). (1975). *The New Columbia Encyclopedia, Fourth Edition.* Columbia University Press, p. 1850.

2. H. Alford. (2005, August 21). Not a word. *The New Yorker.*

3. J. Jordan. (2020, July 17). Hunting for mountweazels: Eley Williams on the fun – and responsibility – of dictionaries. *The Guardian.*

4. Feist Publications, Inc. v. Rural Telephone Service Company, Inc., 499 U.S. 340 (1991).

5. L. Greenhouse. (1991, March 28). Court limits copyright protection. *The New York Times*, p. D1.

6. R. Hughes. (1903). *The Musical Guide, Volume One.* McClure, Phillips & Co., p. 306.

7. P. M. Cohen. (1976). What's the good word? *Word Ways, 9*(4), pp. 195–198.

8. W. F. Buckley. (1971, December 19). The Compact Edition of the Oxford English Dictionary. *The New York Times*, p. 7.

9. N. Bierma. (2005, September 21). Dictionary sets a trap with an invented word. *Chicago Tribune.*

10. R. Lefort. (2009, October 31). Mystery of Argleton, the "Google" town that only exists online. *The Telegraph.*

11. The strange story of Agloe, NY. (2016, October 30). *Times-Record Herald.*

12. D. Bramwell. (2020, May 3). The imaginary American town that became a tourist attraction. *The Guardian.*

13. M. Byko. (2001). Designers make their mark with computer chips. *Journal of the Minerals, Materials, & Metals Society, 53*(6), pp. 12–13.

14. K. T. Jensen. (2016, August 1). Cool images hidden on silicon chips. *PCMag.*

15. C. Alden. (2001, February 28). Spot the difference. *The Guardian.*

16. T. Suárez. (1992). *Shedding the Veil: Mapping the European Discovery of America and the World.* World Scientific Publishing Co.

17. Plagiarism case won. (1944, December 14). *The New York Times*, p. 30.

18. P. M. Boffey. (1988, April 19). Two critics of science revel in the role. *The New York Times*.
19. P. J. Hilts. (1992, January 7). Plagiarists take note: Machine's on guard. *The New York Times*.
20. P. Gray. (1993, April 26). The purloined letters. *Time*.
21. S. B. Oates. (1977). *With Malice toward None: The Life of Abraham Lincoln*. New American Library.
22. Kohn, G. C. (2000). *The New Encyclopedia of American Scandal*. Facts on File / Infobase Publishing.
23. E. McDowell. (1991, April 21). Lincoln scholar rebuts charges of plagiarism. *The New York Times*.
24. Historians rebut plagiarism charge. (1991, May 1). *The New York Times*.
25. E. Eakin. (2002, January 26). Stop, historians! Don't copy that passage! Computers are watching. *The New York Times*.
26. D. Streitfeld. (1993, December 17). Plagiarism ruling has it both ways. *The Washington Post*.
27. J. Swan. (1994). Sharing and stealing: Persistent ambiguities. *Journal of Information Ethics*, 3(1), pp. 42–47.
28. P. J. Hilts. (1993, March 29). When does duplication of words become theft? *The New York Times*.
29. J. Mervis. (1993, April 22). NIH takes Stewart and Feder off the misconduct beat. *Science*, 362, p. 686.
30. P. J. Hilts. (1993, June 1). Fraud sleuth on a fast over a halt to inquiries. *The New York Times*.
31. P. J. Hilts. (1993, June 4). U.S. agency to review case of scientist on hunger strike. *The New York Times*.
32. P. J. Hilts. (1993, June 13). Inspector ends a hunger strike against agency. *The New York Times*.
33. F. Hoke. (1995, February 5). On their own: Stewart and Feder persist with misconduct inquiries. *The Scientist*, 9(3), pp. 3–4.
34. C. Gross. (2016). Scientific misconduct. *Annual Review of Psychology*, 67, pp. 693–711.
35. L. Widdicombe. (2012, February 5). The plagiarist's tale. *The New Yorker*.
36. E. Mustich. (2012, January 10). Salon debate: What is plagiarism? *Salon*.
37. J. Bosman. (2011, November 8). Little Brown pulls novel, citing plagiarism. *The New York Times*.
38. Widdicombe. The plagiarist's tale.
39. J. Bosman. (2011, December 8). Is it plagiarism? Publisher says no. *The New York Times*.
40. A. Flood. (2011, November 21). Lenore Hart rejects plagiarism accusations. *The Guardian*.
41. N. Thayer. (2013, March 4). 25 Years of slam dunk diplomacy. *NK News*.
42. J. Duns. (2013, March 7). Nate Thayer is a plagiarist. www.jeremy-duns.com/blog/2014/5/30/nate-thayer-is-a-plagiarist

43. J. Coscarelli. (2013, March 7). Did Nate Thayer plagiarize in the article "The Atlantic" wanted for free? *New York Intelligencer.*
44. S. Morrison. (2013, March 8). Nate Thayer: freelance plagiarist? *Columbia Journalism Review.*
45. S. Beasley. (2013, April 26). Nice poem; I'll take it. *The New York Times.*
46. A. Flood. (2013, January 14). Poetry competition winner exposed as plagiarist. *The Guardian.*
47. T. Fitch. (2013, September 22). Plagiarism scandal has revealed an ugly side of Australian poetry. *The Guardian.*
48. C. Hartman. (2013, June 6). On being plagiarised. *London Review of Books* blog. https://www.lrb.co.uk/blog/2013/june/on-being-plagiarised
49. A. Flood. (2013, May 22). Another plagiarism scandal hits poetry community. *The Guardian.*
50. W. Storr. (2017, September 9). "Plagiarists never do it once": Meet the sleuth tracking down the poetry cheats. *The Guardian.*
51. Storr. "Plagiarists never do it once."
52. I. Lightman. (2020, November 7). How the wordsmith of Oz took other people's poetry without credit. *The Telegraph.*
53. I. Lightman, personal communication.
54. P. Wasley. (2006, August 11). The plagiarism hunter. *The Chronicle of Higher Education.*
55. OU strips master's degree in plagiarism investigation. (2007, March 29). *The Columbus Dispatch.*
56. I. Chen. (2021, June 23). How a sharp-eyed scientist became biology's image detective. *The New Yorker.*
57. E. Bik. (2022, November 2). Science has a nasty photoshopping problem. *The New York Times.*
58. D. Hruby. (2021, September 10). The "plagiarism hunter" terrorizing the German-speaking world. *The New York Times.*
59. Reuters. (2021, January 10). Austrian Labour Minister quits over plagiarism allegations.
60. P. Oltermann. (2021, June 30). German Greens say plagiarism claims are "character assassination." *The Guardian.*
61. A. Zimmerman. (2021, July 8). German Greens' Baerbock admits mistakes in plagiarism row. *Politico.*
62. J. Alvarez. (2022, May 28). "I was careless": Plagiarism allegations: Diana Kinnert admits mistakes. *DailyNews.*
63. Hruby. The "plagiarism-hunter" terrorizing the German-speaking world.
64. Chen. How a sharp-eyed scientist became biology's image detective.
65. Hruby. The "plagiarism hunter" terrorizing the German-speaking world.
66. T. Bostian. (2000, April 20). A professor at Tennessee cites academic abuses. *The New York Times.*
67. R. Lipsyte. (2000, August 20). The continuing battle inside and outside the lines. *The New York Times.*
68. R. Lipsyte. (2000, July 20). What happens after the whistle blows? *The New York Times.*

69. R. Lipsyte. (2002, July 7). Maligned and marginalized at Tennessee, a whistle-blower endures. *The New York Times.*
70. S. Ganim. (2014, January 9). Women who blew whistle in student-athlete cases and what happened next. *CNN.*
71. S. Lyall. (2014, April 26). Reporter digging into scandal hits a university's raw nerve. *The New York Times.*
72. D. Kane. (2011, July 17). UNC honor court failed to find McAdoo's obvious plagiarism. *The News & Observer.*
73. M. Brooks. (2012, October 23). Report: UNC receiver Erik Highsmith plagiarized 11-year-olds. *The Washington Post.*
74. All Things Considered (2015, January 1). Four UNC-Chapel Hill employees out in the wake of cheating scandal. National Public Radio. Transcript: https://www.npr.org/2015/01/01/374417450/four-unc-chapel-hill-employees-out-in-wake-of-cheating-scandal
75. J. Neff. (2015, September 16). N&O reporter wins award for courage in journalism. *The News & Observer.*
76. M. McIntire. (2017, September 1). Football favoritism at F.S.U.: The price one teacher paid. *The New York Times.*
77. M. Bonesteel. (2017, September 1). Report alleges plagiarism, other academic misconduct at Florida State during 2013 title season. *The Washington Post.*
78. McIntire, Football favoritism at F.S.U.
79. J. Glatzer. (2019, June 22). Ashton Kutcher didn't give the graduate speech at a W.Va. school, but the words sure were familiar. *The Washington Post.*
80. Glatzer. Ashton Kutcher didn't give the graduate speech.
81. M. Erb. (2019, May 31). DeMoss issues apology, statement for graduation speech. *The Parkersburg News and Sentinel.*
82. M. Hunt. (1989, May 14). Did the penalty fit the crime? *The New York Times.*
83. R. A. Mackinnon. (1988, December 16). Was plagiarism-case professor treated fairly? *The New York Times.*
84. Hunt. Did the penalty fit the crime?
85. L. K. Altman. (1988, November 29). Eminent Harvard professor quits over plagiarism, university says. *The New York Times.*
86. Hunt. Did the penalty fit the crime?
87. Mackinnon. Was plagiarism-case professor treated fairly?
88. Different standards? (1988, December 16). *The New York Times.*
89. Hunt. Did the penalty fit the crime?
90. L. K. Altman. (1988, December 2). Psychiatrist's downfall spurs debate. *The New York Times.*
91. M. Arlen. (1988, December 7). Much ado over a plagiarist. *The New York Times.*
92. The Cornell presidency. (1885, July 8). *The New York Times.*
93. Prof. Adams's writings. (1884, July 13). *The New York Times.*
94. Cornell University. (1885, July 15). *The New York Times.*
95. Dr. Adams's plagiarism. (1884, August 24). *The New York Times.*

96. Professor Charles Kendall Adams. (1902, August 2). *The Publishers' Weekly*, No. 1592.
97. Scientific notes and news. (1902, August 1). *Science, 16*(396).
98. D. Goleman. (1989, February 11). Doctor forced out for plagiarism is reappointed to the hospital's staff. *The New York Times*.
99. B. Marquard. (2015, March 12). Shervert Frazier, 93: Catalyst in mental illness field. *The Boston Globe*.
100. S. Vehviläinen, E. Löfström & A. Nevgi. (2018). Dealing with plagiarism in the academic community: Emotional engagement and moral distress. *Higher Education, 75*, 1–18.
101. T. Holland. (2015, September 26). Why I won't use Turnitin to check my PhD thesis. *Medium*.
102. Y. Gorenko. (2019, December 13). 4 common ways students avoid plagiarism detection. *TeachThought*. https://www.teachthought.com/technology/4-common-ways-students-avoid-plagiarism-detection/
103. A. Wick. (2021, August 27). 6 ways to identify if students are using text spinners to plagiarize. *The Cengage Blog*. https://blog.cengage.com/6-ways-to-identify-if-students-are-using-text-spinners-to-plagiarize/
104. M. Aaron. (2019, October 23). Joe Biden's campaign has spent at least $4,200 on anti-plagiarism software. *Slate*.
105. I. Bogost. (2024, January 4). The plagiarism war has begun. *The Atlantic*.
106. K. Chuck. (2013, May 31). Can I use the same paper for multiple college courses? *The New York Times*.
107. M. Sullivan. (2013, June 6). Who does the ethicist think he is? *The New York Times*.
108. J. Dempsey. (2011, February 22). German Defense Minister defies calls to quit over plagiarism. *The New York Times*.
109. Universität kassiert Guttenbergs Doktortitel. (2011, February 23). *Zeit Online*. https://www.zeit.de/politik/deutschland/2011-02/guttenberg-doktorarbeit-bayreuth
110. M. Kimmelman. (2011, March 14). In Germany, uproar over a doctoral thesis. *The New York Times*.
111. "Youth Word of the Year" shows "problem" of trendy English. (2011, December 6). *The Local*. https://www.thelocal.de/20111206/39325
112. D. D. Guttenplan. (2011, March 6). A folly that can cost a reputation – or not. *The New York Times*.
113. D. Weber-Wulff. (2014). *False Feathers: A Perspective on Academic Plagiarism*. Springer-Verlag.
114. C. F. Schuetze. (2011, April 24). The whiff of plagiarism again hits German elite. *The New York Times*.
115. G. Danneman. (2018). Crowd-based documentation of plagiarism: The VroniPlag Wiki experience. In F. M. Dobrick, J. Fischer, & L. M. Hagen (Eds.), *Research Ethics in the Digital Age*. Springer, pp. 45–67.
116. Schuetze. The whiff of plagiarism.
117. CDU-Parlaentarier Pröfrock verliert Doktorgrad. (2011, June 7). *Spiegel Panorama*.
118. German MEP Silvana Koch-Mehrin quits in plagiarism row. (2011, May 11). *BBC*.

119. C. Penfold. (2011, June 15). A doctor no more. *Deutsche Welle.*

120. C. Cottrell. (2013, February 5) University revokes German official's doctorate. *The New York Times.*

121. N. Kulish & C. Cottrell. (2013, February 9). German fascination with degrees claims latest victim: Education Minister. *The New York Times.*

122. A. Abbott. (2015, September 29). German minister accused of plagiarism in medical dissertation, *Nature.*

123. H. von der Burchard. (2016, March 9). German Defense Minister to keep her doctorate. *Politico.*

124. P. Oltermann. (2021, May 22). German politicians suffer higher degree of embarrassment from plagiarism than from sex scandals. *The Guardian.*

125. C. Dankbar. (2021, June 10). SPD mayoral candidate Franziska Giffey loses her doctorate for good. *Berliner Zeitung.*

126. Associated Press. (2021, December 21). Former German Minister becomes new mayor of Berlin.

127. B. Knight. (2021, May 25). German politicians are dogged by claims of PhD plagiarism. *Deutsche Welle.*

128. J. Dempsey. (2011, February 21). Old doctoral thesis haunts a top German minister. *The New York Times.*

129. Kulish & Cottrell. German fascination with degrees claims latest victim.

130. P. Cohen. (2011, August 23). Thinking cap: The seemingly persistent rise of plagiarism. *The New York Times.*

131. Schuetze. The whiff of plagiarism.

132. The Daily Dish. (2008, August 20). Putin's thesis (raw text). *The Atlantic.*

133. I. Danchenko & C. Gaddy. (2006, March 30). The mystery of Vladimir Putin's dissertation. Foreign Policy Program panel presentation. https://www.brookings.edu/wp-content/uploads/2012/09/Putin-Dissertation-Event-remarks-with-slides.pdf

134. Danchenko & Gaddy. The mystery of Vladimir Putin's dissertation.

135. D. Volchek. (2018, March 7). Cut-and-paste job: My father wrote Putin's dissertation. *Radio Free Europe.*

136. L. Neyfakh. (2016, May 22). The craziest black market in Russia. *Slate.*

137. S. Shuster. (2013, February 28). Putin's PhD: Can a plagiarism upend Russian politics? *Time.*

138. N. MacFarquhar. (2016, July 22). By Russian standards, Melania Trump would be a plagiarism amateur. *The New York Times.*

139. Neyfakh. The craziest black market.

140. O. Khvostunova. (2013, May 7). Plagiarism-gate. *Institute of Modern Russia.* http://imrussia.org/en/society/453-plagiarism-gate

141. MacFarquhar. By Russian standards.

142. A. Osipian. (2019, April 5). Putin's plagiarism, fake Ukrainian degrees and other tales of world leaders accused of academic fraud. *The Conversation.*

143. Q. Schiermeier. (2012, June 21). Romanian prime minister accused of plagiarism. *Nature, 486,* p. 305.

144. R. Marinas. (2014, December 16). Romanian PM gives up doctorate after years of plagiarism allegations. Reuters.

145. Oprea reported for plagiarism: Interim Prime Minister says author is a "source of lies" against him. (2015, July 1). *Nine O'Clock.* https://nineoclock.ro/2015/07/01/oprea-reported-for-plagiarism-interim-prime-minister-says-author-is-a-"source-of-lies"-agains t-him/

146. Associated Press. (2016, August 1). Romanian council rules ex-minister plagiarized thesis.

147. A. Fota. (2022, January 18). Romania's prime minister accused of plagiarism as rivals demand probe. *Politico.*

148. M. Robinson. (2014, June 4). UK-based Serbian academics vow to expose "dubious degrees." Reuters.

149. S. Rakic. (2019, September 25). Students end blockade of Belgrade University. *Serbian Monitor.*

150. J. Bailey. (2020, September 30). The ongoing Albanian plagiarism crisis. *Plagiarism Today.*

151. Reuters. (2019, November 21). Serbia's Finance Minister plagiarized his doctoral thesis, university says.

152. Bailey. The ongoing Albanian plagiarism crisis.

CHAPTER 3 UNCONSCIOUS PLAGIARISM

1. D. C. Broaddus. (1999). *Genteel Rhetoric: Writing High Culture in Nineteenth-Century Boston.* University of South Carolina Press.

2. The Holmes breakfast. (1880, February). *The Atlantic Monthly Supplement,* pp. 1–24.

3. D. Ketterer. (1986). "Professor Baffin's Adventures" by Max Adeler: The inspiration for "A Connecticut Yankee in King Arthur's Court"? *Mark Twain Journal, 24*(1), pp. 24–34.

4. O. W. Holmes. (1862). *Songs in Many Keys.* Ticknor and Fields.

5. J. J. Kilpatrick. (1987, October 10). "I too have committed plagiarism." *The Washington Post.*

6. B. Michelson. (1977). Mark Twain the tourist: The form of "The Innocents Abroad." *American Literature, 49*(3), p. 385.

7. M. Twain. (1910). *Mark Twain's Speeches.* Harper & Brothers.

8. Holmes. *Songs in Many Keys.*

9. M. Twain. (1869). *The Innocents Abroad, or The New Pilgrims' Progress.* American Publishing Co.

10. Twain. *Mark Twain's Speeches.*

11. Acquitted of plagiarism. (1890, December 20). *The New York Times.*

12. Unconscious assimilation: A leading Chicago preacher's explanation of an alleged plagiarism. (1879, October 19). *The New York Times.*

13. The Rev. Dr. Lorimer dead. (1904, September 9). *The New York Times.*

14. P. Gay. (1998). *Freud: A Life for our Time.* W. W. Norton.

15. J. W. Beach. (1942). Coleridge's borrowings from the German. *English Literary History*, *9*(1), pp. 36–58.

16. L. L. Whyte. (1960). *The Unconscious before Freud*. Basic Books, p. 66.

17. H. Keller. (1903). *The Story of My Life*. Doubleday.

18. H. Keller. (1892). The Frost King. *The Mentor*, *2*(1), pp. 13–16.

19. M. Anagnos. (1892). Editorial notes. *The Mentor*, *2*(3), pp. 117–118.

20. M. T. Canby. (1889). The Frost Fairies. In *Birdie and His Fairy Friends: A Book for Little Children* (2nd ed.). Wm. Fell.

21. Canby. The Frost Fairies, p. 113.

22. Keller. The Frost King, p. 14.

23. A. W. Sullivan. (1892). How Helen Keller acquired language. *American Annals of the Deaf*, *37*(2), pp. 127–154.

24. Anagnos. Editorial notes.

25. J. K. Love. (1934). The childhood of Helen Keller. *British Medical Journal*, *1*(3811), p. 115.

26. Keller. *The Story of My Life*, p. 66.

27. Keller. *The Story of My Life*.

28. Keller. *The Story of My Life*, pp. 67–68.

29. Keller. *The Story of My Life*, p. 106.

30. Keller. *The Story of My Life*, p. 68.

31. A. Whitman. (1968, June 2). Triumph out of tragedy: Helen Keller, blind and deaf writer, traveler and humanitarian, is dead at 87. *The New York Times*.

32. N. Shoenberg. (2003, August 13). Where have you gone, Helen Keller? *Chicago Tribune*.

33. R. L. Stevenson. (1986). My first book – Treasure Island. *The Courier*, *21*(2), p. 81.

34. Stevenson. My first book, p. 83.

35. Stevenson. My first book, p. 84.

36. Stevenson. My first book, p. 84.

37. W. Irving. (1894). *Tales of a Traveler*. American Book Co.

38. F. W. C. Hersey. (1911). Introduction to Stevenson's "Treasure Island." Ginn and Co.

39. S. Schiff. (1999). *Véra (Mrs. Vladimir Nabokov)*. Modern Library.

40. K. Curtis. (2005, September 25). "Lolita," still the fire of readers' eyes. *The Washington Post*.

41. S. Weinman. (2019). *The Real Lolita: The Kidnapping of Sally Horner and the Novel That Scandalized the World*. HarperCollins.

42. D. Nabokov. (1986, September 3). Nabokov was glad "The Enchanter" survived. *The New York Times*.

43. E. Jong. (1988, June 5). Time has been kind to the nymphet: "Lolita" 30 years later. *The New York Times*.

44. C. Caldwell. (2004, May 23). Who invented Lolita? *The New York Times*.

45. M. Maar. (2005). *The Two Lolitas*. Verso Books.

46. Maar. *The Two Lolitas*.

47. Maar. *The Two Lolitas*, Kindle location 435.

48. N. Paton. (2004, April 2). Novel twist: Nabokov family rejects Lolita plagiarism claim. *The Guardian.*

49. E. Flock. (2017, August 1). Was Nabokov's "Lolita" inspired by a little-known story by Salvador Dalí? PBS News Hour.

50. J. R. R. Tolkien. (2000). (Humphrey Carpenter, Ed.). *The Letters of J. R. R. Tolkien.* Houghton Mifflin, p. 131.

51. D. Ungureanu. (2017, October 30). The surreal sources of "Lolita": Nabokov and Dalí. *Los Angeles Review of Books.*

52. Ungureanu. The surreal sources of "Lolita."

53. S. Len. (2006). *While My Guitar Gently Weeps: The Music of George Harrison.* Hal Leonard, p. 67.

54. S. Vaidhyanathan. (2001). *Copyrights and Copywrongs: The Rise of Intellectual Property and How It Threatens Creativity.* New York University Press.

55. G. Thomson. (2013). *George Harrison: Behind the Locked Door.* Omnibus Press.

56. Thomson. *George Harrison.*

57. Thomson. *George Harrison.*

58. K. Womack & J. Kruppa. (2021). *All Things Must Pass Away: Harrison, Clapton, and Other Assorted Love Songs.* Chicago Review Press.

59. Richard Owen. (2015, November 26). *The New York Times.* https://archive.nytimes.com/query.nytimes.com/gst/fullpage-9B03E3D8103AF935A15752C1A9639D8B63.html

60. George Harrison guilty of plagiarizing, subconsciously, a '62 tune for a '70 hit. (1976, September 8). *The New York Times.*

61. N. Genzlinger. (2018, January 15). Edwin Hawkins, known for the hit "Oh Happy Day," is dead at 74. *The New York Times.*

62. Vaidhyanathan. *Copyrights and Copywrongs,* p. 127.

63. A. C. Yen & J. P. Liu. (2008). *Copyright Law: Essential Cases and Materials.* Thomson/West.

64. Bright Tunes Music Corp. v. Harrisongs Music, Ltd., 420 F. Supp. 177 (S.D.N.Y. 1976).

65. ABKCO Music, Inc. v. Harrisongs Music, 508 F. Supp. 798 (S.D.N.Y. 1981).

66. A. Krebs & R. McG. Thomas Jr. (1981, February 27). Less damage. *The New York Times.*

67. S. Soocher (2015). *Baby You're a Rich Man: Suing the Beatles for Fun & Profit.* ForeEdge.

68. A. Kozinn. (2001, November 30). George Harrison, former Beatle, dies at 58. *The New York Times.*

69. "Good Morning Dearie" a hit. (1921, November 21). *The New York Times.*

70. Court lets song go on. (1922, April 29). *The New York Times.*

71. C. B. Jaeger. (2008). Does that sound familiar: Creators' liability for unconscious copyright infringement. *Vanderbilt Law Review, 61*(6), pp. 1903–1934.

72. H. Finkelstein. (1963). Review: Cases on copyright, unfair competition, and other topics bearing on the protection of literary, musical and artistic works. *The Yale Law Journal, 72*(4), pp. 844–852.

73. Fred Fisher, Inc. v. Dillingham 298 F. 145 (S.D.N.Y. 1924).

74. Fred Fisher, Inc. v. Dillingham 298 F. 145 (S.D.N.Y. 1924).

75. Fred Fisher, Inc. v. Dillingham 298 F. 145 (S.D.N.Y. 1924).

76. R. K. Walker. (2017). Ghosts in the hit machine: Musical creation and the doctrine of subconscious copying. *Landslide* 9(4), pp. 48–53.

77. J. E. Cohen, L. P. Loren, R. L. Okediji, & M. A. O'Rourke. (2019). *Copyright in a Global Information Economy.* Aspen Publishing.

78. N. Coleman. (2019, July 31). Katy Perry's copyright case may sound familiar to these stars. *The New York Times.*

79. J. S. Hollingsworth. (2000). Stop me if I've heard this already: The temporal remoteness aspect of the subconscious copying doctrine. *Hastings Communications and Entertainment Law Journal, 23*(2), p. 473.

80. Isley feels vindicated in Bolton case. (2001, February 20). *Billboard.*

81. Hollingsworth. Stop me if I've heard this already.

82. T. English. (2016). *Sounds Like Teen Spirit.* Timothy English, p. 323.

83. T. Cateforis. (2011). *Are We Not New Wave? Modern Pop at the Turn of the 1980s.* University of Michigan Press, p. 148.

84. A. Decurtis. (2005, November 1). John Fogerty is closer to peace with a label. *The New York Times.*

85. A. Sweeting. (2000, July 10). The saddest story in rock. *The Guardian.*

86. J. Montgomery. (2009, July 27). Think Kelly Clarkson's "Already Gone" sounds like Beyoncé's "Halo"? So Does Kelly . . . . MTV.

87. L. Rohter (2009, August 3). Songs are too similar, Kelly Clarkson says. *The New York Times.*

88. B. D. Fisher. (2005). *Puccini's Madam Butterfly.* Opera Classics Library series. Opera Journeys Publishing.

89. D. Schickling & R. Vilain. (1998). Puccini's "work in progress": The so-called versions of "Madama Butterfly." *Music & Letters, 79*(4), pp. 527–537.

90. J. Levin. (2012, June 19). Why did Jonah Lehrer plagiarize himself? *Slate.*

91. M. Moynihan. (2012, July 30). Jonah Lehrer's deceptions. *Tablet.*

92. J. Kahn. (2012, August 1). Fabrication acknowledged, a bestseller is withdrawn. *The Boston Globe.*

93. G. Baverstock. (1997). *Tell Me about Enid Blyton.* Evans Brothers.

94. R. Druce. (1992). *This Day Our Daily Fictions: An Enquiry into the Multi-million Bestseller Status of Enid Blyton and Ian Fleming.* Rodopi, p. 29.

95. F. MacShane. (Ed.). (1981). *Selected Letters of Raymond Chandler.* Columbia University Press, p. 334.

96. E. Mitchell. (2003, February 21). Never too late to have an adolescence. *The New York Times.*

97. Swipe File. (1996, February). *The Comics Journal,* No. 184, p. 5.

98. M. K. Johnson, S. Hashtroudi, & D. S. Lindsay. (1993). Source monitoring. *Psychological Bulletin, 114*(1), pp. 3–28.

99. A. S. Brown & D. R. Murphy. (1989). Cryptomnesia: Delineating inadvertent plagiarism. *Journal of Experimental Psychology: Learning, Memory, and Cognition, 15*(3), pp. 432–442.

100. L. Stark & T. J. Perfect. (2007). Whose idea was that? Source monitoring for idea ownership following elaboration. *Memory, 15*(7), pp. 776–783.
101. R. L. Marsh, J. D. Landau, & J. L. Hicks. (1997). Contributions of inadequate source monitoring to unconscious plagiarism during idea generation. *Journal of Experimental Psychology: Learning, Memory, and Cognition, 23*(4), pp. 886–897.
102. T. J. Perfect, A. Defeldre, R. Elliman, & H. Dehon. (2011). No evidence of age-related increases in unconscious plagiarism during free recall. *Memory, 19*(5), pp. 514–528.
103. Brown & Murphy. Cryptomnesia.
104. C. N. Macrae, G. V. Bodenhausen, & C. Guglielmo. (1999). Contexts of cryptomnesia: May the source be with you. *Social Cognition, 17*(3), pp. 273–297.
105. Johnson et al. Source monitoring.
106. D. P. McCabe, A. D. Smith, & C. M. Parks. (2007). Inadvertent plagiarism in young and older adults: The role of working memory capacity in reducing memory errors. *Memory & Cognition, 35*(2), pp. 231–241.
107. Perfect et al. No evidence of age-related increases.
108. A. C. Gingerich & M. C. Sullivan. (2013). Claiming hidden memories as one's own: A review of inadvertent plagiarism. *Journal of Cognitive Psychology, 25*(8), pp. 903–916.
109. A. C. Gingerich & C. S. Dodson. (2013). Sad mood reduces inadvertent plagiarism: Effects of affective state on source monitoring in cryptomnesia. *Motivation and Emotion, 37*, pp. 355–371.
110. A. G. Greenwald & M. R. Banaji. (1989). The self as a memory system: Powerful, but ordinary. *Journal of Personality and Social Psychology, 57*(1), pp. 41–54.
111. A. Defeldre. (2005). Inadvertent plagiarism in everyday life. *Applied Cognitive Psychology, 19*(8), pp. 1033–1040.

CHAPTER 4 PLAGIARISM IN POLITICS

1. B. Franklin. (1970, May 1). Nixon may name mines director. *The New York Times.*
2. Nixon fills four cabinet posts during 1970. (1971). *Congressional Quarterly Almanac 1970*, 26th ed. Congressional Quarterly Inc.
3. B. A. Franklin. (1970, May 26). Senate test on mines official delayed by plagiarism dispute. *The New York Times.*
4. U.S. Congress. *Congressional Record.* Vol. 116, Part 19: 25412–25413.
5. S. Blakeslee. (1970, October 14). New director of mines. *The New York Times.*
6. E. Shanahan. (1971, March 3). Senate reopens Casey hearing; information on '65 suit received. *The New York Times.*
7. E. Shanahan. (1971, March 1). Judge challenges memory of Casey, S.E.C. nominee. *The New York Times.*
8. E. Shanahan. (1971, February 26). 3rd suit disclosed by S.E.C. nominee. *The New York Times.*
9. E. Shanahan. (1971, March 10). Committee backs Casey for 2d time. *The New York Times.*

10. J. Conaway. (1983, September 7). Spy master: The file on Bill Casey. *The Washington Post*.

11. A. Liptak. (2008, July 4). Copying issue raises hurdle for Bush pick. *The New York Times*.

12. Liptak. Copying issue.

13. Liptak. Copying issue.

14. C. Johnson & D. Q. Wilber. (2003, July 8). Court nominee accused of plagiarism won't withdraw. *The Washington Post*.

15. M. Feldstein. (2010). *Poisoning the Press: Richard Nixon, Jack Anderson, and the Rise of Washington's Scandal Culture*. Farrar, Straus and Giroux, p. 42.

16. Feldstein. *Poisoning the Press*.

17. D. Greenberg. (2008, February 24). Friends, Romans, countrymen, lend me your speech. *The New York Times*.

18. *The Rachel Maddow Show*. (2014, October 28). Transcript. MSNBC.com.

19. A. Kaczynski. (2013, October 29). Rand Paul has given speech plagiarized from Wikipedia before. *BuzzFeed News*.

20. J. W. Peters. (2013, October 30). Senator Rand Paul is accused of plagiarizing his lines from Wikipedia. *The New York Times*.

21. A. Kaczynski. (2013, November 2). Three pages of Rand Paul's book were plagiarized from think tanks. *BuzzFeed News*.

22. A. Kaczynski. (2013, November 7). More instances of plagiarism in Rand Paul's book. *BuzzFeed News*.

23. A. Kaczynski. (2013, November 8). The last two cases of Rand Paul plagiarism that we are going to post. *BuzzFeed News*.

24. J. Martin. (2013, November 4). Senator Rand Paul faces new charges of plagiarism. *The New York Times*.

25. J. McElhatton. (2013, November 5). Washington Times ends Sen. Rand Paul column amid plagiarism allegations. *The Washington Times*.

26. A. Blake. (2013, October 31). Rand Paul denies charges, blames "haters." *The Washington Post*.

27. B. Knowlton. (2013, November 3). Rand Paul muses about "dueling" with his accusers. *The New York Times*.

28. J. R. Carroll. (2013, November 6). Rand Paul admits his plagiarism "is my fault." *USA Today*.

29. J. Rutenberg & A. Parker. (2013, November 5). Though defiant, Senator accused of plagiarism admits errors. *The New York Times*.

30. J. Rutenberg. (2013, November 12). A Senator lays out his positions on the military, very carefully. *The New York Times*.

31. J. Rutenberg. (2013, November 7). Rand Paul may have had his own writings plagiarized. *The New York Times*.

32. J. Frank. (2013, November 8). Brannon says he reviewed lifted passages, will revise campaign site. *Raleigh News & Observer*.

33. J. Martin. (2014, July 23). Senator's thesis turns out to be remix of others' works, uncited. *The New York Times*.

34. J. Martin, J. Keller, M. Ericson, & N. Corasaniti. (2014, July 23). How Senator John Walsh plagiarized a final paper. *The New York Times.*
35. N. Coransniti & J. Martin (2014, July 24). Army War College starts plagiarism inquiry of Senator John Walsh's thesis. *The New York Times.*
36. D. McCabe. (2014, October 30). NRSC was behind Walsh plagiarism leak. *The Hill.*
37. E. Osnos. (2014, July 29). Why politicians plagiarize so often. *The New Yorker.*
38. A. Rosenthal. (2014, July 25). John Walsh's campaign sinking under plagiarism. *The New York Times.*
39. K. Wehr & G. S. Stolberg. (2014, July 25). Plagiarism scandal tests a Senator still forming a rapport with Montanans. *The New York Times.*
40. J. Martin. (2014, August 7). Senator quits Montana race after charge of plagiarism. *The New York Times.*
41. J. Martin. (2014, October 10). Plagiarism costs degree for Senator John Walsh. *The New York Times.*
42. M. Volz. (2014, August 16). Montana Democrats choose a new Senate candidate. *The Washington Post.*
43. J. Gerstein. (2004, October 26). Researcher alleges potential plagiarism in 11 passages of Kerry's writings. *The New York Sun.*
44. W. Safire. (1996, August 15). October surprises. *The New York Times.*
45. U.S. Government Accountability Office. (n.d.). Copyright & terms of use. https://www.gao.gov/copyright
46. J. Wilgoren. (2004, May 5). Veterans group criticizes Kerry on his record in Vietnam. *The New York Times.*
47. M. R. Gordon. (2013, January 29). Kerry sails through the Senate as Secretary of State. *The New York Times.*
48. D. Weiner. (2008, April 15). McCain "family recipes" lifted from the Food Network. *The Huffington Post.*
49. E. Bumiller. (2008, April 16). Family recipes, passed down from one site to another. *The New York Times.*
50. D. Weiner. (2008, April 29). Cindy McCain responds to recipe theft on "The View." *The Huffington Post.*
51. M. D. Shear. (2008, April 16). Bloggers find something fishy in McCain's "family recipes." *The Washington Post.*
52. Wikinews investigates claim McCain plagiarized speech from Wikipedia. (2008, August 23). Wikinews.org. https://en.wikinews.org/wiki/Wikinews_investigates_claim_McCain_plagiarized_speech_from_Wikipedia
53. T. Goddard. (2008, August 11). Did McCain plagiarize his speech on the Georgia crisis? *Congressional Quarterly.*
54. A. Romano. (2008, August 12). McCain gets Wiki. *Newsweek.*
55. J. Martin. (2008, August 12). McCain camp dismisses plagiarism rap. *Politico* blog. https://www.politico.com/blogs/jonathanmartin/0808/McCain_camp_dismisses_plagiarism_rap.html

56. Stealing policy ideas from Wikipedia. (2008, August 13). *The New York Times* Laugh Lines blog. https://archive.nytimes.com/laughlines.blogs.nytimes.com/2008/08/13/stealing-policy-ideas-from-wikipedia/

57. Mr. Sam changes his mind. (1964). *The Reporter, 30*, p. 18.

58. D. K. Shipler. (1970, March 10). Agnew, in suburb speech, borrowed from memo. *The New York Times.*

59. D. Greenberg. (2008, February 24). Friends, Romans, countrymen, lend me your speech. *The New York Times.*

60. N. P. Lewis. (2010). The myth of Spiro Agnew's "nattering nabobs of negativism." *American Journalism, 27*(1), pp. 89–115.

61. Agnew quits vice presidency and admits tax evasion in '67. (1973, October 11). *The New York Times.*

62. Campaign becomes confrontation with past: Privilege, wealth shaped Quayle. (1988, August 21). *Los Angeles Times.*

63. A. Lewis. (1988, September 15). What is Quayle hiding? *The New York Times.*

64. B. Woodward & D. S. Broder. (1992, January 7). Quayle's reputation vs. the record. *The Washington Post.*

65. J. Witcover. (1999, September 28). Quayle abandons race for GOP nomination. *The Baltimore Sun.*

66. M. Schwartz & J. R. Dickenson. (1987, May 31). Not with my punchline you don't! *The Washington Post.*

67. B. Weinraub. (1988, April 27). Disappointed, Gore is taking stock. *The New York Times.*

68. F. Kwarteng. (2017, January 11). Saint Akufo-Addo in the web of the moral shame of new-age plagiarism. *GhanaWeb.*

69. M. M. Bigg. (2017, January 8). Ghana president faces outcry over plagiarism in inaugural speech. Reuters.

70. M A. Thiessen. (2016, July 21). Mike Pence's "time for choosing" moment. *The Washington Post.*

71. A. Blake. (2016, July 20). Mike Pence's speech draws on phrases from Reagan, the Bible – and Bill Clinton? *The Washington Post.*

72. K. D. Harris, with J. O'C. Hamilton. (2009). *Smart on Crime: A Career Prosecutor's Plan to Make Us Safer.* Chronicle Books, p. 10.

73. A. Haley. (1965, January). Playboy interview: Martin Luther King. *Playboy, 12*(1), pp. 117ff.

74. K. Harris. (2019). *The Truths We Hold: An American Journey.* Penguin Press, p. 8.

75. A. C. Ford. (2021, January 20). Kamala Harris is officially Vice President of the United States. *Elle.*

76. L. Giella. (2021, January 5). Fact check: Did Kamala Harris plagiarize a story from Martin Luther King Jr.? *Newsweek.*

77. N. Ibrahim. (2021, January 6). Did Kamala Harris plagiarize Martin Luther King Jr.? Snopes.com. https://www.snopes.com/fact-check/kamala-harris-plagiarize-mlk/

78. G. Mason. (1776). *The Virginia Declaration of Rights*, Section 1. U.S. National Archives and Records Administration.

79. From John Adams to Thomas Jefferson, 22 June 1819. Founders Online, National Archives. https://founders.archives.gov/documents/Adams/99-02-02-7158

80. D. Fleming. (2023). *Who's Your Founding Father?* Hachette Books.

81. C. L. Hunter. (1877). *Sketches of Western North Carolina, Historical and Biographical.* The Raleigh News Stream.

82. S. Syfert. (2014). *The First Declaration of Independence?* McFarland & Co.

83. H. A. Bruce. (1906). New light on the Mecklenburg Declaration of Independence. *The North American Review, 183*(596), p. 48.

84. From John Adams to William Bentley, 21 August 1819. Founders Online, National Archives. https://founders.archives.gov/documents/Adams/99-02-02-7224

85. A. Henderson. (1918). The Mecklenburg Declaration of Independence. *The Mississippi Valley Historical Review, 5*(2), pp. 207–215.

86. Fleming. *Who's Your Founding Father?*

87. From Thomas Jefferson to John Adams, 9 July 1819. Founders Online, National Archives. https://founders.archives.gov/documents/Jefferson/03-14-02-0491

88. From Thomas Jefferson to James Madison, 30 August 1823. Founders Online, National Archives. https://founders.archives.gov/documents/Jefferson/98-01-02-3728

89. From Thomas Jefferson to Henry Lee, 8 May 1825. Founders Online, National Archives. https://founders.archives.gov/documents/Jefferson/98-01-02-5212

90. Morning Edition. (2007, January 25). Jimmy Carter defends "Peace Not Apartheid." National Public Radio.

91. B. Goodman. (2007, January 12). Carter Center advisers quit to protest book. *The New York Times.*

92. B. Goodman. (2006, December 9). Commentator says work was copied. *The New York Times.*

93. D. Ross. (2007, January 9). Don't play with maps. *The New York Times.*

94. G. Ini. (2006, December 9). Carter admits to ignoring key source. Committee for Accuracy in Middle East Reporting and Analysis. https://www.camera.org/article/carter-admits-to-ignoring-key-source/

95. H. Friel. (2008, January 1). Get Carter. https://fair.org/extra/get-carter/

96. D. Greenberg. (2008, February 24). Friends, Romans, countrymen, lend me your speech. *The New York Times.*

97. C. Grady. (2017, March 2). What the Obamas' $65 million book advance actually means. *Vox.*

98. A. Lawson. (2010, November 16). Pakistani journalist upset by George Bush "plagiarism." *BBC News.*

99. A. Rashid. (2004, February 12). The mess in Afghanistan. *The New York Review of Books.*

100. R. Grim. (2010, November 12). George Bush book "Decision Points" lifted from advisers' books. *The Huffington Post.*

101. Grim. George Bush book "Decision Points" lifted from advisers' books.

102. Lawson. Pakistani journalist upset by George Bush "plagiarism."

103. J. Bailey. (2010, November 16). The George W. Bush plagiarism controversy. *Plagiarism Today*.

104. M. Lacey. (2000, August 6). Bush accused of stealing Clinton's oratory. *The New York Times*.

105. M. Dowd. (1987, September 12). Biden's debate finale: An echo from abroad. *The New York Times*.

106. M. Kaus. (1987, September 28). Biden's belly flop. *Newsweek*, p. 23.

107. UK General Election 1987 Campaign – Kinnock the Movie. YouTube. https://www.youtube.com/watch?v=SFg-CP6qpfU

108. C-Span. Democratic presidential candidates debate at the 1987 Iowa State Fair. https://www.c-span.org/video/?3685-1/democratic-presidential-candidates-debate-1987-iowa-state-fair

109. A. Rosenthal. (1987, October 1). Two top aides to Dukakis resign as one admits role in Biden tape. *The New York Times*.

110. J. Risen & R. E. Meyer. (1987, September 13). No time to cite source, he says: Biden stirs row by using lines from Briton's talk. *Los Angeles Times*.

111. E. J. Dionne, Jr. (1987, September 18). Biden admits plagiarism in school but says it was not "malevolent." *The New York Times*.

112. M. Dowd. (1987, September 16). Biden is facing growing debate on his speeches. *The New York Times*.

113. J. Margolis & E. Povich. (1987, September 24). Biden admits errors, drops out. *Chicago Tribune*.

114. A. Entous. (2022, August 15). The untold history of the Biden family. *The New Yorker*.

115. M. Cooper. (2008, January 4). Iowa results lead Dodd and Biden to quit race. *The New York Times*.

116. M. Viser, D. Grandoni, & J. Stein. (2019, June 4). Joe Biden's campaign acknowledges lifting language from other groups for its policy plans. *The Washington Post*.

117. D. Broyer & A. Swoyer. (2020, October 7). Mike Pence-Kamala Harris VP debate dominated by coronavirus. Associated Press.

118. D. Smith. (2020, September 7). Neil Kinnock on Biden's plagiarism "scandal" and why he deserves to win: "Joe's an honest guy." *The Guardian*.

119. Mr. Disraeli's originality. (1852, November 20). *The Age*, p. 2.

120. Echoes of the week. (1878, October 5). *The Illustrated London News*, p. 318.

121. A. Lindey. (1952). *Plagiarism and Originality*. Harper Brothers.

122. I. Dale. (2020). *The Prime Ministers*. Hodder & Stoughton.

123. K. Stuart. (2010, September 9). "Queen" scribe calls Tony Blair a plagiarist. *The Hollywood Reporter*.

124. Theresa May battles a sore throat and prankster in conference speech. (2017, October 4). BBC.

125. M. Smith. (2017, October 4). Theresa May accused of plagiarising The West Wing in keynote speech to Conservative Party conference. *Daily Mirror*.

126. A. Woodcock. (2019, December 2). Boris Johnson accused of "copying and pasting" legal thread about London Bridge from a blog. *The Independent*.

127. L. Buchan. (2018, May 18). Labour frontbencher ridiculed for copying Barack Obama's acceptance speech. *The Independent*.
128. Labour's Kate Osamor resigns as shadow minister. (2018, December 1). BBC.
129. T. Kaushal. (2023, November 6). The women who made modern economics – review. The London School of Economics and Political Science. https://blogs.lse.ac.uk/lser eviewofbooks/2023/11/06/book-review-the-women-who-made-modern-economics-r achel-reeves/
130. S. Keynes & G. Parker. (2023, October 26). New book from UK Shadow Chancellor Rachel Reeves lifts from Wikipedia. *Financial Times*.
131. B. Morton. (2023, October 26). Rachel Reeves says she "should have done better" amid plagiarism row. BBC.

CHAPTER 5 CONSEQUENCES

1. H. G. Leach. (1910, February 6). Was "Tom Sawyer" Danish or American? *The New York Times*.
2. M. Twain. (1917). *Tom Sawyer Abroad and Tom Sawyer, Detective*. Harper & Brothers, p. 126.
3. H. S. Nielsen. (2013). The ethics of literary borrowing: Risks and rewards. In J. Lothe & J. Hawthorn (Eds.), *Narrative Ethics*. Rodopi.
4. A. B. Benson. (1938). Mark Twain's contacts with Scandinavia. *Scandinavian Studies and Notes, 14*(7), pp. 159–167.
5. D. Rachels. (1998). Oliver Hillhouse Prince, Augustus Baldwin Longstreet, and the birth of American literary realism. *The Mississippi Quarterly, 51*(4), pp. 603–604.
6. Puzzles of Hardy solved at Colby. (1936, October 11). *The New York Times*.
7. Rachels, Oliver Hillhouse Prince, Augustus Baldwin Longstreet, and the birth of American literary realism.
8. Charges Jack London with plagiarism. (1906, November 24). *The New York Times*.
9. Against Jack London. (1907, February 23). *The New York Times*.
10. E. R. Young. (1907, March 9). My dogs in the north land. *The New York Times*.
11. The retriever and the dynamite stick – a remarkable coincidence. (1902, August 16). *The New York Times*.
12. J. London. (1990). *The Call of the Wild, White Fang, and Other Stories*. Oxford University Press, p. xix.
13. K. Kopelson. (2008, May 22). Confessions of a plagiarist. *London Review of Books, 30* (10). https://www.lrb.co.uk/the-paper/v30/n10/kevin-kopelson/diary
14. "Author" now in jail; just "copies" stories. (1949, October 15). *The New York Times*.
15. B. Cerf. (1953, February 7). Heroine of the month. *The Saturday Review of Literature, 36* (7), p. 7.
16. Convict purloins book and receives royalties of $600. (1953, January 6). *Evening Star* (Washington, DC).
17. Whodunit critic spots plagiarism. (1956, December 14). *The New York Times*.

18. A. Narvaez. (1984, May 19). Rutgers professor resigning after plagiarism accusation. *The New York Times*.

19. No censure for stolen words. (2007, July 20). *The New York Times*.

20. C. Ross. (1982). The great script tease. *Film Comment*, *18*(6), p. 15.

21. Ross. The great script tease, p. 16.

22. B. Chase-Riboud. (2014). *Everytime a Knot Is Undone, a God Is Released*. Seven Stories Press.

23. Oral history interview with Barbara Chase-Riboud. (2019, June 7–11). Smithsonian Archives of American Art.

24. R. Cohen. (1991, August 15). Judge says copyright covers writer's ideas of a Jefferson affair. *The New York Times*.

25. B. Weinraub. (1998, February 10). Plagiarism suit over "Amistad" is withdrawn. *The New York Times*.

26. M. Loke. (1997, December 19). Writer who cried plagiarism used passages she didn't write. *The New York Times*.

27. S. Brown. (2022, December 2). At 91, Adrienne Kennedy is finally on Broadway. What took so long? *The New York Times Style Magazine*.

28. O. Barrios. (2003). From seeking one's voice to uttering the scream: The pioneering journey of African American women playwrights through the 1960s and 1970s. *African American Review*, *37*(4), pp. 611–628.

29. J. Green. (2022, December 8). Review: Who committed the "Ohio State Murders"? Who didn't? *The New York Times*.

30. S. Carson. (2019, June 10). Swan dives into past upon release of eighth novel. *Midland Mirror*.

31. C. De León. (2020, February 7). New literary prize will award over $100,000 to a female novelist. *The New York Times*.

32. S. Abu-Baker Hussein. (2012). *The Image of Man in Selected Plays of August Wilson*. AuthorHouse.

33. C. Bigsby (Ed.). (2007). *The Cambridge Companion to August Wilson*. Cambridge University Press.

34. Playwright August Wilson on blackness and the blues. (1988, October 20). BillMoyers .com. https://billmoyers.com/content/august-wilson/

35. Bigsby. *The Cambridge Companion to August Wilson*.

36. S. Kuta. (2022, April 22). How playwright August Wilson captured the highs and lows of Black America. *Smithsonian Magazine*.

37. D. Malehorn. (2011, October 8). How I found August Wilson's Carnegie "diploma." *Pittsburgh Post-Gazette*.

38. G. Garcia. (1994, December 11). Nely Galán. *The New York Times*.

39. O. Blanco. (2016, July 15). Latina media exec's secret to success: "Don't be a wimp." CNN.

40. Garcia. Nely Galán.

41. Two Charlemagne plays. (1908, January 5). *The New York Times*.

42. A. Riding. (1991, December 22). A nonagenarian in Paris, a conversation with Julian Green. *The New York Times*.
43. M. O'Dwyer. (1998). The quest for identity in the Civil War novels of Julien Green. *The Georgia Historical Quarterly, 82*(3), 575–593.
44. The plagiarism racket. (1929, October 23). *The Nation, 129*(3355), p. 456.
45. P. Bogdanovich. (2011, October 27). Places, everyone! *Condé Nast Traveler*.
46. Sandemo:på nettet. (1999, April 23). *Dagbladet*.
47. P. Klass. (2015, May 9). The plagiarism jitters. *The New York Times*.
48. P. Klass. (1987, April 5). Turning my words against me. *The New York Times*.
49. By the book: Donna Leon. (2019, March 7). *The New York Times*.
50. L. Rogak. (2009). *Haunted Heart: The Life and Times of Stephen King*. Thomas Dunne Books.
51. P. McIntyre. (2006). Paul McCartney and the creation of "Yesterday": The systems model in operation. *Popular Music, 25*(2), pp. 201–219.
52. R. Coleman. (1996). *McCartney: Yesterday … and Today*. Dove Books, p. 6.
53. Coleman. *McCartney*, p. 6.
54. Coleman. *McCartney*, p. 7.
55. A. L. Dixon. (2011). *When Night Turns into Morning*. Xlibris Corp, p. 77.
56. Coleman. *McCartney*, p. 17.
57. J.-M. Guesdon & P. Margotin. (2013). *All the Songs: The Story behind Every Beatles Release*. Black Dog & Leventhal.
58. P. McIntyre & P. Thompson (2021). *Paul McCartney and His Creative Practice: The Beatles and Beyond*. Palgrave Macmillan, p. 79.
59. S. A. Holmes (1991, September 4). Thomas Backers' ad faults Senators. *The New York Times*.
60. A. R. Hunt. (1991, October 17). Tales of ignominy, beyond Thomas and Hill. *The Wall Street Journal*, p. A22.
61. D. Garner. (1996, July 22). Beg, borrow, or …. Salon.com. https://www.salon.com/1996/07/22/plagiarism_4/
62. A. L. Bardach. (1992, January). Nina Totenberg: Queen of the leaks. *Vanity Fair*, pp. 46–57.
63. J. Mayer. (2010, August 23). Covert operations. *The New Yorker*.
64. J. Dwyer. (2015, January 26). What happened to Jane Mayer when she wrote about the Koch brothers. *The New York Times*.
65. A. Pareene. (2011, January 6). Tucker Carlson's attempt to smear the New Yorker. Salon.com. https://www.salon.com/2011/01/06/jane_mayer_smears/
66. S. Schoenberg. (2012, May 21). Elizabeth Warren responds to false accusations of plagiarism with fundraising email. *MassLive*.
67. K. Trinko. (2012, May 18). Correction on Warren, in The Corner. National Review. https://www.nationalreview.com/corner/correction-katrina-trinko/
68. J. M. Pasachoff. (2015). Simon Marius's *Mundus Iovialis*: 400th anniversary in Galileo's shadow. *Journal for the History of Astronomy, 46*(2), pp. 218–234.

69. G. G. Cole. (2022). Evolution according to Matthew. Review of *Science Fraud: Darwin's Plagiarism of Patrick Matthew's Theory* by M. Sutton, Curtis Press. *Evolution*, 76(9), pp. 2218–2221.

70. M. Walker. (1995). *Nazi Science: Myth, Truth, and the German Atomic Bomb*. Plenum Press.

71. A. Heard. (2018, December 18). Amber Heard: I spoke up against sexual violence – and faced our culture's wrath. That has to change. *The Washington Post*.

72. D. Evon. (2022, May 5). Did Amber Heard steal "Talented Mr. Ripley" lines during Depp trial? Snopes.com. https://www.snopes.com/fact-check/amber-heard-johnny-depp-trial/

73. M. Haberman & M. Barbaro (2016, July 19). How Melania Trump's speech veered off course and caused an uproar. *The New York Times*.

74. E. Brown. (2016, July 21). How a freelance journalist broke the Melania Trump plagiarism story in 3 tweets. *Vox*.

75. D. Hochman. (2016, July 21). Jon Favreau on speechwriting, life after D.C. . . . and Melania Trump. *The New York Times*.

76. A. Whiting. (2016, July 19). The likelihood that Melania Trump accidentally copied Michelle Obama is "less than 1 in a trillion." *Washingtonian*.

77. A. Blake. (2016, July 19). 93 percent different: The Trump team's brazenly bad defense of Melania's alleged plagiarism. *The Washington Post*.

78. M. Haberman, A. Rappeport, P. Healy, & J. Martin. (2016, July 19). Questions over Melania Trump's speech set off finger-pointing. *The New York Times*.

79. Blake. 93 percent different.

80. Haberman & Barbaro. How Melania Trump's speech veered off course and caused an uproar.

81. R. Lizza. (2016, July 20). Three problems with the Melania Trump plagiarism admission. *The New Yorker*.

82. J. Horowitz. (2016, July 20). Behind Melania Trump's cribbed lines, an ex-ballerina who loved writing. *The New York Times*.

83. D. Evon. (2016, October 10). Melania Trump copied statement from Hillary Clinton. Snopes.com. https://www.snopes.com/fact-check/melania-trump-copied-statement-from-hillary-clinton/

84. D. Mikkelson. (2017, August 13). Melania Trump criticizes Charlottesville violence, plagiarizes Michelle Obama? Snopes.com. https://www.snopes.com/fact-check/melania-tweet-charlottesville/

85. D. Evon. (2017, September 23). Did Melania Trump steal her United Nations speech from Michelle Obama? Snopes.com. https://www.snopes.com/fact-check/melania-trump-united-nations-obama/

86. D. Evon. (2018, January 15). Did Melania Trump copy Michelle Obama's MLK Day message? Snopes.com. https://www.snopes.com/fact-check/melania-michelle-mlk-message/

87. D. Evon. (2018, March 5). Did Melania Trump plagiarize Michelle Obama's statement on Women's History Month? Snopes.com. https://www.snopes.com/fact-check/melania-trump-plagiarise-michelle-obamas-statement-womens-history-month/

88. K. Rogers. (2018, May 8). As Melania Trump faces plagiarism claims, her staff lashes out at news media. *The New York Times.*

89. K. LaCapria. (2018, May 29). Did Melania Trump plagiarize a Memorial Day tweet from Michelle Obama? Snopes.com.

90. J. Lanzendorfer. (2016, May 23). The forgotten Dust Bowl novel that rivaled "The Grapes of Wrath." *Smithsonian Magazine.*

91. S. Babb. (2004). *Whose Names Are Unknown: A Novel.* University of Oklahoma Press.

92. M. J. Meyer. (2007). Whose Names Are Unknown (review). *Steinbeck Review, 4*(1), pp. 135–139.

93. J. Steinbeck. (1961). *The Winter of Our Discontent.* Viking Press, p. 308.

94. P. Kael. (1971, February 12 & 19). Raising Kane – I; Raising Kane – II. *The New Yorker.*

95. P. Bogdanovich. (1972, October). The Kane mutiny. *Esquire,* pp. 99–105, 180–190.

96. B. Kellow. (2011). *Pauline Kael: A Life in the Dark.* Viking.

97. N. Bowers. (1997). *Words for the Taking: The Hunt for a Plagiarist.* Southern Illinois University Press.

98. Bowers. *Words for the Taking,* p. 54.

99. N. Bowers. (1994). A loss for words: Plagiarism and silence. *The American Scholar, 63* (5), pp. 545–555.

100. W. Grimes. (1994, October 25). What rhymes with, uh, plagiarism? *The New York Times.*

101. F. Chevaillier. (2019). Experiment with textual materiality: Page, author, and medium in the works of Steve Tomasula, Michael Martone, and Eduardo Kac. *College Literature, 46*(1), pp. 179–203.

102. J. Quinn. (1998, February 23). Nora Roberts: A celebration of emotions. *Publishers Weekly.*

103. B. Lang. (2011, November 10). Howard Suber on Pauline Kael's research theft: "It felt like rape." *The Wrap.*

CHAPTER 6 COPYRIGHTS AND CONTEXTS

1. T. Wu. (2008, May 5). Fan feud. *The New Yorker.*

2. E. Pilkington. (2008, April 16). Emotions run high at Harry Potter's A to Z trial. *The Guardian.*

3. Warner Bros. Entertainment Inc. v. RDR Books, 575 F. Supp. 2d 513 (SDNY 2008).

4. M. Rich. (2008, April 13). J.K. Rowling to testify over Potter encyclopedia. *The New York Times.*

5. A. Hartocollis & A. O'Connor. (2008, April 14). J.K. Rowling, in court, assails Potter Lexicon. *The New York Times.*

6. A. Hartocollis. (2008, April 16) Sued by Harry Potter's creator, lexicographer breaks down on the stand. *The New York Times.*

7. J. Eligon. (2008, September 8). Rowling wins lawsuit against Potter Lexicon. *The New York Times.*

8. D. Itzkoff. (2008, December 5). Potter Lexicon is said to have publishing date. *The New York Times.*

9. B. Beebe. (2020). An empirical study of U.S. copyright fair use opinions updated, 1978–2019. *New York University Journal of Intellectual Property and Entertainment Law, 10*(1), pp. 1–40.

10. TV lampoon cleared. (1955, December 10). *The New York Times*, p. 41.

11. M. C. Albin. (1985). Beyond fair use: Putting satire in its proper place. *UCLA Law Review, 33*(2), p. 526.

12. J. Pareles. (1993, November 13). Parody, not smut, has rappers in court. *The New York Times*.

13. L. Greenhouse. (1994, March 8). Ruling on rap song, high court frees parody from copyright law. *The New York Times*.

14. H. Mitgang. (1989, March 10). Old copyright treaty; new shield for artists. *The New York Times*.

15. Z. S. Rosen. (2024). Who Framed Mickey Mouse? *Kansas Law Review, 73*, pp. 44–111.

16. B. Barnes. (2002, December 27). Mickey's copyright adventure: Early Disney creation will soon be public property. *The New York Times*.

17. D. Traxel. (1999, April 4). Hollywood and Vine. *The New York Times*.

18. H. Martin. (2022, May 11). Republicans took away Disney's special status in Florida. Now they're gunning for Mickey himself. *Los Angeles Times*.

19. D. Itzkoff. (2010, January 28). For the heirs to Holmes, a tangled web. *The New York Times*.

20. R. Charles. (2014, July 18). Sherlock Holmes and the vanishing copyright. *The Washington Post*.

21. Klinger v. Conan Doyle Estate, Ltd., No. 14–1128 (7th Cir. 2014).

22. R. Schwartz. (2023, January 10). Why Sherlock Holmes can finally smile. IGN. https://www.ign.com/articles/why-sherlock-holmes-can-finally-smile#

23. A. Flood. (2020, December 22). Lawsuit over "warmer" Sherlock depicted in Enola Holmes dismissed. *The Guardian*.

24. A. Cullins. (2020, November 2). "Enola Holmes" producers blast copyright infringement suit from Conan Doyle estate. *The Hollywood Reporter*.

25. E. Gardner. (2020, December 21). Netflix settles "Enola Holmes" lawsuit with Conan Doyle estate. *The Hollywood Reporter*.

26. A. M. Jiménez. (2019, March 21). Cervantes y el "Quijote" apócrifo: ¿Quién fue Avellaneda? *The Conversation*.

27. C. Bacon-Smith. (1986, November 16). Spock among the women. *The New York Times*.

28. C. Aragon & K. Davis. (2019). *Writers in the Secret Garden: Fanfiction, Youth, and New Forms of Mentoring*. MIT Press.

29. A. Harmon. (1997, August 18). In TV's dull summer days, plots take wing on the net. *The New York Times*.

30. https://www.fanfiction.net

31. https://archiveofourown.org

32. ems023. (2018, August 7). Those that remain. https://www.fanfiction.net/s/9663671/1/Those-that-Remain

33. H. C. Cuccinello. (2017, February 10). Fifty shades of green: How fanfiction went from dirty little secret to money machine. *Forbes.*
34. G. Aviles. (2019, December 20). "Fifty Shades of Grey" was the best-selling book of the decade. *NBC News.*
35. Cuccinello. Fifty shades of green.
36. C. Grady. (2016, April 5). Hamlet, The Divine Comedy, and 3 other pieces of classic literature that are also fan fiction. *Vox.*
37. L. W. Dorsett & M. L. Mean (Eds.). (1985). *C. S. Lewis Letters to Children.* Touchstone, p. 99.
38. A. Romano. (2020, August 18). Lovecraftian horror – and the racism at its core – explained. *Vox.*
39. A. E. Cha. (2003, June 18). Harry Potter and the copyright lawyer. *The Washington Post.*
40. A. Vargas. (2020, September 29). Stephenie Meyer appreciates fanfiction but urges writers to "go do something you can claim too." *Showbiz Cheatsheet.*
41. A. Romano. (2021, June 2). 10 famous authors who write fanfiction. *The Daily Dot.*
42. C. Coker. (2011, March). The "Contraband" incident: The strange case of Marion Zimmer Bradley. *Transformative Works and Cultures, 6.* https://journal.transformative works.org/index.php/twc/article/view/236/191
43. A. J. McDougall. (2022, October 23). Is it time to rethink the rules of fanfiction? *Daily Beast.*
44. K. Hess. (1973, October 14). Still the bible of the American kitchen. *The New York Times.*
45. W. E. Farrell & W. Weaver Jr. (1984, July 6). Tales from the kitchen. *The New York Times.*
46. L. Barron. (2018, March 27). Today's Google Doodle celebrates Hannah Glasse, the Julia Child of the 18th century. *Time.*
47. M. Brown. (2006, June 1). Mrs. Beeton couldn't cook but she could copy, reveals historian. *The Guardian.*
48. J. Maslin. (1997, July 1). White gloves off, dishing the dirt. *The New York Times.*
49. What's the matter with Martha? (1989, March 16). *South Florida Sun Sentinel.*
50. M. Burros. (1983, December 8). An author is accused of plagiarizing recipes. *The New York Times.*
51. N. Jenkins. (1984, September 12). Food notes: Culinary dispute settled. *The New York Times.*
52. P. C. Richman. (1984, September 16). "Stolen" recipes suit settled. *The Washington Post.*
53. M. Rich. (2007, October 19). How to get Junior to eat his veggies turns out to be (too) common knowledge. *The New York Times.*
54. J. 8. Lee. (2007, October 31). Seinfeld attacks wife's cookbook rival. *The New York Times.*
55. K. S. Lombardi. (2007, November 25). In kids' stealth foods, similar strategies dished. *The New York Times.*
56. M. Rich. (2008, January 8). An author sues the Seinfelds, for a cookbook and for barbs. *The New York Times.*
57. S. Clifford. (2009, September 10). Judge rejects copyright suit against Jessica Seinfeld. *The New York Times.*

58. A. Gendar. (2010, April 29). Jerry Seinfeld's wife, Jessica, wins cookbook lawsuit against "The Sneaky Chef" Missy Chase Lapine. *New York Daily News*.

59. D. Gregorian. (2011, February 25). Judge throws out defamation suit against Jerry Seinfeld. *New York Post*.

60. E. Heil. (2021, October 11). Publisher pulls Singaporean cookbook "Makan" amid plagiarism allegations. *The Washington Post*.

61. L. K. Peterson. (2020, September 13). What we talk about when we talk about recipe ownership. *Los Angeles Times*.

62. M. Schmich. (1997, June 1). Advice, like youth, probably just wasted on the young. *Chicago Tribune*.

63. A. Raghunathan. (2005, June 29). Duval gets reprimand for plagiarizing speeches. *Tampa Bay Times*.

64. T. Marshall. (2007, April 21). Principal is fined over two speeches. *Tampa Bay Times*.

65. K. Yi. (2015, June 5). West Boca principal faces debate over second speech. *Sun Sentinel*.

66. S. Travis. (2015, February 8). State orders plagiarizing principal to attend creative writing class. *Sun Sentinel*.

67. CBS New York. (2011, June 29). Principal accused of plagiarism at esteemed Manhattan school for writers and artists.

68. CNN Wire. (2014, June 11). Colorado principal resigns after admitting plagiarism in graduate speech. *Fox 4*.

69. M. B. W. Tabor. (1991, July 15). Boston dean quits in plagiarism case. *The New York Times*.

70. L. Heron. (2010, May 25). Columbia University valedictorian plagiarizes Patton Oswalt. *ABC News*.

71. K. Ferguson & A. Stuhlman. (2015, June 9). Walpole High valedictorian plagiarized "Chipotle" graduation speech. *Times Advocate*.

72. Valedictorian admits plagiarizing commencement speech. (2008, June 5). 10 WBNS.

73. Circleville, graduate settle fight over speech. (2008, June 19). *The Columbus Dispatch*.

74. D. Emery. (2017, May 17). Did President Trump plagiarize his commencement speech from "Legally Blonde"? Snopes.com. https://www.snopes.com/fact-check/trump-legally-blonde-speech/

75. P. J. Cardwell & J. Odermatt. (2023, May 5). Eurovision: Even before the singing starts, the contest is a fascinating reflection of international rules and politics. *The Conversation*.

76. The rules of the contest. https//eurovision.tv/about/rules

77. D. Wyatt. (2013, February 19). Germany's Eurovision entry Cascada accused of plagiarising last year's winner "Euphoria." *The Independent*.

78. B. Waterfield. (2007, March 30). Eurovision entry is like my song, claims Swede. *The Telegraph*.

79. B. Royston. (2007, March 28). We never heard of Pandora. *ESCToday*.

80. T. Stephens. (2008, May 22). Swiss hope for Eurovision wonder. Swissinfo.ch. https://www.swissinfo.ch/eng/culture/swiss-hope-for-eurovision-wonder/6665658

81. G. G. Yazıcıtunc. (2021, March 5). Eurovision 1999: Germany's Sürpriz in focus. *EuroVisionary*.
82. S. Bakker. (2001, March 1). Almost 70 percent: "This is plagiarism"! ESCToday.com. https://esctoday.com/32/almost_70_percent_this_is_plagiarism_/
83. C. Jensen. (2021, January 18). Eurovision battle: Belgium 1996 vs Sweden 2001. *EuroVisionary*.
84. A. Marshall. (2019, February 7). Jack White wins Eurovision. Kind of. *The New York Times*.
85. J. Korn & N. Brown. (2023, April 25). Jury selected in Ed Sheeran music copyright case. *CNN Business*.
86. A. Ross. (2016, April 14). The unoriginal originality of Led Zeppelin. *The New Yorker*.
87. B. Sisario. (2019, September 22). Original or copied? "Stairway to Heaven" is back in court. *The New York Times*.
88. A. Kim. (2020, March 10). Led Zeppelin wins major copyright battle for "Stairway to Heaven." *CNN Entertainment*.
89. B. Sisario & N. Smith (2015, March 10). "Blurred Lines" infringed on Marvin Gaye copyright, jury rules. *The New York Times*.
90. E. Gardner. (2015, July 14). Judge rejects new "Blurred Lines" trial, trims damages to $5.3 million. *The Hollywood Reporter*.
91. B. Sisario. (2019, March 31). "Blurred Lines" on their minds, songwriters create nervously. *The New York Times*.
92. D. M. Bagdade. (1992). Digital sound sampling: A re-evaluation after "Grand Upright Music." *DePaul-LCA Journal of Arts and Entertainment Law*, 3(1), pp. 1–6.
93. J. Runtagh. (2016, June 7). Songs on trial: 12 landmark music copyright cases. *Rolling Stone*.
94. R. Harrington. (1992, December 24). The groove robbers' judgement. *The Washington Post*.
95. L. Van Gelder. (2004, September 9). Arts briefing. *The New York Times*.
96. C. Richards. (2012, July 6). The court case that changed hip-hop – from Public Enemy to Kanye – forever. *The Washington Post*.

CHAPTER 7 PLAGIARISM PAST, PRESENT, AND FUTURE

1. H. McIntyre. (2015, April 15). After 14 weeks at number 1, "Uptown Funk!" finally steps aside. *Forbes*.
2. N. Messitte. (2014, December 22). How "Uptown Funk" proves Bruno Mars is exactly like Coldplay. *Forbes*.
3. D. Kreps. (2016, October 30). Bruno Mars, Mark Ronson face lawsuit over "Uptown Funk." *Rolling Stone*.
4. E. Christman. (2015, May 4). Inside the new royalty split for "Uptown Funk": Who gets paid what. *Billboard*.
5. Kreps. Bruno Mars, Mark Ronson face lawsuit over "Uptown Funk."
6. J. Monroe. (2018, April 13). Bruno Mars and Mark Ronson settle one of three "Uptown Funk" lawsuits: Report. *Pitchfork*.

7. M. Kaminsky. (2017, December 30). Bruno Mars and Mark Ronson's "Uptown Funk" faces (yet another) copyright infringement suit. *Forbes*.

8. N. Yoo. (2018, July 2). Mark Ronson settles "Uptown Funk" Zapp copyright lawsuit. *Pitchfork*.

9. Kaminsky. Bruno Mars and Mark Ronson's "Uptown Funk" faces (yet another) copyright infringement suit.

10. M. Hassan. (2017, April 20). Charly García claims Bruno Mars owes him $2 million for stealing "Uptown Funk." *Remezcla*.

11. J. Shepherd. (2015, August 12). Mark Ronson and Bruno Mars accused of plagiarising Uptown Funk, again. *The Independent*.

12. C. Hodgson. (2015, January 15). Uptown Funk and The Really Wild Show theme are actually the same song. *Cosmopolitan*.

13. In:Demand. (2015, January 21). Mark Ronson Hears "The Really Wild Show" theme for the first time. https://www.youtube.com/watch?v=8NXip7d2yJc

14. "The Spider" sued for fourth time. (1927, October 6). *The New York Times*.

15. J. R. Chambers. (2008). Explaining false uniqueness: Why we are both better and worse than others. *Social and Personality Psychology Compass*, 2(2), pp. 878–894.

16. D. K. Simonton. (2004). *Creativity in Science: Chance, Logic, Genius, and Zeitgeist*. Cambridge University Press.

17. N. Guicciardini. (2017). The Newton–Leibniz calculus controversy, 1708–1730. In E. Schliesser & C. Smeenk (Eds), *The Oxford Handbook of Newton*. Oxford Handbooks Online.

18. B. Nyhan & J. Reifler. (2010). When corrections fail: The persistence of political misperceptions. *Political Behavior*, 32(2), pp. 303–330.

19. M. Puente. (2015, November 12). Judge "shakes off" lawsuit against Taylor Swift . . . by quoting Taylor Swift. *USA Today*.

20. C. Cooke. (2022, March 1). Taylor Swift gets lesser known Shake It Off lawsuit dismissed – again. *Complete Music Update*.

21. J. F. Clarity & W. Weaver Jr. (1986, January 16). To Teflon or not to Teflon. *The New York Times*.

22. M. Osborne. (2023, March 17). National Audubon Society votes to keep the name of an enslaver. *Smithsonian Magazine*.

23. E. H. Burtt Jr. & W. E. Davis Jr. (2013). *Alexander Wilson: The Scot Who Founded American Ornithology*. Belknap Press.

24. E. Stringham. (1953). Audubon and Wilson: Artist vs. scientist. *Southwest Review*, 38(1), pp. 44–52.

25. S. Levingston. (2013, March 19). Jane Goodall's "Seeds of Hope" contains borrowed passages without attribution. *The Washington Post*.

26. S. Levingston. (2014, April 2). Jane Goodall's "Seeds of Hope" reissued a year after being pulled from the shelves. *The Washington Post*.

27. Time 100 Leadership Series. (2019, April 17). *Time*.

28. Hardcover nonfiction. (2021, November 7). *The New York Times*.

29. B. Crader. (2002, January 18). A historian and her sources. *The Weekly Standard*.

30. P. H. King. (2002, August 4). As history repeats itself, the scholar becomes the story. *Los Angeles Times.*

31. D. D. Kirkpatrick. (2002, February 23). Historian says borrowing was wider than known. *The New York Times.*

32. D. D. Kirkpatrick. (2002, February 28). Writer leaves "NewsHour" in furor over book. *The New York Times.*

33. D. D. Kirkpatrick. (2002, June 1). Author Goodwin resigns from Pulitzer board. *The New York Times.*

34. Best sellers: January 8, 2006. (2006, January 8). *The New York Times.*

35. P. Rucker. (2008, November 19). Obama inspired by, compared to Lincoln. *The Washington Post.*

36. A. Jones. (2009, May 7). Prof denies contact regarding plagiarism. *Tuscaloosa News.*

37. Associated Press. (2009, April 22). Lawsuit says Jacksonville State University president plagiarized doctoral dissertation. *Advance Local.*

38. J. Stripling. (2009, June 2). In living color. *Inside Higher Ed.*

39. H. Greene. (n.d.). Dr. William A. Meehan to retire after holding JSU's third longest presidency. Jacksonville State University. https://www.jsu.edu/meehan-legacy/biography.html

40. B. Lockette. (2023, February 17). Professor emeritus honored for lifetime achievement. Jacksonville State University. https://www.jsu.edu/news/articles/2023/02/president-emeritus-honored-for-lifetime-achievement-.html

41. S. Kerr. (2000, March 12). Diva. *The New York Times.*

42. D. Smith. (2000, November 16). Sontag is among winners of National Book Awards. *The New York Times.*

43. D. Carvajal. (2000, May 27). So whose words are they, anyway? A new Sontag novel creates a stir by not crediting quotes from other books. *The New York Times.*

44. Carvajal. So whose words are they, anyway?

45. N. Siegal. (2019, September 15). A new biography of Susan Sontag digs to find the person beneath the icon. *The New York Times.*

46. L. Gutkin. (2019, October 11). A tale of two plagiarists. *The Chronicle of Higher Education.*

47. P. S. Menell. (2022). Reflections on music copyright justice. *Pepperdine Law Review, 49* (3), pp. 533–614.

48. Did Bob Dylan lift lines from Dr. Saga? (2003, July 8). *The Wall Street Journal.*

49. G. Susman. (2003, July 8). Did Bob Dylan plagiarize a Japanese book? *Entertainment Weekly.*

50. I. Crouch. (2014, May 20). Bob Dylan, fanboy. *The New Yorker.*

51. M. Rich. (2006, September 14). Who's this guy Dylan who's borrowing lines from Henry Timrod? *The New York Times.*

52. M. Wood. (2012, October 25). The Bob Dylan interview. *Rolling Stone.*

53. M. Diehl. (2010, April 22). It's a Joni Mitchell concert, sans Joni. *Los Angeles Times.*

54. R. Sheffield. (2016, October 13). Why Bob Dylan deserves his Nobel Prize. *Rolling Stone.*

55. A. Pitzer, (2017, June 13). The freewheelin' Bob Dylan. *Slate*.

56. Crouch, Bob Dylan, fanboy.

57. D. Kinney. (2014). *The Dylanologists: Adventures in the Land of Bob*. Simon & Schuster.

58. R. Falco. (2022, October 17). How Bob Dylan used the ancient practice of "imitatio" to craft some of the most original songs of his time. *The Conversation*.

59. A. Lindey. (1952). *Plagiarism and Originality*. Harper & Brothers, p. 253.

60. A. Pora. (2022, February 2). Plagiarism and bogus degrees: The rampant cheating in Romanian schools. *Radio Free Europe*.

61. Lindey. *Plagiarism and Originality*, p. 254.

62. T. Mallon. (1989). *Stolen Words*. Harcourt.

63. R. Durst, G. Katz, A. Teitelbaum, J. Zislin & P. N. Dannon. (2001). Kleptomania: Diagnosis and treatment options. *CNS Drugs*, 15(3), pp. 185–195.

64. J. S. Maxmen & N. G. Ward. (1995). *Essential Psychopathology and Its Treatment* (2nd edition revision for DSM-IV). W. W. Norton.

65. D. Smith. (2006, April 26). Aggrieved publisher rejects young novelist's apology. *The New York Times*.

66. M. Rich & D. Smith. (2006, April 28). Publisher to recall Harvard student's novel. *The New York Times*.

67. G. J. Curtis & K. Tremayne. (2021). Is plagiarism really on the rise? Results from four 5-yearly surveys. *Studies in Higher Education*, 46(9), pp. 1816–1826.

68. American Psychiatric Association. (2013). *Diagnostic and Statistical Manual of Mental Disorders: DSM-5*, 5th ed. American Psychiatric Publishing.

69. A. Kaczynski. (2014, September 29). Tennessee Democratic Senate nominee plagiarized almost everything written on his website. *BuzzFeed News*.

70. J. Keller. (2002, February 25). Doris Kearns Goodwin: Truth takes more hits. *Chicago Tribune*.

71. I. B. Siaputra. (2013). The 4PA of plagiarism: A psycho-academic profile of plagiarists. *International Journal for Educational Integrity*, 9(2), pp. 50–59.

72. Associated Press. (1995, March 12). Chicago Sun-Times editorial editor admits plagiarism, quits. *Los Angeles Times*.

73. A. Ross. (2004, May 24). Das Lied von der Brad. *The Rest is Noise*. https://www.therestisnoise.com/2004/05/symphony_of_bra.html

74. N. Kulish. (2010, February 11). Author, 17, says it's "mixing," not plagiarism. *The New York Times*.

75. H. J. Jackson. (1975). Sterne, Burton, and Ferriar: Allusions to the "Anatomy of Melancholy" in volumes five to nine of "Tristram Shandy." *Philological Quarterly*, 54 (2), pp. 457–470.

76. G. Hurlburt. (2017). Shining light on the dark web. *Computer*, 50(4), pp. 100–105.

77. R. C. Baker. (2011, April 6). The misbegotten career of Roy Lichtenstein. *The Village Voice*.

78. B. O'Doherty. (1963, October 27). Lichtenstein: Doubtful but definite triumph of the banal. *The New York Times*.

79. D. Alberge. (2023, April 9). "It's called stealing": New allegations of plagiarism against Roy Lichtenstein. *The Observer.*

80. D. Shields. (2010). *Reality Hunger: A Manifesto.* Vintage Books, p. 100.

81. Shields. *Reality Hunger,* p. 209.

82. J. Lethem. (2007, February). The ecstasy of influence. *Harper's Magazine.*

83. A. Callard. (2019, December 10). In defense of plagiarism, sort of. *The Chronicle of Higher Education.*

84. T. S. Eliot. (1998). *The Sacred Wood and Major Early Essays.* Dover Publications, p. 72.

85. M. Gladwell. (2004, November 14). Something borrowed. *The New Yorker.*

86. S. Fish. (2010, August 9). Plagiarism is not a big moral deal. *The New York Times.*

87. S. Fish. (2010, August 16). The ontology of plagiarism: Part two. *The New York Times.*

88. J. A. Mott-Smith. (2017, May 23). Bad idea about writing: Plagiarism deserves to be punished. *Inside Higher Ed.*

89. Ecclesiastes 1:9. (2011). *Holy Bible: New International Version.* Biblica.

90. K. Knibbs. (2023, September 4). The battle over Books3 could change AI forever. *Wired.*

91. A. Reisner. (2023, September 25). What I found in a database Meta uses to train generative AI. *The Atlantic.*

92. A. Resiner. (2023, September 25). These 183,000 books are fueling the biggest fight in publishing and tech. *The Atlantic.*

93. R. Roberts & R. Kreuz. (2015). *Becoming Fluent: How Cognitive Science Can Help Adults Learn a Foreign Language.* MIT Press.

94. Z. Small. (2023, July 10). Sarah Silverman sues OpenAI and Meta over copyright infringement. *The New York Times.*

95. Associated Press. (2023, September 21). John Grisham and George RR Martin among authors suing OpenAI for "systematic theft on a mass scale." *The Independent.*

96. M. M. Grynbaum & R. Mac. (2023, December 27). The Times sues OpenAI and Microsoft over A.I. use of copyrighted work. *The New York Times.*

97. W. Cho (2024, February 13). Sarah Silverman, authors see most claims against Open AI dismissed by judge. *The Hollywood Reporter.*

98. W. Oremus & E. Izadi. (2024, January 4). AI's future could hinge on one thorny legal question. *The Washington Post.*

99. K. Robertson. (2024, May 22). OpenAI strikes a deal to license News Corp content. *The New York Times.*

100. T. Spangler. (2024, May 29). OpenAI inks licensing deals to bring Vox Media, The Atlantic content to ChatGPT. *Variety.*

101. One-third of college students used ChatGPT for schoolwork during the 2022–23 academic year. (2023, September 5). Intelligent.com. https://www.intelligent.com/one-third-of-college-students-used-chatgpt-for-schoolwork-during-the-2022-23-academic-year/

102. I. Bogost. (2023, May 16). The first year of AI college ends in ruin. *The Atlantic.*

103. D. Weber-Wulff, A. Anohina-Naumeca, S. Bjelobaba, T. Foltýnek, J. Guerrero-Dib, O. Popoola, . . . & L. Waddington. (2023). Testing of detection tools for AI-generated text. *International Journal for Educational Integrity, 19*(1), p. 26.

104. AI Phrase Finder. (2024, March 9). The 10 most common ChatGPT words. https://aiphrasefinder.com/common-chatgpt-words/

105. S. Philip. (2024, March 31). Delving into "delve." https://pshapira.net/2024/03/31/delving-into-delve/

EPILOGUE

1. B. Fehr & J. A. Russell. (1984). Concept of emotion viewed from a prototype perspective. *Journal of Experimental Psychology: General, 113*(3), pp. 464–486.

2. Decotelli nega plágio no mestrado, explica doutorado e diz: "Sou ministro." (2020, June 29). UOL.com. https://educacao.uol.com.br/noticias/2020/06/29/decotelli-nega-plagio-no-mestrado-explica-doutorado-e-diz-sou-ministro.htm

3. J. Torbati. (2007, October 4). Law prof. borrows text for book. *Yale Daily News.*

4. J. McWhorter. (2024, January 23). We need a new word for "plagiarism." *The New York Times.*

5. S. K. Maynard. (2007). *Linguistic Creativity in Japanese Discourse.* John Benjamins.

6. D. Kim, Y. Pan, & H. S. Park. (1998). High- versus low-context culture: A comparison of Chinese, Korean, and American cultures. *Psychology & Marketing, 15*(6), pp. 507–521.

7. T. R. Robinson & N. H. Shah. (2023, December 14). Harvard president faces additional plagiarism allegations. *The Harvard Crimson.*

8. K. Long. (2024, January 4). Neri Oxman admits to plagiarizing in her doctoral dissertation after BI report. *Business Insider.*

9. A. De Palma. (1990, November 10). Plagiarism seen by scholars in King's Ph.D. dissertation. *The New York Times.*

10. M. D. Shear, K. Rogers, & A. Karni. (2021, May 14). Beneath Joe Biden's folksy demeanor, a short fuse and an obsession with details. *The New York Times.*

11. A. Flood. (2019, March 28). Plagiarism, "book-stuffing," clickfarms . . . the rotten side of self-publishing. *The Guardian.*

12. N. Powelson. (2023, November 15). A.I. has taken self-publishing by storm: Writers and publishers weigh in on how to cope. *The Observer.*

13. E. Creamer. (2023, September 20). Amazon restricts authors from self-publishing more than three books a day after AI concerns. *The Guardian.*

14. H. Brewis. (2023, December). Plagiarism and you. YouTube.com. https://www.youtube.com/watch?v=yDp3cB5fHXQ

15. S. Elbeshbishi. (2022, April 24). Inspiration or infringement? Songwriters clashing in court more often after "Blurred Lines." *USA Today.*

16. T. Buckley. (2023, February 15). Winnie-the-Pooh horror film is a scary sight for copyright holders. *Bloomberg.*

17. D. Victor. (2017, July 13). As "Game of Thrones" returns, is sharing your HBO password O.K.? *The New York Times.*

18. S. Frenkel & S. A. Thompson. (2023, July 15). "Not for machines to harvest": Data revolts break out against A.I. *The New York Times.*

Index